S0-ADS-476

Microsoft® Works for the PC

Robert Cowart

Osborne **McGraw-Hill**
Berkeley, California

Osborne **McGraw-Hill**
2600 Tenth Street
Berkeley, California 94710
U.S.A.

For information on translations and book distributors outside of the U.S.A., write to Osborne **McGraw-Hill** at the above address.

A complete list of trademarks appears on page 434.

Microsoft Works® for the PC

567890 DODO 90

ISBN 0-07-881272-0

Jeffrey Pepper, Acquisitions Editor
Elizabeth Fisher, Associate Editor
Rick Grimm and Gail Todd, Technical Reviewers
Lyn Cordell, Project Editor
Judy Wohlfrom and Robert Cowart, Text Designers

CONTENTS

This book is dedicated to Dr. John W. Mauchly and Dr. J. Presper Eckert for inventing the first electronic digital computer. Without their efforts and successes, the computer revolution, with its extraordinary contributions in the areas of human productivity, scientific discovery, and communications, may not have been possible.

ACKNOWLEDGMENTS

When I agreed to take on the project of writing a book about a soon-to-be-released product from the software giant Microsoft, all involved assumed that the enterprise would take only three or four months. But monolithic projects have nasty appetites. Nine months later, you could smell the midnight oil burning at Osborne/McGraw-Hill in Berkeley, California, and up at Microsoft in Redmond, Washington. However, not to be undone by unexpected program design changes (that demanded a seemingly endless number of chapter rewrites) and ship-date setbacks, we persevered. The results are what you hold in your hand — an introduction to a unique and powerful tool designed for "the rest of us" (at least the rest of us who prefer PCs!).

Throughout the laborious process, certain individuals stood by steadfastly, providing moral, technical, and editorial support, and I want to offer thanks. For her interest in having me work with Osborne/McGraw-Hill in the first place, I salute editor-in-chief Cindy Hudson. In addition, my appreciation goes to those at Osborne who worked so assiduously and professionally on this project: acquisitions editor Jeff Pepper and associate editor Liz Fisher; technical editor Gail Todd; project editor Lyn Cordell; and proofreading coordinator Madhu Prasher.

I feel particularly indebted to the helpful folks at Microsoft who not only reviewed every chapter of this book (often in short order) but who also remained constantly available to answer questions by phone. First and foremost, thanks to Rick Grimm for never raising his voice even when I phoned him at home on a Sunday night. Next, to Pam Stanton-Wyman for her thoughtful comments and suggestions about word processing; to Gary Jackson for his help with the communications chapter; and finally to Bruce Jacobsen, product manager for Works, for his cooperation in establishing an amiable working relationship between Microsoft and Osborne/McGraw-Hill.

Finally, some credits for artistic and technical production assistance are in order. Many thanks to Judy Wohlfrom, art director for Osborne/McGraw-Hill, who, along with Ted Nace, helped develop the book design. Thanks also to Renee Benoit for her illustrations. Numerous manufacturers deserve credit for their loans of equipment and software which I used in the layout, design, and preparation of this book. Manuscript pages were written using PC-Write from Quicksoft and printed on a QMS PS-800+ laser printer for editing. Screen shots for most of the figures were captured using HOTSHOT from SYM-SOFT. Page layout was done using Xerox's Ventura Publisher running on an AST Premium 286 computer in conjunction with Moniterm Viking-1 and Sigma Designs LaserView 19-inch video monitors. Final pages were printed on a Qume ScripTEN laser printer. Typefaces used were Times, Optima, and Courier from Adobe Systems.

PREFACE

Microsoft Works for the PC is a brilliant and timely program. It wraps all the essential computer programs into one package and makes them easy to use, much like the Macintosh version of the same program. Now almost anybody can use a PC-compatible computer to get real work done quickly. There's only one problem left — learning to use it! If you're one of those many customers who opened your new copy of Works, looked at the 700+ page manual and heaved a heavy sigh, you know what I mean. You expected a little lighter reading with a program that was supposed to be so simple.

It's not that the supplied manual is incomplete. In fact it contains a great deal of useful information. It's just that large portions of the information can't help much until you know what you're doing. Like lots of other things about computers it's sort of a Catch 22, leaving you — who just need to write a letter, prepare a budget, or print a mailing list — at the short end of the stick. That's where this book comes in.

This book is a direct, compact introduction to all the essentials of Microsoft Works for the PC. Conveyed in a concise, step-by-step approach, the information in each of the 12 chapters makes learning Works relatively painless. Each section is presented in bite-sized chunks and is meant to be read as you operate your computer. As a result, you will produce practical results as you learn, and these results can later be applied to your own tasks. You will learn by creating real-world documents such as a business letter, a name and address list, a retail store invoice, and a company budget. Then you'll be shown how to pull all these together into a single document, or to create form letters, mailing labels, and business charts from your data.

As either a training manual for classroom instruction or for use as a self-paced tutorial, this book attempts to take the computer novice from the first steps of installing Works on a computer through the creation of and understanding of complex documents that integrate word processing, spreadsheets, databases, and charts all through the use of examples. There's even a little humor thrown in to soften the technicality.

HOW TO USE THIS BOOK

Here's a basic explanation of the book's organization, to help you use it more efficiently and to get an idea of what's covered.

Even if you're not new to computers, you should read Chapter 1. Here, you'll encounter a short description of what the four tools of Works are all about. Word processing, spreadsheets, databases, and communications are explained — in general and as they pertain to Works. It's basically a good all-around introduction to what microcomputers are good for and what you can expect to do with Works.

Then, if you're one of those who ran to the bookstore even before installing Works on your computer, follow the instructions in Chapter 2. Here you'll create the working disks from which you'll run Works on your computer by running the Setup program supplied with Works. If you've already run the Setup program, you might as well skip this chapter and jump to Chapter 3.

Beginning with Chapter 3, you'll be running the Works program as you read along. This chapter explains the basics of the Works user interface, that is, how you interact with the program and tell it what you want it to do. Here you'll learn about special keys on the PC keyboard, what you'll see on the screen, and how to use your mouse, if you have one.

Then, in Chapter 4, you'll begin creating your own documents. You'll learn how to type in a business letter, fix typographical errors in it, and, if you have a printer, print it out on paper. Likewise, Chapter 5 introduces you to the Works spreadsheet, where you'll design a simple invoice for a retail store, fill it in, and watch as Works automatically performs mathematical calculations on the numbers. Chapter 6 then takes you through the steps of creating a simple database: a telephone book / mailing list containing names, addresses, and phone numbers. You'll learn how to add data (names, addresses, and so on) into the database, how to look up a specific bit of information by searching, and how to edit your data to keep it up-to-date.

If you have a modem, you'll find Chapter 7 especially useful. It introduces you to the world of electronic communications whereby you can contact other computers to exchange and retrieve information such as airline schedules or stock quotes.

The next three chapters — 8, 9, and 10 — are extensions to Chapters 4, 5, and 6, building on what you learned in those sections. Thus, you'll learn to take advantage of more sophisticated capabilities of Works, such as copying data between documents, building a moderately complex budget spreadsheet, and printing professional-looking database reports from the database.

Chapter 11 stands on its own, showing you how to produce a wide range of charts from numbers in the budget spreadsheet you created in Chapter 9. You'll create eight basic types of charts, each with several variations, and learn how to print them out as well as how to view them on the screen.

In Chapter 12, you'll learn how to pull all of your documents together, integrating them in various ways. Here you'll learn how to pull a chart into a business letter, how to print mailing labels and form letters from a database mailing list, and how to exchange information between spreadsheets, databases, and communications documents.

Two appendixes provide additional reference material. Appendix A lists in one convenient location all of the editing commands, special keystrokes, and other pertinent information for each of the Works tools. System requirements for running Works are also covered there. Appendix B details what you need to know about exporting and importing documents to and from other programs such as Lotus 1-2-3, WordStar, Word-Perfect, and Microsoft Word.

Finally, when you need to refresh your memory on a given topic, use the complete index and well-organized table of contents to look up specific step-by-step techniques.

Chapter

Introducing Works

One

Microsoft Works is an easy-to-use computer program designed for your IBM PC or PC-compatible computer. Works is a powerful, productive tool that incorporates four of the most popular types of PC programs in one convenient package. These four components, or tools, are word processing, spreadsheet, database management, and telecommunications. With Works, even if you are a newcomer to personal computing, you can quickly get up to speed and begin putting your PC to practical use for everything from writing letters to creating professional-looking business charts.

Despite its relatively low price and attempt to be all things to all people, Works is a complete and competent program. In many respects it will perform as well as more expensive stand-alone programs, but without the cost of numerous separate programs and the headache of learning to use each one with its own peculiarities.

The key advantage is that Works is an *integrated* program. This means that the modules of Works were designed to interact with one another, thereby allowing you to move data from one section into another fairly easily. For example, you can copy a graph, spreadsheet, or database into a word processing document. Or you can take some data received through the communications module and make a chart out of it. Without an integrated program like Works, this can be a tedious chore (if it is possible at all), often requiring the use of several different

1

programs and some technical expertise. The ability to transfer data from module to module easily is what integrated software is all about, and it can prove to be a great boon, particularly for businesses.

USER INTERFACE ADVANTAGES

Integration has another advantage. One thing that has popularized Apple's Macintosh, particularly for newcomers to the microcomputer, is the consistency of its *user interface* — the way you interact with the computer's programs. Once you know how to use one program on the Mac, it's a fairly easy task to learn almost any other, since many of the commands and general program layout (called the *environment*) are consistent from program to program.

But things aren't so simple on the PC, at least not until Works arrived on the scene. If you have tried using a number of different PC programs for a given task, such as word processing, you will have noticed little consistency among their appearance, commands, and features. Try learning Word-Star, Microsoft Word, and Xywrite and you will see what we mean. Each program uses an entirely different set of commands for even the simplest of maneuvers, such as moving a block of text or deleting a word.

Microsoft Works offers the advantage of a consistent Macintosh-style user interface to the PC, eliminating this type of difficulty. Since many of the commands in Works are identical from module to module, moving around through the various parts of the program will be easy to learn as well as to remember.

FILE COMPATIBILITY ADVANTAGES

Another problem computer users have had to face is that of incompatible file formats (ways of storing information on disk) between programs. This is a prevalent problem on the Macintosh as well as the PC. What it means is that more often than not, you will find it difficult to use a document in a program other than the one in which it was created.

In fact even today, aside from a few programs similar to Works, only ad hoc standards exist for defining the way in which PC programs should store their data, and whether that data can be shared by other programs. These standards have arisen primarily in response to the popularity of a handful of programs rather than from any consensus of industry committees or from conscious attempts to create standards.

Within each primary category of microcomputer software, at least one predominant way of formatting the associated data has emerged and taken hold. In some cases, more than one has. In databases for example, the popularity of dBASE II and dBASE III (from Ashton-Tate) and pfs:File (Software Publishing) has prompted many database vendors to provide some level of compatibility with these programs' data files. Word processing programs rely heavily on ASCII (American Standard Code for Information Interchange). Those developed recently rely as well on the Microsoft Word, Microsoft Interchange Rich Text Format (RTF), and the IBM Document Content Architecture (DCA) formats. Lotus Development Company's success with 1-2-3 has popularized the WKS (worksheet) format for storing spreadsheet data. Other standards such as DIF (originated by Software Arts for use with VisiCalc) and SYLK files (developed by Microsoft for use by its programs Chart and Plan) thrown into the ring add up to a marketing struggle among manufacturers. Unfortunately, it's the user who ends up the loser.

Realizing the need and desire of many computer users to transfer data from one program to another, software manufacturers now often feature built-in import/export capabilities to aid in this process. As an example, the database program Paradox (Ansa) can import and export as many as seven different file types. But even with such utilities and the existence of popular standards for data storage and sharing, problems often arise during the process of translating or transferring data between programs. This is especially likely with word processing documents, for which intricate formatting information such as tab size, indentation, justification, and headers and footers are usually lost in the translation from one word processor to another.

WHY USE AN INTEGRATED PACKAGE?

Many PC users who do more than one type of work with their PCs have had to choose a favorite package for each task and learn the different commands and user interface for each one. Then they have had to learn to live with whatever problems may be endemic to data sharing between these programs. Finally, they have had to cope with the inconvenience of the numerous steps involved to ship information from one program to the other.

As a typical example, to move some accounting data from a spreadsheet into a database, you first have to get into the spreadsheet program and load the particular accounting spreadsheet containing the desired information. Then you mark the block of data you want to copy into the database and issue the command to save that portion on your floppy or hard disk temporarily. Next, you exit the spreadsheet program and load the database program. Then you bring up the database you want to import into. You may have to redesign the database's layout before reading the temporary file into it;

otherwise, it might not fit properly, and data will be lost. Finally, assuming your database can read the format of the data you want to read in, you issue the import command, and the task is finished. Sound laborious? It is.

On the positive side, though, this arrangement allows you to pick the programs best suited to each task, or at least the ones you like the most — to mix and match. But clearly an integrated program, if it contains the elements you need for your daily work, is a simpler solution. With a good integrated program, facilities for "cutting and pasting" bits of information from one module to another are usually right at your fingertips. Works, for example, allows you to keep several documents simultaneously open in different windows, switch between them at will, and move information from one document to another quickly.

Often, this type of convenience has its price. Like an automobile with power steering, power brakes, and air-conditioning, there's usually a trade-off in performance. The trade-off inherent in many integrated programs is in their power. Expensive and comprehensive stand-alone programs such as Microsoft Word, dBASE III, Crosstalk, or Paradox are designed to supply a high level of performance for one specific task. Integrated packages such as Symphony, Jazz, First-Choice, Quartet, Ensemble, Microsoft Works (for the Mac), and Microsoft Works (for the PC) all trade some of this power for the convenience of data compatibility and a common user interface.

The extent of this trade-off is beginning to wane, however, as microcomputer technology matures. Microsoft Works is a prime example of this development; several of its modules are quite competent even when compared to stand-alone products. Without a doubt, for many people the power and convenience of Works will more than compensate for its few shortcomings.

THE FOUR TOOLS OF WORKS

With this understanding of the nature and advantages of an integrated productivity program in mind, we will now take a quick look at the four primary tools in Works to see generally what they are and what they can do for you. The details of how to use each tool will be discussed in upcoming chapters.

About Word Processing

A common occurrence in the computer arena is the replacement of everyday language with confusing computerese. The term *word processing* is a case in point. A word processor is actually just a clever typewriter that lets you fix mistakes and rearrange your text in various ways before you type it out — that capability is what the "processing" is. If you type a lot, a word processor alone can justify the expense of your entire computer system and software.

With a word processor you can write and edit business letters, form letters, lists, company reports, contracts, invoices, magazines, and books. Some word processors even let you write in different languages. The big advantage of a word processor over a typewriter is that you don't have to worry about making mistakes. This means you can throw away your eraser and forget about "white-out" forever. If you make a mistake using a word processor, you just back up and fix it.

Until the advent of the microcomputer, word processors were expensive, single-purpose machines found principally in large businesses. Although they used computer technology, these machines could not be used for any other tasks. In computer parlance, they were *dedicated word processors*. That is, they were dedicated to the purpose of word processing. Now, thanks to decreasing costs of microcomputer technology, anyone who can afford a color TV can buy a word processor. Furthermore, microcomputers are not dedicated machines but general-purpose machines, limited only by the software you plug into them.

Using a word processor amounts to typing on your computer's screen instead of on a piece of paper. At first this experience can feel a little foreign, but you will soon get used to it. Then it won't be long before a typewriter seems like an antique (though you may still keep one around for typing addresses on envelopes). As you type on the computer's keyboard, the letters are displayed on the screen, and are simultaneously stored in the computer's memory. When you get to the end of a line, you don't have to press the carriage return key, either. Word processors do that for you automatically. Nor do you have to worry about typing too fast, since a computer can easily keep up with even the fastest typist.

It is by virtue of the fact that your words are in the computer's memory (sometimes called *RAM*, for *Random Access Memory*) that you can move the words around right on the screen and make revisions until you are satisfied with the way your document looks. The computer, responding to your commands, simply shifts the words around within RAM. When you are happy with the revisions, you then instruct the computer to print out your document on paper, using your printer.

Another important feature of word processors (and this is true of most other computer programs as well) is that your work is not lost when you turn off the computer. You can save your documents for later printing or revisions by storing them on floppy disks or a hard disk (if your computer has one). Word processing programs, with the help of your computer's *DOS (Disk Operating System),* store your work on your disk as files. Each file is stored separately, and can later be reloaded into the computer's RAM, revised (edited), and printed again. It can even be joined with other files to create new documents. This way you can cut and paste various versions of, say, a contract for different clients without having to retype each component part of the contract again and again. This will increase your productivity and decrease your typos at the same time.

Many word processors feature a search and replace capability that will hunt down occurrences of a particular word in your document and alter it automatically, while readjusting the surrounding text to fit the line. This feature is useful if you find you have made a misspelling repeatedly, or if you want to abbreviate a long word to speed your typing and let the computer replace it later with the full word.

The ability of word processors to mark blocks of text and then move them or copy them within a single document is a real time saver, too. Most programs offer means for such block moves. Typically you have to mark the beginning and end of the block in question; then you simply insert the block in its final destination using a move or copy command.

Some of the better word processors are beginning to feature built-in spelling checkers and a few even boast a thesaurus. Typically, a spelling checker works after the fact; it proofreads your entire document once you have finished writing. When it finds a mistake, it lets you correct the error. Some spelling checkers actually work as you type, causing the computer to make a beeping sound if you spell a word wrong; then, if you like, they can make suggestions for correcting the spelling. A built-in thesaurus can be very handy when you find yourself stuck for a word. With Borland's Turbo Lightning, for example, you simply place the *cursor* (the blinking underline on the PC screen) on the word you want a synonym for, press a key, and — *voilà* — its synonyms appear. Press another key and the word drops into your document without your even having to type it.

Finally, most modern word processors allow you to decide exactly how your text will appear on the printed page. Such details as margins, tabs, headers and footers, page numbering, bold and italic printing and so forth can usually be controlled with the aid of various formatting commands that you type in. Depending on the program, the effects of these formatting commands on your printed pages may or may not be displayed directly on the computer screen. The popular term for programs that display formatting effects is *WYSIWYG* (for What You See Is What You Get, pronounced wiz-e-wig). Non-WYSIWYG word processors, sometimes called *style guide* programs, don't display the effects until you actually print the document.

About the Works Word Processor

The word processor in Works is very capable. In fact, next to the spreadsheet tool, it is the strongest module of Works. Even when compared to other stand-alone word processors, Works' word processor shines. If you are familiar with Microsoft Word, you will recognize the Works word processor since it is essentially Microsoft Word 2.0 minus a few of Word's more advanced features such as style sheets.

The Works word processor lets you create, edit, and print documents of any length easily. Formatting is one of its strongest points. The Works word processor sports a full complement of formatting commands for altering individual characters (such as bold, underlining, and italic), setting tabs, setting paragraph indents and margins, and defining your page headers. Many word processors only let you create a single set of paragraph and tab formats for each document. But the Works word processor lets you define individual formats for every paragraph. This powerful and convenient feature makes the creation of complex documents, such as a technical manual or any document with tabbed columns, indented quotations, and so on, much simpler.

You can also work with the Works word processor in *split-screen mode*, which lets you see and edit more than one document at a time. Each document gets its own portion of the screen, letting you easily cut and paste from one to the other. This feature is particularly useful for piecing together form letters, contracts, press releases, and so forth from existing documents.

Works can print out form letters or mailing labels using information from a Works database. In the case of form letters, the word processor inserts information from a database into predetermined spots in each letter as it is printed. Typically this would be used to personalize a letter with the recipient's name and address at the top of the letter, and perhaps elsewhere in the body. However, many other variations are possible, such as printing personalized invoices with lists of charges, a total amount due, terms of payment for each customer, and so forth.

The Works word processor is to some degree a WYSIWYG program. You will see on the screen just where each page begins and ends, and bold letters and underlining will appear as well. You can freely move blocks of text, insert text, and delete text, leaving the job of repagination to the program. And, incidentally, unlike Microsoft Word for the PC, page breaks are accurately calculated and shown on your screen so you know where the end of each page is. But there are a few things which will not display on your screen in the same way that they will print on paper. In particular, various typefaces and character attributes (italic, bold, underline), though indicated on-screen to some degree, will not appear until you actually print your documents.

To help uncover hidden typos, the Works word processor includes a rather intelligent built-in spelling checker. The checker can locate not only blatant spelling errors but mishyphenations, accidental word repetition (the the), and irregular or incorrect capitalizations as well. To supplement the large dictionary supplied with Works, you can create a personal dictionary that the word processor will reference when searching for misspellings.

One feature that all good word processors should have is an *undo* button — a sort of panic button. If you accidentally erase something or make a major change to a document that turns out for the worse, Works' undo command can reverse the change. It undoes the last change you made to your document's text or formatting.

Finally, when it comes to printing out your documents, the Works word processor can interact successfully with many different types and brands of printers, including some popular laser printers. Moreover, it will support the use of additional fonts (different kinds of typefaces such as Times, Courier, or Helvetica) if your printer is capable of producing different styles of type. This feature gives you a significant amount of control over the final look of printed documents.

Now that you have an overview of the Works word processor, let's take a look at what a spreadsheet can do.

About Spreadsheets

If you have ever seen an accountant poring over a wide notebook of green-ruled paper that has lots of columns and rows, you know what a spreadsheet is. Many businesses use these charts for keeping records of transactions, budgets, receivables, payables, general ledgers, and the like. Just as word processors are the electronic counterpart to the typewriter, computerized spreadsheets are the electronic version of an accountant's or manager's multicolumn accounting paper. Of course, the computation capabilities of the computer add some interesting twists.

Most spreadsheets are used to store numbers, and those numbers are usually part of some overall mathematical formula. Take a column of expenses, for example. Chances are the column is to be added, with a total appearing at the bottom. To arrive at the total, an accountant would normally sit down with a calculator and manually punch in the numbers to arrive at a total. But since a computer likes nothing better than to sit around adding, subtracting, and multiplying numbers, why not have the computerized spreadsheet do all the calculations? This is precisely what a microcomputer spreadsheet program does.

Introduced on microcomputers in the late 1970s, spreadsheets caught on like wildfire. VisiCalc on the Apple II became an overnight success and set the standard for some time. This program was largely responsible for the success of Apple Computer and their Apple II. Soon other spreadsheets such as SuperCalc, Microplan, and PerfectCalc appeared, each with its own merits. With the release of the IBM PC in 1981, and the introduction of Lotus 1-2-3 not long after, the third generation of spreadsheets was well underway.

A spreadsheet appears on the computer as a table of columns and rows. Each intersection of a column and a row creates a box called a *cell*. Cells are referenced by their location on the spreadsheet, such as A1 (column A, row 1) or G3 (column G, row 3). Each cell can hold a number and an optional formula. The formula is used to calculate the cell's numerical value with reference to other cells in the spreadsheet. For example, consider the following cells:

Columns			

	A	B	C	D
Row 1	12			
2	24			
3	56			
4	76			
5	21			
6	189			

Formula in cell A6 = A1+A2+A3+A4+A5

By entering the formula shown into cell A6, the spreadsheet could easily calculate the total of cells A1 through A5 and place the result into cell A6. Notice that formulas always reference other cells by their location. Also, spreadsheet programs generally do not display the formula in a cell but rather the result of the numerical calculation performed by the formula. Some programs will let you see both the formula and the value simultaneously. This useful feature serves as a reminder of the relationships between cells.

Beyond simple mathematical computations, the real power of the newer electronic spreadsheets derives from their many more advanced built-in functions. These functions allow the numbers in the spreadsheet to be used in analytical, trigonometric, and statistical modeling computations. Some perform date calculations as well. With the appearance of these additional capabilities, spreadsheets began to be used as what-if tools for sophisticated and rapid business analysis. As an example, if you change the data in any of cells A1 through A5 in the spreadsheet, the total in A6 will automatically change to reflect the alterations. With a complex spreadsheet containing many cells and formulas, say, a proposed annual budget for a business, you could quickly experiment with the bottom-line effect of altering key variables. This can be an invaluable aid in the corporate or even small-business decision-making process. This is precisely why electronic spreadsheets such as Lotus 1-2-3 have become so popular.

Spreadsheet programs vary widely in the number and type of functions they offer. Some are designed for business and financial analysis. Others excel at scientific and engineering problem solving. Some programs will let you link multiple spreadsheets together via formula cell references in each sheet. And some really expensive programs (often costing tens of thousands of dollars) let you hook your PC up to a mainframe computer to perform statistical analysis of very large databases.

Most spreadsheets will let you decide how you want the numbers in each cell to be displayed. For example, you may want dollar amounts to display the $ symbol. Or you may want figures to show a certain number of decimal places. Cells can also contain text information (called *labels*) rather than just numbers. Usually such labels would be the names of columns or rows. Without labels it is easy to forget what each cell's contents represent.

Spreadsheets also vary in the number of cells allowable. By and large, the spreadsheet size is dictated by the amount of RAM in your computer, since most programs require that your entire spreadsheet reside in RAM while you work with it.

About the Works Spreadsheet

The Works spreadsheet is Lotus 1-2-3 compatible in that it can directly read and work with spreadsheet files created with or for Lotus 1-2-3. The converse is also true; the Works spreadsheets can be transferred to 1-2-3. However, Works will not read in 1-2-3 macro or PIC (graph) files, though it does have its own internal charting to pick up the slack here. Also, Microsoft has a macro package designed to integrate nicely with Works so that you can repeat complex commands with a single keystroke.

In addition, the Works spreadsheet supports all the functions of 1-2-3 Version 1 and offers a few other functions as well, adding up to a total of 59. Other features such as numeric alignment and the use of different fonts and styles (such as bold, italic, and underline) when printing reports from spreadsheets are icing on the cake. Works spreadsheets can be as large as 256 columns by 4096 rows.

There are a few advanced features that the Works spreadsheet does not have. These include tables, distribution ranges, and automatic series and label-range justifications.

The Works spreadsheet includes a full range of editing commands similar to those in the word processor. You can add or delete columns or rows, or change their sizes or positions within the spreadsheet's matrix. You can sort the spreadsheet according to data in specific rows, and scroll though large spreadsheets (since all the data may not fit on the screen at the same time) while "freezing" the column and row names so as not to lose your reference points. You can also alternate between seeing the numeric values or the formula contents of cells.

As an aid while working on larger spreadsheets, you can split the screen to display up to four sections of the same worksheet simultaneously. Another command lets you decide whether to have the spreadsheet automatically recalculate its formulas every time you alter a cell's value or to wait until you have made all your changes first.

Finally, you can print out a wide variety of reports from your spreadsheets that can include all or just part of a given matrix of cells; can incorporate titles or descriptive phrases; and can use various typefaces and font sizes, as well as other printer attributes such as boldface, italics, and underlining on dot matrix, daisywheel, or laser printers. And, of course, as with 1-2-3, Works can print charts. Bar, line, pie, and scatter charts can be viewed on screen or printed with borders, legends, and labels of various types.

About Databases

A database is really nothing more than a list of items you want to remember. In fact, most of us use databases everyday, but we just don't call them by that name. Encyclopedias, telephone books, and shopping lists are examples of everyday databases. Just as with electronic spreadsheets and word processors, the difference between a computer database and one on paper is convenience. With a computer you can rearrange the items in the list by sorting them or you can quickly search through the list to find specific items. The computer is very fast at this kind of searching, even with a big database.

Computer databases are typically used in business environments for customer lists, inventory management, transaction records, and the like. However, there is no reason not to use a database for household tasks such as organizing phone numbers or holiday card mailing lists.

Information in a database is stored in columns and rows, a layout similar to that of a spreadsheet. The main difference is that the columns are called *fields* and the rows are called *records*. You might think of each field as a category, and each record as a separate entry in the list. For example, consider a typical telephone book. The fields and records of a database are laid out in a manner similar to the illustration on the next page.

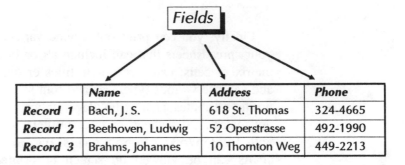

	Name	Address	Phone
Record 1	Bach, J. S.	618 St. Thomas	324-4665
Record 2	Beethoven, Ludwig	52 Operstrasse	492-1990
Record 3	Brahms, Johannes	10 Thornton Weg	449-2213

In this example, the three fields are Name, Address, and Phone. Each entry (or person) in the book constitutes one record.

As opposed to the cells in spreadsheets, database fields are designed to let you easily find a particular piece of information quickly. If you need to look up a particular phone number or see a list of everyone who lives in a certain city, a computerized database can quickly provide you with the correct information. A database's fields are simply pigeonholes for storing information rather than for performing calculations as the cells of a spreadsheet. Think of a database as analogous to a filing cabinet, whereas a spreadsheet is more like a sophisticated calculator.

Database programs vary widely in their capacities for holding data. Some can handle enormous quantities of information. Others have strict limitations. Also, the maximum size of each record and the size of each field may be constrained by certain limitations. Some more sophisticated programs will allow you to link or join separate databases temporarily or permanently, to achieve the effect of a larger database, or to pull out only selected subsets of data from one database to create an entirely new one altogether. Finally, a few database programs include what is called a programming language. With a programming language, you can design database systems to perform very specific tasks such as managing your business accounts or recording sales as they are transacted in a store. Ashton-Tate's well-known dBASE II and III include programming languages, as do Microrim's R:base and Ansa's Paradox, to name a couple.

Of course, any database program worth its salt will allow you to print out your data on paper in a variety of formats, selectively showing only desired records and fields and even performing calculations such as totals and subtotals in the process of creating the report.

About the Works Database

The Works database allows you to have up to 4096 records in each document. In addition, you may have up to 256 fields in each record. For everyday uses, 256 fields is quite a lot. Unfortunately, 4096 is a relatively small number of records compared to other databases for the PC which will typically allow 64,000 or even one million records.

As is common practice among database programs, Works gives you two ways of working with and viewing the data in a document: a *forms* view, where you look at one record at a time in a layout of your own design, and a *list* view, where you see records and fields displayed in columns and rows, much like a spreadsheet. Custom forms can be up to eight screens long. Entering, editing, and viewing of records can be done in either view, and specific fields can be "locked" to prevent accidental erasure or alteration of important data. Certain fields can also be set up as calculated fields (just like a cell in a spreadsheet), rendering the contents of the field the result of a mathematical calculation based on data in other fields of the same record.

You can sort your data in a wide variety of ways, for instance so that your listings come out in alphabetical or numerical order, and can also query the database. Querying lets you ask Works to search through the database for certain records that meet specific criteria. For example, you may want to list all people whose last names fall between the letters *C* and *M* and who live in Sioux City. The records that fit the search are then displayed while the remainder of the records are hidden from view. Works has some powerful querying capabilities that are relatively easy to master, and queries can be saved for later use as well. If you have used Excel's or Lotus 1-2-3's database, you will find the Works database is similar but slightly more flexible in this regard.

About Communications

The last major tool of Works is *communications*. Communications refers to the ability of computers to send various types of data, whether it be word processing files, spreadsheets, databases, reports, or even graphics to another computer in a different location. This type of transmission is usually achieved via telephone lines hooked up to the computers at each end using special cables and adapters called *modems* (which is short for modulator/demodulator).

With the help of the right software and modems, it is possible to create a report or letter on your computer at home and send it to the office in your same city, or even across the globe in a matter of minutes. In fact, electronic mail services, such as MCI Mail, are being used by thousands of customers in just this way every day. Why wait for the postal service to deliver a letter or pay an overnight courier service ten or twenty dollars to deliver a letter you could send instantly over the phone for less?

In addition, there now exist numerous telephone-based information services that you can tap into using your computer and modem. These services can provide innumerable types of information, from on-line encyclopedias to airline flight schedules. You can even purchase a car or do your banking without leaving your easy chair.

Good communications programs help to make all these processes easier. Since connecting to one of these services usually requires dialing the phone and typing in a password, many programs can set up an automatic dialer to do this for you. This feature, often called *auto log-on,* eliminates having to remember the password and having to type it in each time. Another important feature of communications programs is the ability to perform error checking on files as you send or receive them. Since telephone lines were designed for voice and not computer data, noise on the line can interfere with the information you are sending or receiving. Error checking ensures that your data is transmitted cleanly and without loss of integrity.

Finally, some packages do what is known as *terminal emulation*. This feature temporarily turns your computer into a computer terminal like those used with minicomputers or mainframe computers. A terminal is basically just a keyboard and a TV screen, rather than a full-fledged computer like your PC. Using terminal emulation for one of the popular brands and models of terminals allows you to dial up larger computer systems and work on them just as if you were using the terminal that your computer is emulating.

About Works Communications

The Works communications tool supports binary and text file transmission and terminal emulation. Error checking for file transfers utilizes the popular XModem protocol developed for CP/M computers by the microcomputer folk hero Ward Christensen and placed in the public domain in 1977. Using XModem means that you can effectively insure data integrity when transmitting to or receiving from anyone else using this protocol. Since many other microcomputer communications programs support XModem, the chances are good that you will be able to connect to a remote computer and successfully transfer files. For cases where no error checking is done (for example: MCI Mail or CompuServe in nonprotocol mode), Works lets you turn off the XModem feature.

Auto log-on is supported too, as is terminal emulation of the popular DEC VT 100 and DEC VT 52 terminals. Also, since sending large data files across a modem and telephone line can often take quite a bit of time (particularly when using slower-speed modems), Works lets you start the process of sending or receiving a file and then go back to work using another Works tool. The communications program takes care of the rest.

The nature of the Works environment allows for some other interesting communications capabilities. In addition to being able to send and receive existing files stored on disk, you can also select a document or portion of a document which is currently open and in progress. For example, while working on a spreadsheet, database, or word processing document, you can select just a portion of it to be sent to another computer.

MOVING AHEAD

Don't be alarmed if some of the details just discussed went over your head. The purpose of this book is to explain and give you hands-on experience with all the features and capabilities just mentioned. In the following chapters, you'll be introduced to the Works tools one at a time, and then you will learn how to use them together.

At this point you at least have a general idea of what Works can do, and may already have some ideas about what you want it to do for you. However, if you're like the many users who looked at the 700-page Works manual and balked, chances are you haven't yet installed Works into your computer. If this is the case, you should now move on to Chapter 2, "Getting Set Up." Chapter 2 will take you through the steps of setting up Works for your computer and making working disks of the program. It also covers the essential details of printer installation and "mouse" installation.

If you have already installed the program according to instructions in the manual supplied by Microsoft, you may want to skip Chapter 2 and move ahead to Chapter 3, where you will learn the basic skills required for using Works.

Chapter

Getting Set Up

Two

Before you can use Microsoft Works and follow the lessons in this book, you'll have to do a little preparation. In a nutshell, this preparation amounts to the following:

- Running the Setup program

- Making sure your printer — if you have one — is hooked up properly

- Making sure your mouse — if you plan to use one with Works — is connected too

If you have already set up Works for your computer by following the installation procedures described in the manual supplied with Works, you can skip this chapter and move on to Chapter 3, "Getting Oriented." Otherwise you should follow the steps described here.

A note about system requirements: Before going any further, you should make sure that your computer is actually capable of running Works. Please refer to the final section of Appendix A to determine whether your computer meets the necessary requirements. In addition to the hardware requirements listed there, the operating system you are using must be MS-DOS or PC-DOS 2.00 or later. If you are using a pre-2.00 version, you should get an upgrade from your computer dealer before continuing.

RUNNING THE SETUP PROGRAM

Works comes from Microsoft on two sets of disks. One set consists of eight 5-1/4 inch floppy disks. The other set is on four 3-1/2 inch disks. Which disks you'll use depends on the type of disk drive(s) your computer has. The majority of computers use the 5-1/4 inch type of disks; these are labeled as shown in the following table:

Disk Name	Contains
Program disk	The Works program
Setup disk	The Setup program
Learning Works	Computer Based Tutorial disk 1
Learning Works	Computer Based Tutorial disk 2
Learning Works	Computer Based Tutorial disk 3
Spell/Help	Spelling checker and on-screen help files
Text printers	Information that lets Works print text
Chart printers	Information that lets Works print charts

Each disk has elements of the Works program that will need to be assembled onto a working disk from which you will run Works. If your computer has a hard disk, the working disk will be your hard disk. If your computer doesn't have a hard disk, several working disks will be created on floppies.

Luckily, the Setup program makes a simple task of this, with just a little interaction on your part. The Setup program copies the Works program and information about your screen and printer from the various floppy disks onto your working disk. It also copies some other files — notably the spelling checker dictionary, the Help information, and the Computer Based Tutorial information — onto your working disk.

Incidentally, the Setup program also lets you modify an existing working disk in case you decide to use a different screen or printer later on.

Getting Ready to Run Setup

Before you begin, you'll need to gather together a few disks and some information so you can get your computer running and then tell the Setup program what kind of screen and printer you have. First, be sure you have the Works disks and that you know

- ♦ The make and model of your printer

- ♦ The type of screen controller card (video card) your computer has

If you have a floppy disk system, you will also need the following:

- ♦ One blank floppy disk (either formatted or unformatted) for creating your working disk

- ♦ Four formatted disks which you will use to make working copies of the Spelling/Help disk and the three Computer Based Tutorial disks

- ♦ One additional blank formatted floppy disk for storing the documents you will prepare during the course of this book

(If you do not know how to format blank disks, don't worry. The Setup program will format the disks for you if yours aren't formatted. However, since you'll need to format other disks later in order to save the documents you create, you should consult your DOS manual, under the Format command, to learn about this process. Also, the instructions here assume that you are using 5-1/4 inch disks. If your system uses 3-1/2 inch disks, then your steps will be only slightly different. You should refer to the Works manual for details.)

If you have a hard disk, you will not need the extra floppy disks, but you will have to decide what directory you want to store the Works files in. Normally this is C:\WORKS, but you can use another directory if you want.

Starting the Setup Program

The next section is divided into two parts — one part for floppy disk systems, the other for hard disk systems — and explains all the steps necessary for running the Setup program. You should follow only the instructions that apply to your type of computer system.

Floppy Disk Systems

To run the Setup program on a floppy disk system, take the following steps:

1. Turn on your computer and load DOS in the usual way. Consult your computer's manual if you do not know how to do this.

2. Insert the Setup disk, into drive A.

3. Type

   SETUP ↵

4. The Setup program will begin. Because the Setup program is self-explanatory, there's not much sense in covering each step here. We'll just touch on some general points.

   ♦ When prompted, choose floppy drive B as the drive on which you want to create the working disk.

   ♦ Simply follow the instructions that you see on the screen and answer the various questions about your printer and your video card.

   ♦ If you do not have a printer, you still have to choose one from the list. It doesn't matter which one. (If you have questions about selecting a printer, refer to the Works manual's Appendix B, about printers.)

- ♦ You'll also have to choose a printer port. You should probably use LPT1 so you do not interfere with a modem or mouse that may be connected to the COM1 or COM2 port.

- ♦ Insert and remove disks as prompted.

5. When the Setup program is finished, you will have several working disks.

   - ♦ Works program disk

   - ♦ Spell/Help disk

   - ♦ Learning Works disk number 1

   - ♦ Learning Works disk number 2

   - ♦ Learning Works disk number 3

   Label them accordingly, using a felt-tip pen (not a ballpoint pen or pencil since pressing on the disks can damage them).

6. Gather up your eight original Works disks and store them somewhere safe. You'll use the working disks to run the Works program, ensuring that if something should happen to the working copies, you still have the original disks to fall back on.

   Now skip the section about hard disk systems and move ahead to read about hooking up your printer and (if you have one) your mouse.

Hard Disk Systems

If you have a hard disk system, follow these instructions to install Works on your hard disk. (We assume that you have DOS on the hard disk and that your hard disk is drive C. Substitute a different drive letter if necessary.)

1. Turn on your computer and load DOS in the usual way. Consult your computer's manual if you do not know how to do this.

2. Insert the Setup disk, into drive A.

3. Type

   SETUP ↵

4. The Setup program will begin. Because the Setup program is self-explanatory, there's not much sense in covering each step here. We'll just touch on some general points.

   ♦ To accommodate Works, the spelling dictionary, the Help files, and the Computer Based Tutorial, you must have a fair amount of unused space on your hard disk. If you don't have enough space available, the Setup program will tell you. Then you will have to erase some of the files on the hard disk and run Setup again.

   ♦ Choose \WORKS as the directory when that option appears, unless you want to use another directory to store your Works files. Examples in this book assume you've chosen \WORKS.

   ♦ Simply follow the instructions that you see on the screen and answer the various questions about your printer and your video card.

   ♦ If you do not have a printer, you still have to choose one from the list. It doesn't matter which one. (If you have questions about selecting a printer, refer to the Works manual's Appendix B, about printers.) You'll also have to choose a printer port. You should probably use LPT1 so you do not interfere with a modem or mouse that may be connected to the COM1 or COM2 ports.

   ♦ Insert and remove disks as prompted.

5. When finished, you will have created a working disk in the \WORKS directory on drive C, and be returned to the DOS prompt. Now collect all the Works floppy disks and put them away in a safe place.

HOOKING UP YOUR PRINTER

If you intend to follow the printing examples in this book, and to later print out other documents you've created with Works, you'll want to insure that your printer is hooked up correctly before continuing.

If you've already used your printer with other programs and it appears to be operating correctly, then there's nothing to worry about, and you can skip this section. But, if you are in doubt as to whether your printer is functioning properly, try this simple test.

1. Turn on your printer, make sure it has paper, and be certain it is *on-line* (sometimes called *selected*) and hooked up to the printer port of the computer. Most printers have a switch for putting the printer on-line or off-line.

2. Insert your Works program working disk in drive A (if you have a floppy system) or get onto drive C (if you have a hard disk system).

3. Get to either the A> or C> prompt (for floppy or hard disks, respectively) and press CTRL - P. (Hold down the CTRL key and press the P key.)

4. Now type

   DIR ↵

   A directory listing should print out, and it should look like the listing you see on your screen. If it doesn't, your best bet is to refer to the printer appendix in the Works manual where a discussion of ports, cables, configuration switches, and protocols may clear up the problem.

5. Press CTRL-P again to turn off the printing.

HOOKING UP YOUR MOUSE

Works lets you use a mouse with your computer if you have one. Using a mouse with Works simplifies the steps needed to use commands, make selections, and move things around on the screen. If you do not have a mouse, just skip this section and move to Chapter 3, "Getting Oriented."

Mouse Compatibility

Works is compatible with the Microsoft bus mouse or the Microsoft serial mouse or any other brands of mice that are direct replacements for these. For a mouse to work with Works, however, you'll have to see to it that your computer loads the proper mouse *driver* when you boot up the computer. Exactly how this is done depends on the brand of mouse you have, so you should refer to your mouse's instruction manual. If you have already been using a mouse successfully with other programs, then you probably don't have to do anything more.

If you haven't installed your mouse and mouse driver already, generally speaking the technique is as outlined here.

1. Copy the mouse driver (typically called MOUSE.SYS) onto your DOS startup disk using the DOS COPY command.

2. Then, using a word processor, create or modify your startup disk's CONFIG.SYS file to include the line

   DEVICE=MOUSE.SYS

   (This CONFIG.SYS file has to be on your startup disk.)

3. Make sure the mouse is connected to the correct port or connector.

4. Reboot your computer, and the mouse driver is loaded.

When you run Works, it will automatically sense whether you have a mouse connected. It will then alter the screen accordingly to let you scroll through documents, select commands, and so forth. We will present specific tips for using the mouse in each chapter as we go along.

Now you're ready to run Works. Please move ahead to Chapter 3, "Getting Oriented."

Chapter

Getting Oriented

Three

As mentioned in Chapter 1, the four tools of Works are integrated with one another. This integration is achieved through the program's use of a common environment that works the same way for all the tools. The word *environment* refers to the way Works manages your computer's resources such as RAM, disk drives, and printer. And more importantly, it refers to how Works displays information on the screen, and the way you interact with the program, giving it commands and typing in your information. It also means how Works keeps you apprised of what's going on. And of course, as mentioned in Chapter 1, the fact that Works' tools use a common environment also means that you can pull together bits of material that you've created in several tools, producing a single finished document.

In this chapter, you'll be introduced to the Works environment, learning the rudiments of getting around from tool to tool, and understanding the basic feel of the program. You'll also learn about the computer keyboard, how to get help when you need it, how to use menus and dialog boxes, and how to work with files on your floppy or hard disk. Once you have the basics under your belt, you'll be ready to move ahead and begin undertaking useful projects with Works, but you should read this chapter first. Otherwise, you may not understand the instructions in the rest of this book.

THE KEYBOARD

For starters, we'll have to talk about your computer's keyboard and how Works uses the special keys on it. This book uses the IBM PC/XT and Compaq personal computers as its standard for key locations and names and illustrating the keyboard layout. Chances are that your computer's keyboard is very similar, if not identical, to this standard. If you have another kind of keyboard, including those supplied with the IBM AT and compatibles, or are using the newer IBM keyboards, your key placement will differ. Please refer to the operations manual for your computer if you have trouble locating specific keys.

For the most part, Works follows well-established traditions for the PC when it comes to the keys you'll use to control the program. If you've used your PC even a little bit before, and know your way around a few other programs, you'll be able to learn Works quickly, especially with the assistance of the on-screen help and tutorials that are built-in.

Your computer's keyboard is essentially identical to that of a typewriter. All the letter and number keys are in exactly the same locations as you'd expect, though a few punctuation marks might be rearranged a bit (see Figure 3-1). The only real difference between a typewriter and your computer keyboard is the addition of some extra keys, each of which has its own purpose, or in some cases, multiple purposes. If you are not already familiar with your PC's keyboard, please read the following section, which details the use of these extra keys.

Function Keys

On the far left side of the keyboard you will see 10 keys labeled F1 to F10. The F stands for function. The effect of pressing a given function key will vary, depending on which tool you are using at the time, but there are some consistencies between tools. Pressing F1 will always display the *help* index,

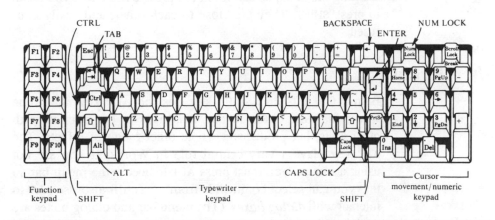

Figure 3-1. *The computer keyboard*

dishing up some helpful information about the process you are currently undertaking. Similarly, F2 is often the *edit* key, which allows you to make changes to database and spreadsheet data.

The CONTROL Key

The CTRL (short for CONTROL) key, located just to the right of the F6 key, is similar in operation to the SHIFT key, in that it is always used in conjunction with some other key on the keyboard. To get a capital letter using the SHIFT key, you have to hold down the SHIFT key, and then press the letter you want capitalized. The CTRL key is used the same way, only with different results. The CTRL key is used extensively within Works. Sometimes the CTRL key is even used with more than one other key at the same time. For example, when using the spreadsheet tool, pressing the CTRL key followed by the SHIFT key and a semicolon (which we write in abbreviated form as CTRL-SHIFT-;) enters the current date into a cell. The important thing to remember is that for the CTRL key to work, you must press it first, and hold it down. Then you press the second and/or third keys, as indicated in whichever exercise you are working on. Also, be careful not to press CTRL when you mean to press SHIFT. They are close to each other, and easily confused.

The ALT Key

Below the left-hand SHIFT key lies the ALT key. This one works just like CTRL, in that it is used in conjunction with other keys, but produces a whole other range of effects. The ALT key plays a very central role in Works. If you are not using a mouse, you must press ALT to access the menu bar so that you can select commands from it. You'll also use ALT to interact with *dialog boxes*. (The menu bar and dialog boxes are explained later in this chapter.)

The ESCAPE key

Just to the right of the F2 key is a key labeled ESC, short for ES-CAPE. Pressing the ESC key lets you back out of, or escape from, a choice you have made in Works. For example, when a menu or prompt is displayed, pressing this key returns you to the previous step. Think of the ESCAPE key as the cancel, or backup key.

The ENTER Key

The ENTER key is located three keys to the right of the *L*. Represented in this book as ⏎, this key has several effects, depending on what you are doing. In general, it tells the computer to accept what you have typed in. Think of it as the "go-ahead" key. A few examples may help clarify its use.

- ♦ If a menu is displayed, press ⏎ to select the menu option you have highlighted (lit up in bright letters).

- ♦ If you are entering data into a cell of a spreadsheet or a field of a database, press ⏎ to finalize the entry.

With the word processor and communications tool, it moves the cursor down one line.

Your ENTER key may be labeled ENTER, RETURN, or CR (Carriage Return), or it may have the bent arrow symbol ↵ on it. When shown as part of your input, it is represented as ↵.

The Cursor Keys

To the right side of the keyboard, there is a block of numbered keys, called cursor keys. The 8, 4, 2, and 6 keys have arrows on them. These keys control the movement of the cursor, letting you move it around on your computer's screen, to highlight menu options, type in commands, or enter data. Thus, you can think of the arrow keys as navigation keys. They are often used in tandem with other keys, particularly the CTRL key, which usually amplifies or exaggerates the effect of the arrow keys, moving you farther or faster in a given direction within a document. In this book, these keys will be referred to as →, ←, ↑, ↓.

The BACKSPACE Key

Not to be confused with the ← key is the BACKSPACE key. This key also usually has a left-pointing arrow on it, though the arrow is hollow and larger than that of the ← key. Unlike the ← key, this key does more than just move the cursor to the left; it also erases the letters you backspace over. It's just like a self-correcting IBM Selectric typewriter. Be careful with this key because it can erase valuable information in your documents if you use it when you don't intend to.

END, HOME, PAGE UP, and PAGE DOWN Keys

Notice that the 1, 7, 9, and 3 keys in the numeric keypad are labeled as END, HOME, PGUP, and PGDN, respectively. These keys move the cursor around in a document in larger jumps than the arrow keys do. Instead of moving one letter at a time, for example, they may move a whole screen at a time or from the beginning to the end of a document. For example, in the word processor, HOME and END move to the beginning and end of a line of text, respectively. CTRL-HOME and CTRL-END move to the beginning and to the end of the document, respectively. PGUP and PGDN simply move the text up or down one screenful at a time, a bit like turning the pages of a book.

If Your Arrow Keys Are Printing Numbers

If you find that your cursor keys do not work properly, and they type numbers instead of having the expected effect, press the NUM LOCK key once. This activates the cursor keys.

Keys Repeat

One final note about the keyboard. Almost all the keys on the keyboard are repeating keys. If you hold down a key more than about one second, it will begin to repeat. You want to be careful not to accidentally press down a key for too long, lest unpredictable results occur, such as the name Sally Smiiiiiith showing up in a document, or even something worse happening if you hold down, say, the BACKSPACE key.

BRINGING UP WORKS

Now let's actually fire up Works and take a look around. Here's how to do it. First make sure you've run the Setup program as explained in Chapter 2. Then, depending upon your system, you follow certain steps. If you have a floppy disk system, do the following:

1. Insert a DOS disk in Drive A and turn on your computer.

2. After you see the A> prompt, remove the DOS disk.

3. Insert the working copy of your Works disk in Drive A and a formatted data disk in Drive B.

4. Type

WORKS ↵.

The Works copyright information and sign-on screen will appear.

If you have a hard disk system, perform the following steps instead:

1. Turn on your computer and wait until you see the C> prompt.

2. Now move to the directory you installed Works into (normally /Works), using the DOS CD command. For instance:

CD/WORKS ↵

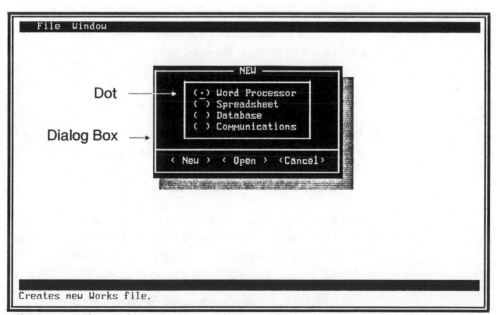

Figure 3-2. *The Works opening screen lets you select a tool*

3. Type

WORKS ↵

The Works sign-on screen will appear as in Figure 3-2.

The sign-on screen is your starting place each time you bring up the Works program for a session or when you want to open a new document. From this screen, you choose which of the four tools you want to work with—word processor, spreadsheet, database, or communications. You choose which of the tools you want by typing the first letter of its name or by pressing the arrow keys until the round dot (o) is positioned in front of the tool you want. After the dot is in the right place, press ↵.

If you are using a mouse, point at your choice and click the mouse's left button to make the selection. Then you have to click on the word <New> in the lower section of the box.

In any case, once you make a choice, the sign-on screen disappears, bringing up the selected tool, with its own screen.

Opening a Word Processing Document

For an example of what happens next, open the word processor tool now by following these steps:

1. Select the word processor tool by pressing the letter **W**.

2. Press ↵ to open a new document. Or, if you are using a mouse, simply click on the space between the ( ) next to the words Word Processor. Then click on < New >. The screen now changes to the image you see in Figure 3-3.

Regardless of which tool you are using, the basic screen layout is the same, and includes four primary elements: the menu bar, work area, the message line, and the status line.

- ◆ **Menu Bar** The menu bar at the top of the screen is central to the operation of PC-Works. It is called a menu bar because each of the words on the bar, when activated, opens up to reveal a list of possible subselections from which you can choose. It's a little like opening up a restaurant menu, perusing the choices, and then ordering something.

- **Work Area**   The work area is where you'll be doing most of your work, such as entering and editing text, creating spreadsheets, and so forth. Everything outside of the work area is used for controlling or modifying your data in the work area, for moving around within it, or to keep you informed of things.

- **Status Line**   The status line always displays information about the file that you are currently working on, such as its name and the mode of operation you are in. At this point, the status line has WORD1.WPS on it, which is temporarily the name of your current word processing document until you rename it. It also displays the message 1/1. We'll cover the meaning of this in Chapter 4, "Using the

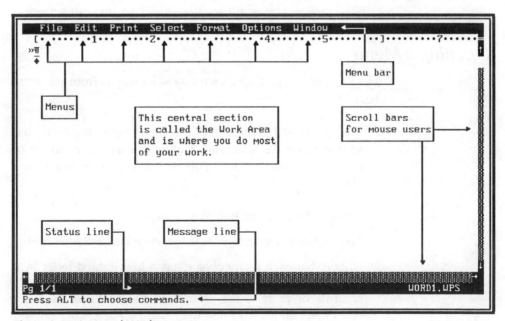

Figure 3-3. *A typical Works screen*

Works Word Processor," but keep in mind that the status line is used by Works to keep you informed of a variety of alterable variables within each of the tools.

◆ **Message Line** Just below the status line lies the message line. Here you will always see a one-line instruction about what commands you can use, and what steps to take next. Sometimes other helpful hints will show up here too. The messages on this line will often change as you move around within Works, so it's a good idea to look at it frequently. It will often help explain what is happening and thus may help prevent possible confusion.

◆ **Scroll Bars** If you are using a mouse, Works will automatically include another feature on your screen: the *scroll bars*. The scroll bars are located on the right and bottom edges of the work area. These are used for quickly and easily moving around within your documents with the mouse. The details of these will be explained in Chapter 4. If you aren't using a mouse, you won't see the scroll bars on your screen.

Opening a Menu

Here's how to open up a menu by selecting it from the menu bar.

1. First press ALT. This moves the cursor up to the menu bar, so you can make selections. Notice that the menu on the far left, File, is highlighted. This means the menu bar is now active.

2. Look at the message line. It now says:

Type highlighted letter of menu or use arrow keys and press ENTER

Notice that each menu choice has a highlighted letter in it. (If it doesn't look that way, try adjusting your monitor's controls or refer to the section on the SETTINGS dialog box in Appendix A.) Press the corresponding letter on your

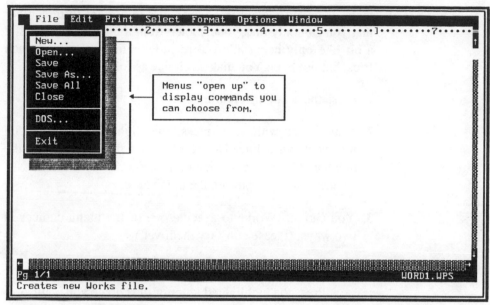

Figure 3-4. A typical menu

keyboard and that menu will open up to reveal a number of commands.

3. Press the F key. The File menu now opens to show the File commands arranged in a vertical list as in Figure 3-4. Now try pressing the → key and notice that you'll see the next menu over, the Edit menu. This is an easy way to see what's on all the menus. If you had wanted to get immediately to the second menu (Edit) without seeing the File menu, you would have just pressed ALT and then E.

If you have a mouse, you open menus in a slightly different way. Simply move the mouse until the square cursor is on the menu choice you want. Then click and hold down the left button.

Making a Menu Choice

Once you have a menu open, how do you order something from it? Selecting something you want Works to do from a menu is called *making a choice*. It's important to remember that you can only make one choice from a menu at a time. It's a bit like only being allowed to order a milkshake or french fries, but not both. You make a choice as follows:

1. Press the ↓ key several times.

2. Notice that with each press, the highlight in the menu moves down a line. Notice also that the message on the message line tells you what each menu choice is for. This is an easy way of exploring the menu choices.

3. You can tell Works to execute one of the menu choices in two ways. (Please don't try them yet.)

   ♦ Highlight it as you just did and then press ↵.

   ♦ Press the highlighted letter of the choice you want. This second technique is much faster, but you don't

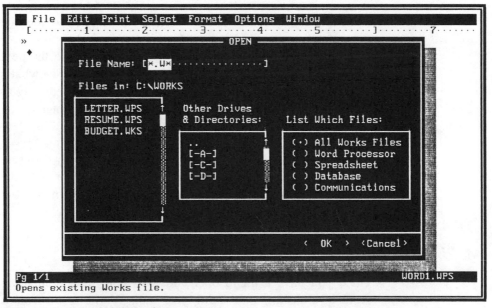

Figure 3-5. *A typical dialog box*

have the advantage of seeing a description of what each command is for before making your choice.

4. If you are using a mouse, notice that as you move the cursor down the choices within the menu, that they become highlighted, one at a time, and a description of what each command is for shows up on the message line. To actually make a choice, you simply move the pointer down to the choice you want and release the button.

Of course, all this may make little sense to you since we haven't yet discussed what all the commands in each menu are for. But don't worry about that now. At this point we're only concerned with learning the steps involved in opening menus and making choices, not what those choices actually do. The whole range of menu names and each menu's command selections will be covered in detail in the chapters covering each tool of Works.

5. Now, using one of the techniques just outlined, make sure you have the File menu showing and then choose the Open command. A large box of information appears, as you see in Figure 3-5. (Your screen may look a little bit different.) This is called a *dialog box*.

ABOUT DIALOG BOXES

Dialog boxes will appear often while you use Works. They typically ask you to make some certain choice about the work you are doing with a tool, and are thus a sort of dialog between you and Works.

Some menu choices use dialog boxes; some do not. Three dots after a command name in the menu (see Figure 3- 4) indicate that there will be a dialog box. Commands without the dots after them do not entail another step.

Dialog boxes come in a variety of types and sizes, and differ in the way you respond to their prompts. But they all have certain elements in common. As you saw in Figure 3-5, a dialog box can have several basic sections. There are five types of dialog box sections each used for controlling Works in different ways. These sections are illustrated in Figure 3-6.

♦ **Text Boxes** These are areas where you are asked to type in some information. This information can be words, such as file names, or numbers.

♦ **Option Boxes** These areas contain choices that are mutually exclusive. That is, you can only have one of the options selected at a time. You may recognize this type of choice from the sign-on screen from which you select the tool you want to work with. You are simply asked to fill certain sets of parentheses ( ) with a dot. Putting a dot between a pair of parentheses is like putting an X in a box on a survey or test form on paper. Thus, a dot means Yes. No dot means No.

♦ **List Boxes** Sometimes there are more items than would fit into a dialog box, or

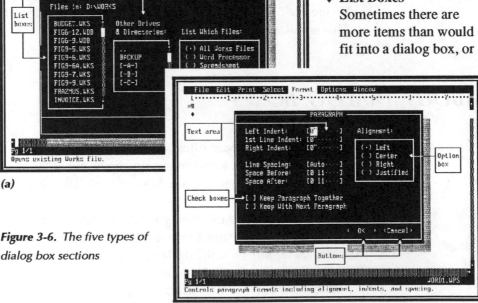

(a)

Figure 3-6. The five types of dialog box sections

(b)

lists of items that change from time to time. Works displays these in a list box. In Figure 3-6(a), there are two list boxes, one for selecting a file and the other for selecting drives and directories. List boxes from other dialog boxes may contain items such as printer fonts and sizes, or the types of printers you can use.

♦ **Check Boxes** These are like on-off switches, letting you decide whether you want Works to do something or not. These are a lot like the options in an option box, but you can set as many on (or off) as you want. This means you can turn on multiple check boxes combining their effects.

♦ **Buttons** Buttons usually appear at the bottom of a dialog box, and ask you whether you want the other settings you've made to be carried out or not. Normally they say <OK> or <Cancel>, though other buttons say things like <Replace All> or <Set>.

How to Move Between Sections of a Dialog Box

Before you can alter a setting in a section, you have to jump the cursor to it. There are two ways to do this.

1. First, if the OPEN dialog box (from the last section) isn't still on your screen, open the File menu and choose Open.

2. The easiest way to jump between sections is by using ALT. Press it now and hold it down. This causes certain letters to become highlighted on your screen.

3. Keeping ALT depressed, press the letter F. Notice that the cursor jumps to the Files section of the box. Press ALT-O and it jumps to the Other Drives section.

4. Try the second approach now. Press the TAB key (to the left of the Q key) to move in a sequential manner from one section to the next. Each time you press TAB, it moves the cursor to the next block of items for selection. This technique is

more clumsy because you can lose track of where the cursor is more easily, and the tabbing order of boxes isn't always intuitively clear.

5. Now type ALT-A to jump to the option box. Once there, you can use the ↓ and ↑ keys or press ALT-W, ALT-S, ALT-D or ALT-C keys to choose which option you want.

Making Choices from Each Section of a Dialog Box

Once you've jumped to the correct section, you'll need to know how to make choices from it. Here is a list explaining how to use the other sections.

- **Text Boxes** Type in the text from the keyboard. Sometimes there will be text already typed in for you. If you want to keep it as is, just jump to another section. If you want to alter it, you can do so by typing in new text. If the word in the text box is highlighted, whatever you type will replace the highlighted text. If it is not highlighted, you can use the arrow keys, the BACKSPACE key, and the DEL key to edit it.

- **Option Boxes** Press ALT plus a letter, or use ↑ and ↓.

- **List Boxes** Press ↓. This highlights the first choice in the box. Then use ↓ and ↑ to move to the item you want. You can jump to the end of the list by pressing END, to the top of the list by pressing HOME. You can jump through the list a section at a time by pressing PGUP or PGDN. You can also jump directly to an item by typing its first letter.

- **Check Boxes** The quickest way to check boxes is to use the associated ALT key. An alternative is to move to the check box and press the spacebar. When turned on, an X appears in between the square brackets, like this: [X]. Press the spacebar again, and the X disappears, indicating that the item is turned off.

♦ **Buttons** Remember, buttons tell Works what to do next. Buttons can be selected several ways. There will always be one button whose brackets < > are highlighted. This is the button that will take effect when you press ↵. There is usually another button called Cancel. This is the button that will be activated when you press ESC. Dialog boxes that have additional buttons can be selected using ALT key combinations.

Additional Notes for Mouse Users

The techniques listed in the previous section will work even if you're using a mouse. However, a mouse makes interaction with dialog boxes easier. Most sections are as simple to use as clicking on them. List boxes, however, are a little more complex. You may note that they have their own little scroll bars that you can use to look through long lists. Position the cursor on the little arrows at either end of the scroll bar, click, and hold. The list will now scroll. Or, you can "grab" the small box in the scroll bar, click, and hold the mouse button down, and "drag" the box up or down in the bar. Then release the mouse button. The list will scroll in an amount proportional to the distance you dragged the box.

SHORTHAND NOTATION FOR MAKING SELECTIONS

From now on, throughout this book, we'll use a shorthand notation for telling you which menus, menu selections, and dialog box selections to make. This will save you time and the hassle of reading through lots of repetitive instructions.

Here's how the shorthand works, illustrated by a simple example.

Instead of saying:

1. Open the File menu now by pointing to it and clicking, or by pressing ALT and then F.

2. Now choose New from the menu by highlighting it and clicking or by pressing ↵.

We'll say this instead:

1. Choose File/New.

This simply means "Open the File menu and select New." This much simpler approach will leave us more room in the book for real exercises and examples with Works rather than cluttering it up with repetition. But it will be up to you to remember the shorthand.

As you know, the exact method you use to make these choices depends on whether you have a mouse or not, and whether you prefer to use the arrow keys or the first letters of the menu names and menu commands. For the remainder of this book, and as you continue to use Works, choose whichever method or methods you feel most comfortable with. Since Works was designed to let you do things a number of different ways, it's really up to you. Even if you do have a mouse, for example, you can use any of the keyboard commands whenever you want. As we work along through the tutorials in each section, you'll soon find what works best for you.

SWITCHING BETWEEN WINDOWS

Up on the menu bar, at the far right, you'll notice the word *Window*. When you have multiple documents open at the same time, each is stored in what's called a window; hence, the menu name. The Window menu lets you jump between various types of documents that you can be working on more or less at the same time. For instance, you can jump from a letter to the database, then into a spreadsheet, do a little communications over the telephone with your modem, then jump back to the word processor right where you left off writing your letter. You could even have several of the same types of document open simultaneously, such as two letters, a report, and a memo. Try these steps to see how you can easily jump back and forth between windows in Works.

1. First, open the Window menu. Notice that in the bottom part of the menu is the line:

   1 WORD1.WPS

   The bottom section of this menu always lists the names of the documents that are currently open, and to which you can jump.

2. There is only one choice here since you only have one document (the WORD1 word processing one) open. Back out of the menu by pressing ESC (or moving up to the top of the menu and releasing the button if you have a mouse).

3. Now let's open a new file to jump to. Select File/New.

4. Choose Word Processor from the dialog box. The new document window opens up, covering the old one. However, the old one is still available to you, as you'll soon see.

5. Open the Window menu again. It should now indicate that you have two possible windows to choose from.

6. Type 1 or highlight WORD1.WPS and press ↵.

You have just jumped from one window into a second window, then back again.

DOING WINDOWS

Having the ability to easily jump around from document to document gives you a great deal of flexibility and convenience while working on a computer. With many computer programs, moving from one document to another requires closing the current one, loading another program into the computer from disk, and then opening the second document. This process would have to be repeated for each additional document. With Works, that's not necessary, but there are certain limitations, and suggestions for managing your use of windows.

Essentially, the idea is to open all the documents you want to work with at a given time, each in a separate window, thus making it easy to move between them. You can have up to eight documents open at a time, but remember that there are limitations to your computer's RAM space, so the realistic number and size of files you can have open simultaneously is dependent upon the size of the files. Works will warn you if any of your files is too large.

ERROR MESSAGES, THE ESC KEY, AND THE BIG BAD BEEP

Even once you become very familiar with Works, there will be times when you'll make mistakes using it. As with any computer program, there are literally thousands of things you can do wrong. The Works interface eliminates many of them by using menus and dialog boxes to execute commands for you. Still, you will sometimes find that you are "stuck" in a certain box or screen, unable to do anything — or so it seems. Worse yet, every time you press a key, you may hear an annoying beep emanating from your computer.

When you hear a beep, Works is doing its best to tell you that you're trying to do something at the wrong time. Sometimes Works will be kind enough to tell you what the problem is by printing an error message on the screen. Even if you don't see a message, more often than not, pressing ESC will get you out of the mess and let you move on. Beeps crop up most often when you are in the middle of some process, such as copying data from one place to another, and then you open a menu and try to choose a command. The best advice is to check out what the status line and the message line are saying. Also, look at the commands on the menus carefully. You can choose a command only when it has a highlighted letter. There are times, due to the nature of Works, when some commands cannot be used. At these times, they have no highlighted letters, and you will hear a beep if you try to use the command. If all the commands seem to be beeping at you, you're probably in the middle of another operation and should either complete it, or press ESC to get out of it. Then the commands should become available to you again.

THE FILE MENU SELECTIONS

Though many of the other menus change from tool to tool, all four Works tools have the File menu in common. The File menu is your connection to your computer's Disk Operating System (DOS) and to the files on your disk drives. There are eight commands on this menu, some of which need to be explained before we move on to the next chapter. This is important reference information and you may want to look back on it later, since it directly affects how all your efforts creating spreadsheets, databases, graphs, and so forth are safely saved on disk. Those commands from the File menu not covered here will be covered elsewhere in the book.

HOW TO MANAGE YOUR FILES

When you are working with and creating documents, at any given point your work is actually being manipulated in your computer's memory chips. As we've mentioned, these chips are called RAM, for Random Access Memory. Because your data is being manipulated in RAM, your PC can work with it very quickly. Unfortunately, RAM chips have volatile memory. That is, the information in them is "forgotten" when you turn off the power to your computer. In order to save your work for later use, such as editing, printing, or for use as the basis for new documents, you have to save your work first.

Works uses your disk drive, whether floppy or hard, as the medium for saving your documents. The important thing to know is that neither Works nor your computer does this automatically. You must remember to save your files before turning off your computer. This is primarily what the File menu is all about. It lets you save your documents before turning off the computer. Then, it lets you retrieve (open) these files later, when you turn your computer back on again.

Saving a File the First Time

You may have noticed that the file names shown in the Windows menu had weird endings tacked to the end of them. Your first file, for example, was listed there as WORD1.WPS. If you know something about your PC's DOS, you'll know that when files are stored on your disks, DOS needs a name to store them under. Without a file name, neither Works nor DOS will be able to find the file again on your disk; the situation would be sort of like a filing cabinet with no names on the folders.

File names used by disks are divided into two sections, the name and the extension. The first part of WORD1.WPS is the name that you get to choose when you create a new file. Works adds the part after the period, the extension, for its own reference. The extensions are used by Works to discern which tool a file belongs to. Here is how Works assigns the extensions, just so you'll know what type of files you see listed in the file boxes and on the Window menu.

Extension	Type
.WPS	Word processing
.WDB	Database
.WKS	Spreadsheet
.WCM	Communications

If you've opened a new document and have been working on it for a while, it's a good idea to save it, even if you're not finished working on it. That way, if the power is interrupted or the computer malfunctions for some reason, you have only lost the work you've done since the last save.

You save a document file by choosing File/Save. The first time you do this, Works will ask you what name you want to

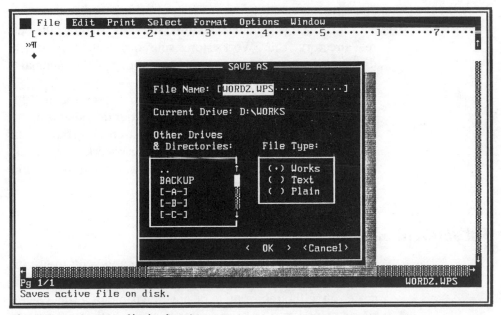

Figure 3-7. *Saving a file the first time*

give the file. The current name of the file (such as WORD1.WPS) will be in the text section of the file box as you see in Figure 3-7.

You can just press ↵ if you want to use the default name. You probably won't want to, though, since a name like WORD2.WPS doesn't really remind you later of what that file was for. It's better to use a descriptive name like LETTER or INVOICE. Unfortunately, with only eight letters in a name, this doesn't leave much room for description.

Saving to Other Drives and Directories

Notice that the SAVE AS dialog box also lets you choose other disk drives and directories to save your file on. Just jump to the box and press ↓ to highlight the drive or directory you want to use. If the current directory (as shown above the list box) has its own subdirectories, those will be available from the list box. Selecting the double periods (..) moves you up one directory on the directory tree. The symbols [-A-], [-B-], [-C-], etc. refer to your other disk drives. You select a drive by choosing one of these.

Note: Once you change the directory, this becomes the current directory. Thus, Works stores subsequent saves in the new directory. Please refer to your PC-DOS or MS-DOS manual if you have questions about subdirectories.

Finally, the word BACKUP refers to a subdirectory that Works creates to store backup copies of your documents. (This is an optional feature that can be turned on or off from the SETTINGS dialog box. To learn about Works' ability to automatically make backups of your data, refer to the Works user's manual.)

Subsequent Saves

After the initial save, Works assumes that you want to use the current name for each subsequent save. That makes sense, since you will rarely want to change the name of a file. Once a file is named the first time, Works won't bother asking you about the name (or present a dialog box) when you save again. Just choose File/Save and it's done.

Important: Once again, we suggest that you save your documents regularly while you are working on them. Saving a file every 15 minutes or so is a very wise idea; it will minimize your lost time should something go wrong.

Using Save As

There are a few times when you'll want to save a document under a new name. For instance, if you want to make a copy of a basic template (sometimes called a *boilerplate*) for use as the basis for other documents, or make a copy of a current document to experiment with, use the Save As command. Here's a typical example:

1. Open the document you want to make a copy of.

2. Choose Save As. The SAVE AS dialog box appears, just as in Figure 3-7.

3. Enter the new name of the file.

4. Works copies the current file on disk under the new name. Then it automatically opens the new file and puts it on the screen. You can switch back to the original file via the Window menu.

Changing File Extensions

If you are experienced with DOS, be careful when copying or renaming files not to alter the extensions in the process. (If you are not experienced, be even more careful!) If you change the extensions, Works may not recognize them as Works files until you rename them properly. All Works documents should at least have a W as the first letter in the extension to appear in the OPEN dialog box.

Opening Files

Opening files is done very much the same way as closing them. Many of the exercises in this book will involve opening files that you have created in earlier chapters, so you will need to know how to do it. It's relatively simple once you know how to use the dialog box.

1. Choose File/Open.

2. The OPEN dialog box appears.

3. You can tell Works what type of files to list by jumping to the options box if you want.

4. Then select the file you want to open from the list box.

5. Then choose < OK > to approve the box.

Alternatively, you can just type in the name of the file you want to open and press ↵.

GETTING HELP WHEN YOU NEED IT

You may have noticed that in addition to listing the currently open documents, the Windows menu has a Help command. The Help command does just what its name implies—it helps you. If you get stuck in the middle of a process and don't understand something about Works, just choose Help Index or Tutorial Index from the Window menu. Works will then help offer relevant help information. For more details about how the Works Help system operates, just try it. The built-in Works help system is self-explanatory. If you have additional questions about the help system, you should consult the Works manual.

EXITING WORKS

Before moving ahead, you should learn how to take a break just in case you'll want to do that between chapters in the future. This will entail exiting from the Works program and returning to DOS. The easiest way to do this is by taking the following steps. These should be done *before* turning off your computer. (If you plan to continue on to the next chapter right now, don't bother with the following steps, though you may want to look at them later.)

1. Choose File/Exit.

2. Works will present you with a series of small dialog boxes, one for each open document. A box might look like this:

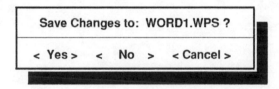

3. In this case we haven't typed in anything worth saving, so you can select No. But once you start creating documents you want to save, be sure to choose Yes. Since Yes is the default, you can simply press ↵ to save the changes. If, for some reason you mess up a document during an editing session and decide to abandon the changes you've made, that's one time you'd choose No at this juncture.

   Works will terminate and you'll be returned to the familiar DOS prompt.

4. You can remove your Works disks now and store them in a safe place for use later.

IF YOU HAVE QUESTIONS

You should now have enough of a basic working understanding of the Works environment to start using it. If you have questions about some things covered in this chapter, don't worry. Chances are that the following chapters will clear things up as you begin to actually use Works. What's important at this point is that you know how to use the special keys on the keyboard, make menu selections, open and close windows, use dialog boxes, and jump between documents. With those things under your belt, you can move ahead to Chapter 4 and learn how to create, edit, and print a document using the word processor. If you forget how to perform some of the basics covered here, just flip back to this chapter and look up the part you need help on.

Chapter

Using the Word Processor

Four

You will recall from the introductory chapter that the word processor is the module of Works that you will use to write letters, reports, or anything that is primarily of a textual nature. The Works word processor lets you create word processing documents of virtually any length, limited only by the capacity of your disk drive, and has many built-in features that you will find useful as you begin creating documents.

In this chapter, you will learn how to create, edit, and print a document. In this case, the document will be a simple business letter. In the process, you will have a chance to experiment with all the major procedures involved in word processing. First you will enter the text from the keyboard. Then you will edit the text, learning how to delete accidental typos, how to move and copy sections of text, and how to change the look, or format, of your letter. Finally, if you have a printer, you will print out the letter on paper.

Recall from the last chapter that every document you create in Works, or any other program, for that matter, is stored by your computer as a file. The first step in creating your letter will be to tell Works that you want to begin a new file. If you took a break after Chapter 3, you'll have to first bring up Works again before continuing. If you've just read Chapter 3, you're all ready to move ahead and learn about the Works word processor.

CREATING YOUR FIRST DOCUMENT

Follow these steps to open a new word processing document:

1. If you're just bringing up Works, choose Word Processor from the NEW dialog box and press ↵.

2. If Works is already running, choose File/New. (Recall from the last chapter that this shorthand notation means to open the File menu, highlight New, and press ↵.)

Works should have gone off and opened a new file for you, presenting you with the blank screen seen in Figure 4-1.

There are several things to notice on your screen. As usual, up at the top you see the menu bar. When you are using the word processor, the menu bar offers options pertinent to writing, editing, and formatting text. Some of these menus you ex-

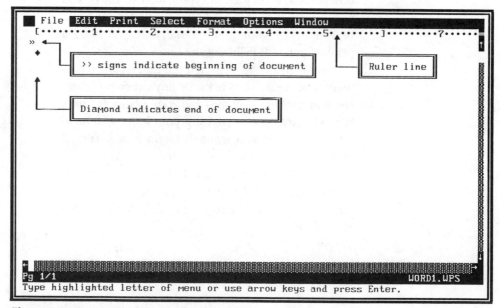

Figure 4-1. *A new word processing document*

perimented with in Chapter 3, so they should be somewhat familiar.

Try pulling down each menu now, just to take a look at the various selections you have at your fingertips. The easiest way to do this is to open the File menu, then press the right arrow key ($\rightarrow$) to see the next menu. You may even want to choose some of the menu choices that have dialog boxes associated with them (as indicated by the "..." after the name, remember?). You can always press ESC (or click on Cancel) to back out of a dialog box.

Referring to your screen or to Figure 4-1, notice that immediately below the menu bar sits the ruler line. The ruler helps you keep track of where you are typing on the page, much like the guide on a typewriter. Each dot on the line represents a column, and every tenth column is marked by an integer. Notice the [and] marks. These indicate the left and right indents (sometimes called margins). Also, though not shown now, the ruler will indicate paragraph indents and the tab settings once you set them. The use of those settings will be explained later.

You can elect to turn off the ruler if you wish to.

1. Choose Options/Ruler to eliminate it.

2. Choose Options/Ruler again to bring the ruler back.

Removing the ruler lets you see an extra line of your text on the screen but, as you'll see later, the ruler is useful to have around.

If you're using a mouse, you'll see scroll bars on the right and bottom edges of the screen. As discussed in Chapter 3, these are used with a mouse to let you move around within your document more quickly.

Notice that the status line (two lines from the bottom) gives WORD1.WPS as the file name since you haven't named the document yet. The status line also says "Pg 1/1," meaning that you are on page 1 of a document one page in length. Finally, notice that the cursor sits blinking up in the upper-left corner of your screen with two other symbols next to it. The >> symbol simply indicates the beginning (top) of the document; the diamond, the end (bottom) of the document. Since you haven't typed in anything yet, the only thing between the top and bottom of the document is the cursor.

ENTERING THE TEXT

With no further ado, let's begin creating the letter. When finished, it will look like that shown in Figure 4-2. The letter contains five different elements: title, address, body, tabular list, and closing. Each of these elements will provide an opportunity to experiment with a different word processor feature. (Don't start typing yet, though.)

Instead of using Figure 4-2 as your guide, use Figure 4-3 as the basis for your typing because it has intentional errors in it that will be used later for learning about editing. Begin entering the text into your new file following the steps outlined here. If you make unintentional mistakes while you are typing, just use the BACKSPACE key (just above the ↵ key) to back up and fix them. If you don't see an error until you are long past it, don't worry. You'll learn how to fix such errors later.

1. Begin by typing in the title on the first line. Do not bother trying to center it yet. We'll do that later.

2. Next, press ↵ key three times to move down a couple of lines to prepare for typing the address. Notice that, as mentioned in Chapter 3, pressing ↵ is necessary for adding new blank lines in a word processing document. Pressing the ↓ key will not move the cursor down a line at this point or create new lines. You will only hear an error beep from your computer if you try this.

3. Enter the first line of the address; then press ↵ to move down to the next line. Repeat this process for the last two

```
                 Product Announcement for Microsoft Works


Efficient Chips
1000 West Goshen Lane
Walla Walla, Washington 98238

Dear Mr. Floyd,

Microsoft Inc. announced today its new integrated
productivity tool for the IBM PC and compatibles, PC-Works.
PC-Works is an integrated product designed to run on low-cost
8086/8088 machines. The key selling points of this program
are ease of learning and immediate business productivity.

PC-Works is a single program with word processing,
spreadsheet, database, and communications built in. The word
processor is quite capable, and is essentially Microsoft
Word version 2.0. Here are some of its features:



Feature                  Notes
----------------------------------------
Document size            Unlimited
Undo                     Yes, from menu
Character formatting     Plain, bold, italic, underline
Fonts                    Depends on printer
Justification            Right, left, center, justified
Paragraph formats        Each paragraph has its own


Of course there are many other useful features included in
the PC-Works word processor that are worth your consideration
as you will see once you try out the evaluation copy of the
program enclosed. Please let us know if you have any
questions.

Sincerely,

Harvey Fledgebog
```

Figure 4-2. *The business letter in final form*

```
Product Announcement for Microsoft Works



Efficient Chips
1000 West Goshen Lane
Walla Walla, Wahshington 98238

Dear Mr. Floyd,

Microsoft Inc. announced today its new integrated
productivity tool for the IBM PC and compatibles, PC-Works.
PC-Works is an inegrated product designed to run on low-cost
8086/8088 machines. The key selling points of this program
are ease of learning and immediate business productivity.

PC-Works is a single program with word processing,
spreadsheet, database, and communications built in. The word
processor si quite capable, and is essentially Microsoft
Word version 2.0. Here are some of its features:



Feeture                     Notes
-------------------------------------
Document size               Unlimited
Undo                        Yes, from menu
Character formatting        Plain, bold, italic, underline
Fonts                       Depends on printer
Justification               Right, left, center, justified
Paragraph formats           Each paragraph has its own


Of coarse there are many other useful features included in
the PC-Works word processor thatare worth your consideration
as you will see once you try out the evaluation copy of the
program enclosed. Please let us know is you have any
questions.

Sinceerely,


Harvey Fledgebog
```

Figure 4-3. The letter with mistakes underlined

lines of the address (including the misspelling). So far this should remind you of using a typewriter.

4. Now press ↵ twice to put in a blank line and type in the greeting.

5. Press ↵ again to skip another line, and begin entering the body of the letter. Don't forget to leave in the spelling mistakes so that we can fix them later on. You don't have to worry about pressing ↵ at the end of each line since the word processor will automatically put in the carriage return there for you. This is called *word-wrapping*. All you have to do is keep typing.

6. When you reach the end of the first paragraph, just move on down and begin the next one by pressing ↵ twice. Stop when you finish that paragraph. Now your letter should look like that in Figure 4-4.

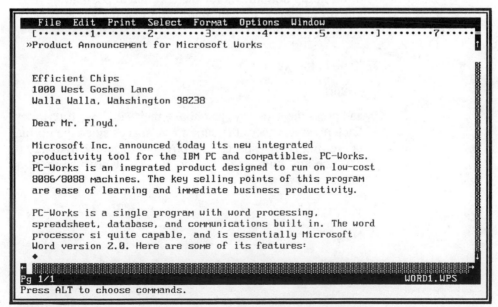

```
 File  Edit  Print  Select  Format  Options  Window
[········1·········2·········3·········4·········5·········]·········7······
»Product Announcement for Microsoft Works                                  ↑


Efficient Chips
1000 West Goshen Lane
Walla Walla, Wahshington 98238

Dear Mr. Floyd,

Microsoft Inc. announced today its new integrated
productivity tool for the IBM PC and compatibles, PC-Works.
PC-Works is an inegrated product designed to run on low-cost
8086/8088 machines. The key selling points of this program
are ease of learning and immediate business productivity.

PC-Works is a single program with word processing,
spreadsheet, database, and communications built in. The word
processor si quite capable, and is essentially Microsoft
Word version 2.0. Here are some of its features:
 ◆                                                                         ↓

Pg 1/1                                                          WORD1.WPS
Press ALT to choose commands.
```

Figure 4-4. *The letter thus far. Note the intentional misspellings*

Using the TAB Key

The next part of the text is a simple table with two columns. Many letters, particularly business letters, will require setting up tables like this one, often with more columns. You use the TAB key to move from column to column, just as you would on a typewriter.

1. First, insert a blank line to separate the table from the previous paragraph. You will soon notice that when you reach the bottom of the screen, Works moves some text up and off the top of the screen in one big jump. You'll suddenly find the cursor (and the last line of the document) in the center of the screen instead of at the bottom. Works has simply scrolled the screen up to let you enter more text. Many word processors scroll the screen one line at a time when you're entering text. Works is a little different in this respect. Although a little disconcerting at first, this jumping to the middle of the screen is a thoughtful feature, since computer screens are usually better focused in the center than they are down at the bottom. As for the text that appears to be missing, don't worry. It's still there, and you'll soon see how to get back to it.

2. Type in the word

   Feeture

   and press the TAB key (just above the CTRL key) four times. Each press advances the cursor five spaces since the normal tab setting is five spaces. It's possible to set the TAB key to advance any number of spaces, but we'll just use them as they are for now.

3. Now type in

   Notes

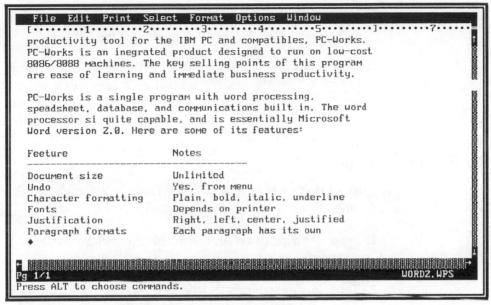

```
 File  Edit  Print  Select  Format  Options  Window
[•••••••••1•••••••••2•••••••••3•••••••••4•••••••••5•••••••••]•••••••••7••••••
productivity tool for the IBM PC and compatibles, PC-Works.
PC-Works is an inegrated product designed to run on low-cost
8086/8088 machines. The key selling points of this program
are ease of learning and immediate business productivity.

PC-Works is a single program with word processing,
speadsheet, database, and communications built in. The word
processor si quite capable, and is essentially Microsoft
Word version 2.0. Here are some of its features:

Feeture                 Notes
_____
Document size           Unlimited
Undo                    Yes, from menu
Character formatting    Plain, bold, italic, underline
Fonts                   Depends on printer
Justification           Right, left, center, justified
Paragraph formats       Each paragraph has its own
♦

Pg 1/1                                              WORD2.WPS
Press ALT to choose commands.
```

Figure 4-5. *The letter with the tabbed columns in place*

4. Drop down to the next line by pressing ↵, and type in the dotted line as it appears in the letter. Remember that all the keys on the PC are repeating keys, so it's easy to type in this line. Just press the hyphen, which is just above P on the keyboard. You don't have to press SHIFT. Hold down this key for a few seconds and it will begin repeating. Let up when your line looks about the right length. If you went too far, just press the BACKSPACE key to back up and erase some of the dashes.

5. Press ↵ again and begin entering the list. Type in

   Document size

   and then press the TAB key three times. This moves the cursor to the Notes column.

6. Then type in

Unlimited

and press ↵. This finishes the first line of the list.

7. Now repeat the process for the remaining five lines, using Figure 4-5 as a guide. Notice that each line will require a different number of tabs to line up the Notes column. If you press too many tabs, use the Backspace key to delete them.

Adding the Ending

Now all that's left to type in is the ending paragraph and the closing.

1. Press ↵ twice to create one blank line before the ending paragraph.

2. Type in the rest of the letter as you see in Figure 4-6. Again, the highlighted words should be entered as shown because you will correct them later as part of the tutorial.

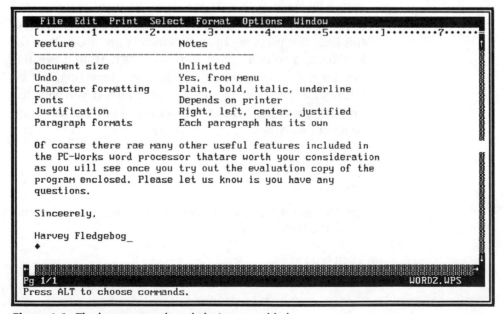

```
 File  Edit  Print  Select  Format  Options  Window
[·········1·········2·········3·········4·········5·········]·········7·····
Feeture                    Notes
------------------------------------------------------
Document size              Unlimited
Undo                       Yes, from menu
Character formatting       Plain, bold, italic, underline
Fonts                      Depends on printer
Justification              Right, left, center, justified
Paragraph formats          Each paragraph has its own

Of coarse there rae many other useful features included in
the PC-Works word processor thatare worth your consideration
as you will see once you try out the evaluation copy of the
program enclosed. Please let us know is you have any
questions.

Sinceerely,

Harvey Fledgebog_
  ◆


Pg 1/1                                                    WORD2.WPS
Press ALT to choose commands.
```

Figure 4-6. *The last paragraph and closing are added*

EDITING YOUR TEXT

Now that you've typed in the basic content of the letter, we can begin editing it. Even if you made some mistakes while typing, don't worry. You'll soon see how to fix those errors, too.

Editing is simply the process of making changes, either major or minor, to your document. Works offers numerous editing features, only some of which we'll explore in this chapter. More advanced capabilities will be discussed in Chapter 8.

Everyone who uses a word processor inevitably develops their own style of editing. Some people like to print out a document and edit on paper, fix the errors, and then print again. Others find editing on the screen more efficient. You will no doubt decide for yourself later. But in the meantime, since we're aware of certain mistakes that need attention, we'll just fix them now.

The first step in editing is learning to move around in the text. While actually entering the text, you seldom found it necessary to move the cursor around to any great extent. For the most part, it moved along by itself as you typed. But now, for editing purposes, you'll want to move up and down quite a bit in order to fix misspelled words and so forth.

Moving Around Within the Document

As you probably have surmised, the cursor marks the position where letters will appear when you begin typing. This is called the *insertion point*. Editing your text involves moving the insertion point to the correct location and then using some commands to fix errors. Moving around within a document is called *navigating*.

The first step in moving the insertion point around is to learn how to *scroll*. Scrolling is necessary when there is more text in your document than can fit on one screen. You could think of a large document as though it were a long scroll, rolled up at both ends. The part that appears on the screen is only a portion of the document. The trick is to scroll the document to the correct spot to make changes.

Scrolling

Practice scrolling by following these instructions:

1. Press the PGUP key (usually located on the 9 key in the numeric keypad). Make sure NUM LOCK is turned off; otherwise pressing PGUP will print the number 9 instead of scrolling the text. Pressing PGUP moves you up one screen toward the beginning of your document.

2. Now press PGDN (on the 3 key). This has the opposite effect. Notice that your document takes up about two full screens. This amounts to about 40 lines of text, which is to say about 4/5 of a standard 8-1/2" x 11" page if printed on a typical printer.

   Sometimes you'll want to move to the very beginning or end of your document. You could use the PGUP or PGDN key, but if you have a long document, there's a faster way. Pressing the CTRL key along with HOME or END achieves this.

1. Press the CTRL key and hold it down with your left hand. While keeping that key down, press END with your right hand. This should move the cursor to the bottom of your document.

2. Now do the same with CTRL and HOME. You should be back at the top of the letter.

   Note: Remember that when you see an instruction such as "press CTRL-HOME" it means to press the CTRL key and the other key (in this case HOME) at the same time. Remember that you press the CTRL key first, and then press the second key, whatever it is.

Scrolling with a Mouse

If you have a mouse connected to your system, the method of scrolling is somewhat different than with the keyboard. Look at the vertical scroll bar on the screen. Notice that there is a dark block somewhere in the bar, called the elevator. This indicates the relative position of the cursor within the document, from top to bottom. By moving the elevator up and down with the mouse you can adjust what part of the text appears on your screen. There are three ways to do this.

1. To scroll a line at a time, position the pointer (the highlighted square block that moves with the mouse) on one of the little arrows either at the top of the bar or at the bottom of the bar, and click the left button. The top arrow moves you toward the top of the document, and the bottom arrow moves you toward the bottom of the document. Each click on the mouse shifts the screen one line in the desired direction. Holding the button down longer causes the scrolling to repeat until you let up.

2. To move to the top or bottom of the document quickly, put the pointer somewhere in the scroll bar itself, either above or below the elevator, and click. Clicking above the elevator moves to the top; below moves to the bottom.

3. Finally, as discussed in Chapter 3, you can "grab" the elevator and pull it to any particular point on the scroll bar. Carefully position the pointer on the elevator. Click and hold the button down this time; don't let up. Now move the mouse up or down. When you release the button, the document will scroll to the relative position in the document. This process is called "dragging" the elevator.

Consider the scroll bars to be a sort of measuring stick for your document, with the top of the bar representing the beginning of your document; and the bottom of the bar, the end. By pulling the elevator to the approximate relative position you want to scroll to you can get close to your desired spot quickly. The horizontal scroll bar works the same way as detailed for the vertical bar, but is only useful if your document is more than a page across.

Note to Mouse Users: Many of the techniques for using the mouse described in this chapter — including use of the scroll bars — work the same way in all four Works tools. If you're using a mouse, you may want to practice these techniques and remember them for use in other chapters of this book. As the chapters progress, we'll make fewer references to mouse techniques, since we assume that you have learned the essentials in the early chapters.

Moving the Cursor

Once you've scrolled to the screen of text you want to edit, the next trick is to move the cursor to the exact location of the word or letter that you want to change. When the cursor is positioned, you can insert text, remove words, fix misspellings, and mark blocks of text for moving, copying, or deletion.

To move the cursor position, just press $\uparrow$, $\downarrow$, $\leftarrow$, and $\rightarrow$ on the number pad on the right side of the keyboard. Here are some exercises to try.

1. You should be at the beginning of the letter now. (If not, press CTRL-HOME.) Press $\rightarrow$ five times. This should put the cursor on the *c* of the word *Product*.

2. Now press $\rightarrow$ again and hold it down for a few seconds. Notice that once the key begins to repeat, the cursor moves faster. When it gets to the end of the first line, it wraps around to the second and third lines. Now press $\leftarrow$ and hold it down. When the cursor gets to the beginning of the document, your computer starts to beep because the cursor can't go any farther.

3. Press $\rightarrow$ a few times until the cursor is on the first line of the address.

4. Now press → again. Hold it down for a while and notice what happens when the cursor reaches the bottom of the screen. The screen scrolls up the same way it did when you were entering text. That is, it jumps to the center of the screen. The reverse happens when the cursor is at the top of the screen and you press the ↑ key.

In addition to the arrow keys, the PGDN and PGUP keys, and the HOME and END keys, there are a few other key combinations that can be used for quickly navigating. Table 4-1 shows a complete list. Try experimenting with the ones you haven't tried yet.

Moving the cursor is particularly easy for mouse users. You simply move the arrow around the screen to the desired point

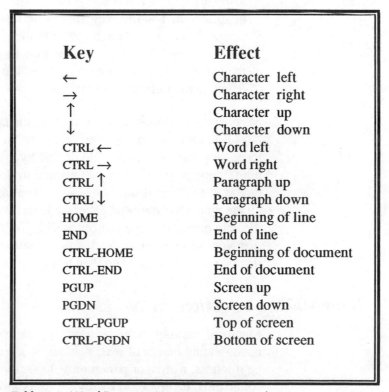

Key	Effect
←	Character left
→	Character right
↑	Character up
↓	Character down
CTRL ←	Word left
CTRL →	Word right
CTRL ↑	Paragraph up
CTRL ↓	Paragraph down
HOME	Beginning of line
END	End of line
CTRL-HOME	Beginning of document
CTRL-END	End of document
PGUP	Screen up
PGDN	Screen down
CTRL-PGUP	Top of screen
CTRL-PGDN	Bottom of screen

Table 4-1. *Word Processor Navigation Commands*

and click. Don't forget to click! Otherwise, you end up making changes in the wrong place, since the text cursor doesn't jump to a new location until you click.

Making Some Changes

Now that you know how to get around, you can begin to correct some of the typos in your letter. Let's start with the third line of the address, where the word *Washington* is spelled wrong.

1. Using the arrow keys or the mouse, position the cursor on the first *h* in *Wahshington.*

2. Now press DEL (the Delete key, usually located at the lower-right corner of the keyboard). This should remove the misplaced *h*. The DEL key always deletes the letter that the cursor is on, rather than the letter to the left of the cursor, as the Backspace key does. Notice also that the space where the *h* was closed up when you deleted the letter, pulling the letters to the right to close the gap.

Many simple errors can be fixed using the DEL or BACKSPACE key. But suppose you wanted to delete an entire word, sentence, or paragraph. You could do this by moving to the beginning or end of the section you wanted to delete, pressing DEL or BACKSPACE until the key began repeating, and waiting for all the words to disappear, letter by letter. But this is an unpredictable method. If you're not careful, you'll often erase more than you intended to. Instead, you can delete a whole block of text by first selecting it and then using the Delete command.

About Making Selections in Works

Much of editing with a word processor centers around manipulating *blocks* of text. A block is a portion of your text, be it letters, words, or paragraphs. In fact a great many of the commands in all Works' tools are based on this idea of manipulating blocks of information, whether they consist of text or other data, such as numbers.

But before a block can be worked with, it must be selected. *Selecting* is the process of telling Works where the beginning and end of the block you want to work with is. In Works, any time you make a selection, it is highlighted on the screen. As long as an area of a document is selected, it will become the center of attention to the Works tool you are using and usually be treated differently than the rest of the document. This remains the case until it is *deselected* by turning off the highlight.

Selecting Portions of Text

The Works word processor has a convenient feature that lets you select a word, sentence, line, paragraph, or even the whole document with just a few key presses. Once selected, a section of text can be manipulated in any number of ways, including being deleted from the document. More about that later. For now, try these exercises to get the hang of selecting. We'll actually do something useful with a selection in a moment.

Selecting with F8   Here's how to select portions of text using the F8 key.

1. Put the cursor on the word *PC-Works* in the first sentence of the second paragraph. Then press F8.

2. Look at the status line, in the lower right-hand corner. Notice the word *EXTEND* there. This means you are in the Extend mode, in which you can extend your selection to include more letters, words, sentences, or paragraphs, or the whole document. The extension begins from the point or word where the cursor was when you pressed F8. This point is called the *anchor point*. Once you get into Extend mode by pressing F8, there are several ways to increase the size of the selection. The first way is by additional presses of F8.

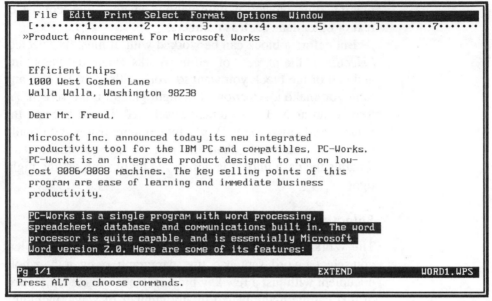

Figure 4-7. Using F8 to Extend the selection

3. Press F8 again. This selects the whole word you are on. Notice that the whole word, *PC-Works*, is now highlighted. This means that word is now selected.

4. Press F8 again to select the entire current sentence, beginning with the word at the anchor point.

5. Now press F8 again. This should select the entire first paragraph. Your screen should now look like that shown in Figure 4-7.

6. Finally, press F8 again to select the entire document. Additional presses have no effect after this point, but notice that you are still in Extend mode as indicated on the status line.

Warning: Be careful not to press keys other than the navigation keys when you've made a selection. If you press, say, the letter *A* the whole selection will be replaced by the letter *A*. If this happens accidentally, choose Edit/Undo from the menu bar before doing anything else and your text will be returned to its previous state.

Extend mode lets you decrease, or shrink the size of the selection too. This is done using the SHIFT-F8 key combination, and works in just the reverse manner as extending.

1. Press SHIFT-F8. The selection shrinks one level, down to just the paragraph.

2. Press SHIFT-F8 again, and you're back to just the first sentence.

3. Press SHIFT-F8 twice more and it looks like you're back where you started — nothing seems to be selected. But the status line indicates that you're still in Extend mode. This is important, as you'll soon see.

Selecting with F8 and the Arrow Keys   There is another way to select an area of text that gives you more control than just pressing the F8 key. You can use any of the navigation controls listed in Table 4-1 to extend or shrink the selection. Here are some examples:

1. Press → several times. As you move the cursor over letters, they become selected. This is because you are still in Extend mode.

2. Press ↓ several times. Notice the similar effect.

3. Press ↑ and see the reverse effect.

4. Try pressing CTRL → and CTRL ← to see the Word Right and Word Left commands work.

5. Now press the ↑ key five times. Notice that as you move up past the anchor point (in this case, at the letter *P* in *PC-Works*), the selection starts from there, moving upward in

the text. So, now text in the first paragraph is selected. This clearly illustrates the action of the anchor point: it's the point around which additional selection, either above or below, originates. It generally doesn't make much sense to select from the bottom up, but it can be done.

Selecting with the SHIFT Key There is a shortcut for selecting. The SHIFT key in combination with the navigation keys can be used in lieu of the F8 key. You may find this easier than using F8. Here's how to use it.

1. First, deselect anything you already have selected by pressing ESC, then pressing any of the arrow keys (careful not to press any keys other than these). This stops the Extend mode, turns off any selection, and returns you to normal typing mode.

2. Move the cursor to the first word in the first paragraph. Now press SHIFT →. The selection advances one letter with each press (unless you hold the key down too long, in which case it moves by itself).

3. Now press SHIFT-CTRL →. The selection advances a word with each press.

4. Release the SHIFT key.

5. Press any of the arrow keys. The highlight disappears, and the selection is now deselected.

Selecting an Area with the Mouse For mouse users, the technique of selecting is a little different. As is the case within all the tools of Works, the keyboard commands work on systems using a mouse, too. But selection is particularly intuitive and simple with the mouse, so you may prefer it. Mouse selection is done using the same technique you learned to drag the elevator for scrolling. Try this:

1. Deselect any possible selections by pressing ESC and then left clicking somewhere in the text. It doesn't matter where.

2. Now move the pointer to the first letter in the word *design* in the first paragraph.

3. Now hold the button down, and move the pointer down several lines. As you move the mouse, the selection extends. When you let up on the button, the selection is finalized.

4. Click again anywhere and the selection is deselected.

The anchor point, as we've described, works similarly to the way it does using keyboard commands. Try this to see.

1. Click in the middle of the first paragraph. This sets the anchor point.

2. Press F8. This starts Extend mode.

3. Click on the first word of the paragraph. This selects all text between the anchor point and the beginning of the paragraph.

4. Click on the last word of the paragraph. This changes the selection. It's now from the anchor to the end of the paragraph.

5. Finally, another convenience is that pressing the right button on the mouse selects the whole word that the pointer is sitting on.

Note: Unless indicated, instructions for "clicking the mouse button" refer to the left button.

MAKING THE CHANGES

Now that you have the idea of selecting, let's get back to editing the letter. For our first change, we want to select the word *si* in order to delete it and then replace it with *is*.

1. First, deselect everything by pressing ESC to get out of Extend mode (if you are in it) and then pressing an arrow key or clicking the mouse.

2. Select the word *si* in the third line of the second paragraph.

3. Open the Edit menu and choose Delete, since we want to delete the currently selected word. Just typing *D* is the easiest way, of course, once the menu is open.

4. The menu disappears and you are returned to your text at just the right spot to type in *is*. (You may have to add a space after the word, depending on how you selected *si*.)

All of this may seem like a lot of work just to eliminate a two-letter word, but for larger selections you will find it's worth the effort.

Let's try another approach. Assume that the addressee's name is really Mr. Freud instead of Floyd. Here's a shortcut for replacing a word or selection with some other text. In this case we'll just change the name in the greeting.

1. Select *Floyd*.

2. With *Floyd* highlighted, type in the word *Freud*. Notice that *Floyd* is deleted the moment you type in the first letter of *Freud*. This saves the extra step of choosing Delete from the Edit menu.

Inserting Letters

Now let's move on to another kind of error — the word *inegrated* in the first paragraph. This word is missing a letter, so the missing letter will have to be inserted into the middle of the word. Missing or dropped letters are probably the third most common form of typos, after misspellings and reversed letters. Here's how to insert a letter.

1. Put the cursor on the first *e*.

2. Type the letter *t*.

Notice that, starting with the *e*, the word opened up to let the *t* in. Unlike on the typewritten page, lines on a computer screen are flexible, letting you insert the letter. In fact so flexible that you may have noticed Works re-forms all the lines of the paragraph almost instantly.

Actually, you could insert any number of letters, words, or even paragraphs wherever you want within a document, and the computer will accommodate. In the world of word processing, this ability is called *inserting*. In Chapter 1, we mentioned that some word processors allow you to to deactivate inserting in favor of the old-style, typewriter-like *overwriting* where newly typed letters overwrite the old ones instead of pushing them to the right. The Works word processor does not let you do this. The advantage is that you will never accidentally type over some text you want to keep. The disadvantage is that you will have to take action to delete unwanted text.

Let's move ahead and make another correction.

1. Move to the *s* of the word *is* on the last line of the last main paragraph. This word is supposed to be *if*.

2. Type the letter *f*, pushing the letter *s* to the right.

3. Press DEL to remove the *s*. (You can use SHIFT-BACKSPACE in lieu of DEL.)

4. Do the same type of repair to the word *Feeture* in the table heading, replacing the second *e* with an *a*.

Fixing the Other Typos

Now that you know how to repair most simple errors, go ahead and correct the remaining ones.

1. In the last paragraph, insert a space between the words *that* and *are*. Put the cursor on the second *a* and press the spacebar.

2. In the same paragraph, the second word, *coarse*, should be spelled *course*.

3. Finally, delete the extra *e* in *Sinceerely* and you're finished editing.

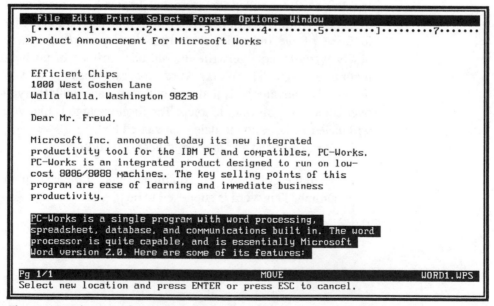

Figure 4-8. Selecting a paragraph in order to move it

Your letter now looks like Figure 4-2, except that you've changed the addressee to Mr. Freud and the heading is not centered. (We'll get to centering in a moment.)

Moving Selected Blocks

The editing process often involves moving larger portions of text, such as sentences and paragraphs, within a document. Rather than inserting a block of text by retyping it, you can pick it up and move it from one place to another using the Move or Copy commands from the Edit menu. This can be a real time saver, and it's easy to do.

To move a block of text, you first select the text you want to move, and then choose the Move command from the Edit menu. Next you move the cursor to the new position and drop it into the text by pressing ↵.

Here's an example of the Move command that will reverse the order of the first two paragraphs in our letter.

1. Press CTRL-HOME to move to the top of the document.

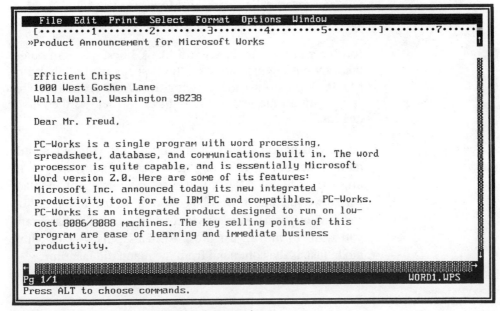

Figure 4-9. Paragraphs reversed but run together

2. Select the entire second paragraph using whatever technique you prefer.

3. Open the Edit menu and choose Move. Your text now looks like Figure 4-8.

   Notice that the status line now says MOVE and the message line instructs you, saying:

   Select new location and press Enter or press Esc to cancel.

4. Now move the cursor to the place where you want to insert the paragraph, which happens to be where the *M* of the word *Microsoft* is, in the first paragraph.

5. Press ↵ (or if using a mouse, just click) and, *voilà!* Now your text looks like Figure 4-9.

6. Notice that the paragraphs have run together. This sort of spacing problem is common when moving blocks of text. You may have to do a little adjusting afterwards, such as inserting or deleting a line or some spaces. But as you know, you can insert a line with ↵. Move to the *M* in *Microsoft* and press ↵ to separate the paragraphs.

   If after a move you have extra blank lines, you can delete them by putting the cursor on the first space of a blank line (the far left margin) and pressing the BACKSPACE key. This "pulls" up all the text to the right of (or below) the cursor one line.

7. After you have things looking right, give yourself a little more practice by returning the second paragraph to its original position. After all, it was obviously out of place where we just put it. Here's a shortcut to use this time. Instead of choosing Edit/Move after selecting the paragraph you want to move, just press F3. This puts you in Move mode just as the command from the menu did last time.

LINE CENTERING

Now there is only one thing that remains to be done before actually printing out the letter: we still have to center the first line in the document. On a typewriter, centering is often a real headache because you have to count the number of letters in the line you want to center, then divide by two, and count outward from the center of the page to find your starting place. But since a computer is first and foremost a calculator, it performs this type of work extremely efficiently. Here's how you do it.

1. Put the cursor anywhere on the first line (the one that begins "Product Announcement . . . ").

2. Select Format/Center. In a split second the line jumps to center stage and your screen looks identical to that shown in Figure 4-10.

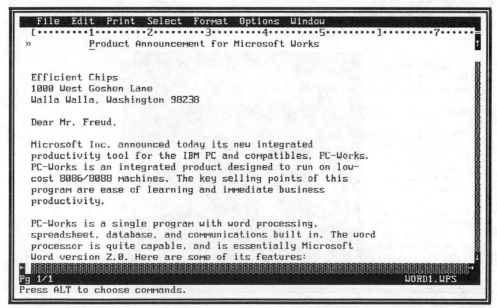

Figure 4-10. *Centering text using Format/Center*

SAVING YOUR WORK

As mentioned in Chapter 3, your computer stores and works with your documents in RAM whenever you are using Works. Unfortunately, RAM is not a permanent storage area; thus your work will be lost when you turn off your computer unless you first save it on disk. Floppy and hard disks, though not completely failure proof, are more permanent storage media and must be used if you intend to keep your documents for future use.

You save your documents via commands on the File menu, specifically the Save and Save As commands. The first time you save a document, Works will ask you for a name to give your document. After the initial save, Works assumes you want to use the current name, unless you indicate otherwise by using the Save As command.

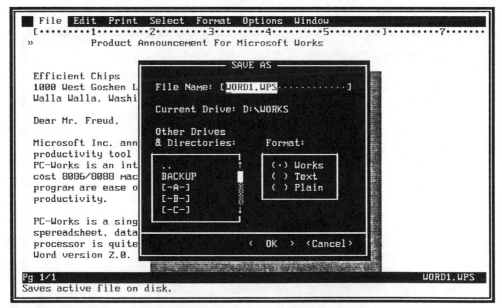

Figure 4-11. *Saving a file the first time*

In general, it's a good idea to save your work anytime you think that losing it would cause undue consternation, or when you have done enough editing that reverting to the last version of your document would be bothersome. We recommend saving writing after each 15 minutes of work. With really important work, set a timer to remind yourself that 15 minutes have passed, so you don't forget to save.

Before printing out our letter, let's save it using the following steps:

1. Choose File/Save. The SAVE AS dialog box appears since this is the first save and Works needs to ask you for the name. Your screen looks like that shown in Figure 4-11.

   The first line indicates the default file name that Works assigned to the document temporarily when we opened it. Thus it says WORD1.WPS. This name is highlighted. You can type in a new name from the keyboard, and it will automatically replace this name. But first you want to be sure that you are going to store the file on the correct disk drive, and that you have a formatted data disk (if you are using floppies) in the drive.

2. Notice that just below the file name, on the line that says "Current Drive" you'll see the drive and directory setting. If you're using a hard disk, this probably reads

   C\WORKS

   This indicates where the file will be saved unless you type a different name into the file name area or change the drive setting by jumping to the Other Drives section and selecting one of the drive designator symbols:

   [-A-] [-B-] [-C-]

   Remember from Chapter 3 that you use the TAB key or ALT key combined with a letter to get to the box. Then you use the arrow keys to move to the drive or directory selection and press ↵ to activate it.

If you are using a two-floppy system, you'd want to save your file on drive B (make sure you have a formatted disk in drive B with some extra room on it). If you are using a hard disk system, use drive C (unless you're using a hard disk of another name).

The File Type box will normally be set to Works, which is fine. Don't alter this setting unless you want to create a file that other word processors or other types of PC programs can read. See Appendix A for details.

So, in short, to save your work:

1. Choose File/Save.

2. Adjust the Current Drive setting if necessary. (Normally this is not necessary.)

3. Move into the File Name section.

4. Type in the file name LETTER1, and press ↵. Your disk drive will make some noise, and the file will be saved.

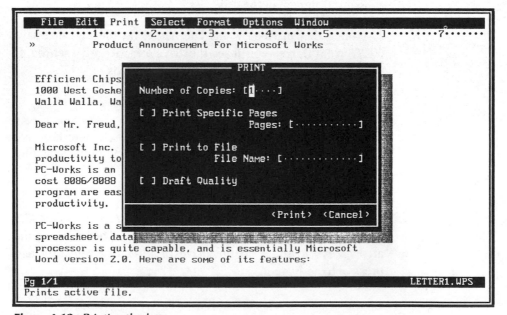

Figure 4-12. Printing the letter

Printing Out the Letter

Assuming you have a printer connected, you can now try printing your letter in its final form.

1. Choose Print/Select Text Printer.

2. A dialog box appears with a list of printer files (.PRD extensions). (You should recognize this dialog box from Chapter 3.) The printer name and other settings should already be the proper ones for your printer, as a result of the installation procedure we did in Chapter 2. If you want to change them, you do that here by selecting the correct PRD file, port number, and page feed settings for your particular printer. However, it's usually not necessary. (In fact, if you know that everything is set correctly you can skip these steps 1, 2, and 3 entirely.)

3. Press ↵ to OK the dialog box.

4. Turn on your printer, make sure it is on-line, and check to see that it is connected to your computer.

5. Choose Print/Print. The dialog box appears as shown in Figure 4-12.

6. Don't worry about all these options. The only thing really necessary here is to indicate how many copies of your document you want to print out. Since you probably only want one, just make sure the 1 is in the Number of Copies section.

7. Press ↵. Your letter should begin printing out.

Congratulations! You've covered the basics of word processing with Works. Using the commands you've learned in this chapter, you can create a wide variety of everyday documents. In Chapter 8, titled "Expanding your Word Processing Skills," we'll cover many of the more advanced features such as altering the paragraph and character formatting, using other fonts, undoing accidental editing errors, and automatically checking your spelling. You may want to turn directly on to that chapter if you need to learn more about word processing immediately. Otherwise, continue with the next chapter, which introduces the Works spreadsheet tool.

IF YOU WANT TO TAKE A BREAK NOW

If you intend to take a break now, you should get out of Works using the following steps:

1. Choose File/Exit. If you have any other files open, Works will ask if you want to save them. Answer accordingly.

2. Works will return you to the DOS prompt (that is, C> or A>).

3. If you are using floppy disks, remove them from the drives and put them in a safe place.

4. Turn off the power to your computer.

Chapter

Using the Spreadsheet

Five

The spreadsheet tool of Works is the electronic version of an accountant's ledger pad, pencil, and calculator. Though you can use spreadsheets to store almost any information that could be placed in columns, they are most often used for keeping track of business expenses of various types in an organized and easily alterable form. Once the numbers are stored in a spreadsheet, Works can quickly perform a variety of mathematical, statistical, and financial computations on them to quickly produce reports of business activities. Some typical examples might be

- Annual reports

- Budgets

- Tax statements

- Invoices

- Accounts payable and receivable

- Production schedules

Spreadsheets are also heavily used by scientists and engineers for data storage and calculation purposes, and by school teachers for tracking students' grades and activities.

As mentioned in Chapter 1, spreadsheets are often used in a business setting to run "what-if?" calculations that experiment with the effects of altering selected variables. For example, if you wanted to see the effect that hiring a new employee or increasing your inventory would have on your annual profits, it's easy to do so.

Even if you aren't a department manager in a large corporation or the proprietor of your own business, you may want to use the spreadsheet. For example, we keep track of everyday household finances with a spreadsheet, simply because we want our monthly expenses and income to be automatically totaled at the end of each month.

Finally, the Works spreadsheet can draw charts to graphically display the results of your spreadsheet calculations. These reports can even include bar, line, pie and scatter charts to visually display your data in a manner that is more immediate and understandable than is a complex matrix of numbers. (Charting is covered in Chapter 11.)

WHAT YOU WILL LEARN IN THIS CHAPTER

Because the spreadsheet is a powerful tool, it can be complicated. You may find the many statistical and/or business calculations which Works' spreadsheet includes (such as net present value or straight line depreciation) confusing, particularly if you have never used a computer before or are not familiar with statistical or accounting theory.

If you fall into this category, don't be put off, though. Estimates are that only about 10 percent of spreadsheet users need or use the complex functions of spreadsheets. Most people only use about five or six of the simplest functions. Besides, within the scope of this book, it's not possible to cover them in any great detail. This chapter will introduce you to the basics of spreadsheets by having you build, edit, calculate, and print an example spreadsheet. Then, in Chapter 9, "Expanding Your Spreadsheet Skills," you'll learn some more tricks and techniques.

GETTING STARTED

Because spreadsheets are powerful and can be complex, some careful consideration is necessary in the planning stages. What kind of information do you intend to put in the spreadsheet? How should it be arranged? What types of solutions are you attempting to reach through the calculations? What types of reports do you need to produce? These are all questions you should ask yourself as you create a new document.

Once you've answered these questions, you next determine which formulas and/or mathematical functions you'll incorporate into your spreadsheet and where they'll go. Finally, you move on to the easy part — typing in your data and watching the results. When you're done, you'll have a working spreadsheet as well as a model, or *template,* you can use again and again or modify for use in a particular application.

Elements of a Spreadsheet

In Figure 5-1, you'll see the elements of a typical spreadsheet. Notice that there are markings across the top (A-G) and down the left side (1-20 or 1-19 if you have a mouse). A spreadsheet consists of a series of columns and rows with columns running vertically and rows running horizontally. Each column is named by a letter, and each row by a number. Works allows up to 256 columns and as many as 4096 rows in each spreadsheet. (After reaching column Z, the columns are named as AA, AB, AC, and so on.)

The spot where a column and row intersect is called a cell. A cell is a bit like a pigeonhole or a Post Office box. It has an exact location and address (called the *cell address*) in the spreadsheet and can store information. Thus, the cell in the upper-left corner of Figure 5-1 is called A1 because it sits at the intersection of column A and row 1. Cell names and contents are the basis for all spreadsheet activities.

With 4096 rows and 256 columns, you'd think it possible to have up to 1,048,576 cells. Actually though, the number of possible cells is determined by the amount of memory in your computer, the number of other documents you have open in Works at the time, and the amount of information you put in each cell of your spreadsheet. It has nothing to do with the available storage space on your disk (although you can't store a 400K spreadsheet on a 360K floppy disk).

With so many variables, it's really impossible to say how large your spreadsheets can be, but suffice it to say that for typical spreadsheets, there is ample space.

Cell Contents

Cells can contain two types of data: *labels* and *values*. Labels consist of nonmathematical information and cannot be used in calculations. Labels are typically used to make a spreadsheet easier for the viewer to comprehend. Row and column names are typical examples, as are words like *SUBTOTAL* and *TOTAL*. In Figure 5-1, notice the labels. Though labels more often consist of letters, they can, interestingly, be numbers as well. For example *1987, 10/12/88,* or *July 4* could all be labels. However, unless instructed otherwise, Works will assume that these are numbers, since Works is capable of performing calculations on dates. To tell Works that a number is to be used as a label, you must precede it with a double quotation mark (for example, "1897).

In contrast to labels, values consist of data to be calculated, or show the results of calculations. A list of numbers to be added to get a total would be considered values, as would the total itself. Additionally there are two types of values: *constants* and *formulas*. Constants are directly stated numbers such as 149 and $369.99. Formulas are equations that produce numbers as a result of the formula, such as A1+A2+A3. In either case, the cell holds a numeric value, which explains why formulas are considered values even though they may not look like values.

Formulas have three possible parts to them:

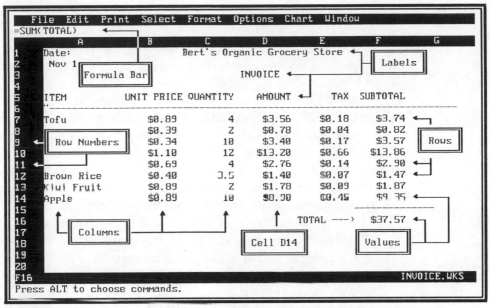

Figure 5-1. *The elements of a typical spreadsheet*

Operators Mathematical statements that perform calculations, such as addition, subtraction, multiplication, and division.

Functions "Canned" equations that perform common calculations for you, such as trigonometry, financial, and date calculations. Works has 59 built-in functions to make complex calculating easier for you.

Cell-References Notations that refer to the values in other cells. For example the formula A1+A2+A3 uses references (joined by operators) to sum the values stored in cells A1, A2, and A3.

STARTING A NEW SPREADSHEET

With no further ado, let's open a new spreadsheet document.

1. If you are already in Works, choose File/New to open the NEW dialog box. If you're just loading Works, the box appears by itself.

2. Choose Spreadsheet from the dialog box and press ↵.

3. A new spreadsheet document is created by Works, and appears on your screen shown in Figure 5-2.

At the right of the status line you see the name of the current file, SHEET1.WKS. Works assigned this name until you choose File/Save and give your spreadsheet a new name. Across the top of the screen you see the familiar menu bar. The formula bar sits just below it. Just below the formula bar you see a row of column names (A, B, C, . . .). Finally, down the left margin of the screen you see the row numbers.

If you are not using a mouse, you'll have 20 rows visible. With a mouse installed, you'll only see 19 rows since the 20th row is used for the horizontal scroll bar. In either case you can see only columns A through G. Getting to other columns and/or rows requires using the arrow keys or mouse to scroll your window around in the spreadsheet.

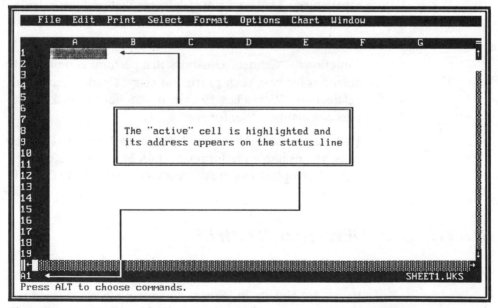

Figure 5-2. A new spreadsheet

The Active Cell

Notice that cell A1 is highlighted. This means it is the *active cell*. There is always one active cell, and its address is indicated on the far left side of the status line. Unless a given cell is active, you cannot enter data into it.

1. Try moving the active cell highlight around the spreadsheet using the ↑, ←, →, and ↓ keys. If you have a mouse, you can just move the pointer and click on the cell you want to activate.

2. Use CTRL in conjunction with →,←,↑, and ↓ to go to the far corners of the entire matrix.

3. You can move directly to a cell by choosing Select/Go To from the menu bar too. When the dialog box appears, type in C4 and press ↵. The highlight will jump to C4. A shortcut to opening this dialog box is to press F5. Note that lowercase letters — such as c1, b3, and so on — are fine to use.

When referencing cells by name, remember to type the letter part first: C1, or FF23, not 1C or 23FF. If you reverse the order, you may get an error message, or sometimes there will be no effect at all.

Though you'll most often use the arrow keys to move within a spreadsheet, there are some other navigation commands you may want to use during this chapter and Chapter 9. Please refer to Appendix A, "Reference," for the complete list of commands for moving around a spreadsheet.

Some Experiments

Before we begin entering a data into the spreadsheet, try some examples to get the idea of how you enter values and labels into cells and to see the effect of a formula.

1. Move to cell A1.

2. Type in the words

This is a test to see what can be typed into a cell ↵.

As you typed the words, they appeared in the formula bar. Not until you pressed ↵ did they appear in the cell. Assuming you hadn't entered anything in other cells of row 1, the whole line of words should now appear across the top line of your spreadsheet. Notice that the formula bar now shows your words with a double quotation mark (") as the first character. This means Works' internal logic has assumed that you intend this cell's contents to be a label, not a value. It assumes this because you typed in words, not numbers. You undoubtedly noticed that the line you entered was longer than the cell and thus it now overlaps columns B, C, D, E, and F. Works will always try to display the contents of a cell, regardless of how long it is. The entire contents of a cell will display on the screen as long as it doesn't run into another cell's display. Since none of the cells adjacent to A1 were filled, Works displayed the entire contents.

3. Move to cell B1.

4. Type in **25** ↵.

Notice the formula bar does not add a double quotation mark. Also notice that only the words *This is a* remain showing in cell A1. Cell contents can overlap other cells on the screen only if the overlapped cells are empty. But if you select A1 again, you'll see that no data was lost.

5. Move to A1. The formula bar shows the entire contents of cell A1. You can use this technique to store little messages to yourself about specific cells in your spreadsheets.

6. Move to C1.

7. Type in **=B1*4** ↵. This is a formula which means "calculate this cell to equal the contents of B1 times 4." The equal sign means that you want this cell to be calculated by Works.

Notice that Works calculates the cell as soon as you press ↵. The number 100 (the result of multiplying 25 times 4) appears in cell C1.

8. Move to B1 and type in **35** ↵. In an instant, C1 recalculates to 140 since a cell in its formula has been altered.

9. Just for fun, let's add one more cell, D1, which will multiply the cell C1 times 4. Move to D1.

10. Type in **=C1*4** ↵. The value 560 appears, which is 140 times 4.

11. Now try altering B1 by typing in different numbers and pressing ↵. Cells C1 and D1 will always recalculate to reflect the changes. This is the basic technique for doing "what-if?" calculations.

Finally, notice that moving to cells C1 and D1 shows the formula in the formula bar, not the current value of the cell. Activating cell B1, on the other hand, displays the current value. This is because cell B1 has no formula.

CREATING AN INVOICE SPREADSHEET

For the bulk of this chapter, we'll build a spreadsheet to be used for invoicing clients of your fictitious company — Uncle Bert's Organic Grocery Store. This spreadsheet will automatically calculate subtotals and totals for a customer, producing a computerized template to be used for other customers as well as printing a hard copy on paper for invoicing purposes.

Clearing the Current Spreadsheet

1. First, close the current spreadsheet by choosing File/Close.

2. When Works asks if you want to save the changes, type N.

3. Now choose File/New and open another new spreadsheet. A new, blank spreadsheet, SHEET2.WKS, appears.

4. Move to C1 and type in

   Uncle Bert's Organic Grocery Store ↵.

5. Move to D2 and type in

   INVOICE ↵.

6. On second thought, those two lines are too close together. Let's move the word *INVOICE* down a line. With D2 still highlighted, choose Edit/Move from the menu bar. MOVE appears in the status line, indicating that you are in the Move mode and Works is waiting for you to move the contents of this cell somewhere.

7. Press ↓ once to highlight cell D3.

8. Press ↵. The spreadsheet blinks off for a moment and reappears with the word *INVOICE* in the new location, D3. (Remember this technique for moving the contents of a cell to another cell.)

   Now that you have a nice looking title and heading in place, we'll enter the first row of the spreadsheet.

1. Move to cell A5.

2. Type in **ITEM** and press ↓ twice. (Using ↓ enters the data and moves down a cell — a little shortcut.)

3. Now you're on A7. Type in **Tofu** ↓.

4. Type in the following list in the same way you entered Tofu:

   Bean Sprouts
   Soy Beans
   Wheat Berries
   Broccoli

Brown Rice
Kiwi Fruit
Apples

5. Now your spreadsheet should look like that shown in Figure 5-3.

Next we'll put in the second column, which will list the price per unit.

1. Move to B5.

2. Type in **UNIT PRICE** and press ↓ twice.

Whoops. It looks like this column is going to cut off some labels in the ITEM column if we keep going. One solution would be to move over to column C and enter the unit price data there. But a better one is to widen column A.

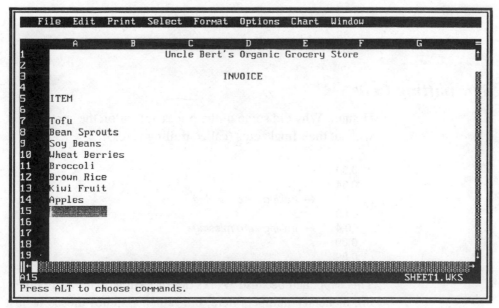

Figure 5-3. *The Item list and the title are entered*

1. Highlight any cell in column A.

2. Now choose Format/ Width.

3. A dialog box appears.

4. Type in **14** and press ↵. Column A widens to accommodate the item names without running into column B.

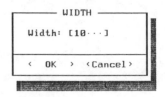

5. Move back to B7, the tofu Unit Price column.

6. Type in **.89** ↓. Notice that Works puts in the leading 0 to display 0.89.

7. Now finish the column with these unit prices:

```
.39
.34
1.10
.69
.40
.89
.89
```

Formatting Cells

Hmmm. Why did some of the prices appear on the spreadsheet without their final zeros (called trailing zeros)?

```
0.39
0.34
1.1    ← trailing zero missing
0.69
0.4    ← trailing zero missing
0.89
0.89
```

This happened because Works doesn't know that you're entering monetary numbers here, but rather assumes these are just any old numbers. Thus, trailing zeros would be superfluous (for example, 1.10 is the same as 1.1) and are removed. So, we're going to have to tell Works to format this column as money. Here's how:

1. Move to any cell in column B.

2. Choose Select/Column. The column highlights.

3. Choose Format/ Dollar. A dialog box appears.

4. Just press ↵ because we want two decimal places.

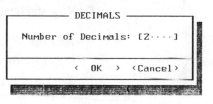

5. The column reforms to look like

UNIT PRICE
$0.89
$0.39
$0.34
$1.10
$0.69
$0.40
$0.89
$0.89

6. Press →. This deselects the column.

7. Move now to C5.

8. Type in **QUANTITY** ↓↓.

Notice that the word *QUANTITY* runs right up against UNIT PRICE.

UNIT PRICEQUANTITY

This is because the title in column B is exactly the width of the column — 10. You could resize column B to add a space or two to it. But here's another solution: since the word *QUANTITY* is only 8 letters long, we have a little room to play with in its cell. You can reformat the look of the cell to push the contents to the right side of the cell.

1. Make sure C7 is the active cell.

2. Choose Format/Style.

3. The Style dialog box appears. This is similar to the one you used in the Word Processor.

4. Choose Right from the alignment box.

5. Now the headings have a space between them.

    UNIT PRICE QUANTITY

You can alter the appearance of any cell (or group of cells) by setting the style to any of the other settings, just as you could alter the format of lines using the word processor in the last chapter. Note that unless you select a larger area, such as a row or column, or group of cells, only the active cell will be formatted in the style you choose from the Format menu. Here are basic cell formats and what they mean.

General   This is the initial style for all cells. Words are formatted left-justified, numbers right-justified, with no assumed decimal places. Additionally, very large and very small numbers are shown in scientific notation.

Left   Lines up the contents with the left side of the cell.

Right   Lines up the contents with the right side of the cell.

Center   Centers the contents of the cell.

Bold, Underline, and Italic change the format of cells when they are printed, and will only show up as a different intensity on your screen, not the final effect. You'll learn what the [X] Locked button means later on.

Entering the Quantity Column

Now enter the Quantity information. This is the column that will change with each customer's order, reflecting how many pounds of each item were purchased.

1. Move to C7.

2. Enter **4** ↓.

3. Now enter the following numbers for the other items:

   2
   10
   12
   4
   3.5
   2
   10

Now your spreadsheet looks like that shown in Figure 5-4.

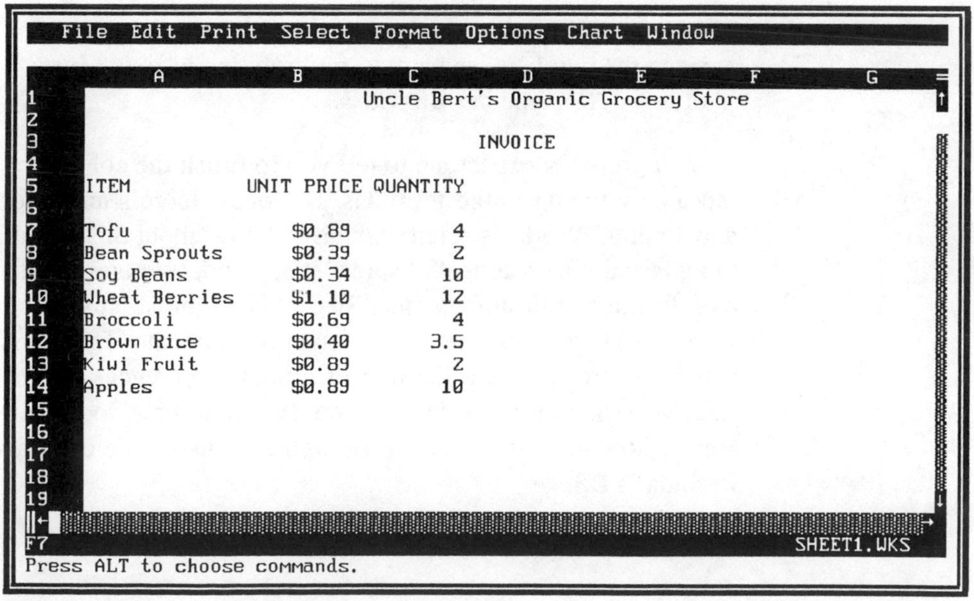

```
 File   Edit   Print   Select   Format   Options   Chart   Window
            A            B         C         D       E       F       G
1                             Uncle Bert's Organic Grocery Store
2
3                                     INVOICE
4
5    ITEM            UNIT PRICE QUANTITY
6
7    Tofu              $0.89         4
8    Bean Sprouts      $0.39         2
9    Soy Beans         $0.34        10
10   Wheat Berries     $1.10        12
11   Broccoli          $0.69         4
12   Brown Rice        $0.40        3.5
13   Kiwi Fruit        $0.89         2
14   Apples            $0.89        10
15
16
17
18
19
F7                                                          SHEET1.WKS
Press ALT to choose commands.
```

Figure 5-4. *Three columns in place*

The next column, AMOUNT, will reflect the unit price times the ordered quantity. Obviously this column will be comprised of calculated cells; that is, cells with formulas in them.

1. Move to D5.

2. Type in **AMOUNT** ↓ ↓.

3. Now you should be on cell D7. The formula for this cell should be B7 times C7, right? So type in =**B7*C7** ↓.

Don't forget to use the asterisk (*) and not a small x to indicate multiplication. You can use either the shifted 8 key or the unshifted PrtSc (Print Screen) key to get an * sign. Also, you don't have to use uppercase letters for the cell references.

4. 3.56 shows up in D7. As you would expect, Works did the calculation.

5. In D8, we'll want a similar formula, only slightly modified since the numbers we want to multiply are in row 8 instead of row 7. So, type in =**B8*C8** ↓.

You probably expect me to tell you to finish the column by repeatedly typing in the formulas. But heck, there's an easier way to do it. Works is smart enough to know about this sort of thing because a great deal of spreadsheet work involves repetitive formula adjustments just like this. Almost any good spreadsheet program lets you quickly replicate formulas, automatically changing the row or column references (called *relative references*) to compensate for their new locations. Here's how to fill in cells D9 through D14 using the existing formula in D8.

1. Make D8 the active cell.

2. Now you have to select the rest of the cells in this section. Press and hold down the SHIFT key to select D8 to D14.

3. With the SHIFT key held down, press ↓ six times until the rest of the column is selected (highlighted).

4. Release the SHIFT key.

5. Choose Edit/Fill Down.

6. The column suddenly fills itself in and calculates the amounts for each item. Not bad, eh? Just to see if the formulas were adjusted correctly, use the arrow keys to move among a few of the cells D8 to D14. You will see that they have been appropriately modified. Remember, though, that the cell at the top of the highlighted selection is the one whose formula will be duplicated.

Of course the formatting for this column needs to be changed to the dollar type to look right.

7. Choose Select/Column.

8. Choose Format/Dollar and two decimal places.

You may have noticed that the nonnumerical words in the column aren't affected by the dollar formatting. All the numerical formats only affect values, not labels. Incidentally, you can restrict a format type to a specific group of cells by selecting only those cells (using SHIFT and the arrow keys), and then choosing the format.

Your screen now should look like Figure 5-5.

Calculating Tax

Just for fun, assume your store is in one of the states where there's a five percent sales tax on groceries. We can add a column to the spreadsheet to calculate tax on each item (though calculating it based on the total amount could be done too) and then come up with a total tax figure to be used in the grand total.

1. In cell E5, enter **TAX.**

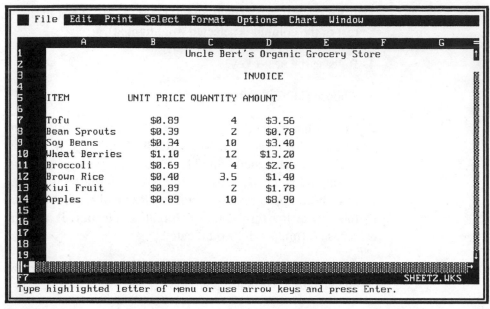

File Edit Print Select Format Options Chart Window

	A	B	C	D	E	F	G
1			Uncle Bert's Organic Grocery Store				
2							
3			INVOICE				
4							
5	ITEM	UNIT PRICE	QUANTITY	AMOUNT			
6							
7	Tofu	$0.89	4	$3.56			
8	Bean Sprouts	$0.39	2	$0.78			
9	Soy Beans	$0.34	10	$3.40			
10	Wheat Berries	$1.10	12	$13.20			
11	Broccoli	$0.69	4	$2.76			
12	Brown Rice	$0.40	3.5	$1.40			
13	Kiwi Fruit	$0.89	2	$1.78			
14	Apples	$0.89	10	$8.90			
15							
16							
17							
18							
19							

F7   SHEETZ.WKS

Type highlighted letter of menu or use arrow keys and press Enter.

Figure 5-5. Four columns in place

2. In cell E7, just enter = (an equal sign). Don't press anything else yet.

3. Press ←. Notice that the cell name D7 appears in the formula bar, and the word *POINT* shows up in the status bar, indicating that you are in Point mode. Using the arrow keys to point to a cell is a shortcut for getting the cell's name into the formula. That way you can visually pick a cell rather than figuring out what its address is.

4. Press ↵ to finalize D7 as the cell address you want in your formula. The highlight jumps back to E7, and waits for the next part of the formula.

5. Type in the next part of the equation, which is ***.05.**

6. Press ↵ to indicate the end of the equation. The equation should read **=D7*.05.**

7. Now select the rest of the column using SHIFT ↓. Then use the Edit/Fill Down command to complete the column as you did before.

   Notice that some of the numbers have more than two decimal places. This is not acceptable in most financial transactions.

8. Set the format of the column to Dollar with two decimal places. If you haven't moved the cursor since the Fill Down you just did, you won't have to reselect the column or cells before this Dollar formatting.

   Works rounds off the figures to the nearest penny.

Summing It All Up

Now create another column showing a subtotal for each item. This will be in column F.

1. In F5 type **SUBTOTAL**.

2. In F7 enter the formula **=D7+E7**. (Use the Point method to get some more practice with it.)

3. With F7 as the active cell, select the cells down to F14 and use the Edit/Fill Down command to complete the formulas in this column.

4. While the cells are still highlighted, choose Format/Dollar to reformat the numbers to dollars. This saves you the step of selecting the entire column. And since you didn't need to format the label cell (SUBTOTAL) it'll work just as well.

   Now your screen looks like that shown in Figure 5-6.

Adding Up the Grand Total

Now add up the figures in the Subtotal column using the Sum function and ranges for an invoice grand total.

1. In cell E16 enter the label **TOTAL ---**. This is just a little label to indicate where the total will show up.

2. In cell F16 enter the formula

   =F7+F8+F9+F10+F11+F12+F13+F14

A pretty long formula, right? You can enter it either by pointing at the cells one by one and pressing ↵, or by typing the whole thing. But once again, you're probably wondering if there's an easier way. Actually there is. A special notation in many spreadsheets exists for indicating a series of cells to be used in formulas or other commands. Such a series of cells is called a *range*. A range is a rectangular group of cells indicated by naming the upper-left and lower-right cells in the range, separated by a colon (:). Thus, the range F7 to F14 could be expressed F7:F14. The range A1:G20 would define the whole screen.

   To cut down on typing in lots of cell names, you could have entered your formulas =SUM(F7:F14). The word *SUM* is a

```
 File  Edit  Print  Select  Format  Options  Chart  Window

         A          B          C          D          E          F          G      =
1                          Uncle Bert's Organic Grocery Store                     ↑
2
3                                   INVOICE
4
5   ITEM          UNIT PRICE QUANTITY AMOUNT      TAX        SUBTOTAL
6
7   Tofu             $0.89        4    $3.56     $0.18        $3.74
8   Bean Sprouts     $0.39        2    $0.78     $0.04        $0.82
9   Soy Beans        $0.34       10    $3.40     $0.17        $3.57
10  Wheat Berries    $1.10       12   $13.20     $0.66       $13.86
11  Broccoli         $0.69        4    $2.76     $0.14        $2.90
12  Brown Rice       $0.40      3.5    $1.40     $0.07        $1.47
13  Kiwi Fruit       $0.89        2    $1.78     $0.09        $1.87
14  Apples           $0.89       10    $8.90     $0.45        $9.35
15
16
17
18
19
G7                                                          SHEET2.WKS
Press ALT to choose commands.
```

Figure 5-6. Five columns in place

built-in function (functions were discussed at the beginning of this chapter) that adds the values of the cells included in the range.

1. Select F16 again and type **=SUM(F7:F14)** ↵. The total of 37.569 appears as before, only the formula is much simpler.

2. Format the cell as Dollars, and the total becomes $37.57. Your screen and spreadsheet now look like that shown in Figure 5-7.

Everything is just about right, except for a few finishing touches. First off, the AMOUNT, TAX, and SUBTOTAL labels should be right-justified to line up with their respective columns.

1. Select the range D5:F5 by moving to D5, pressing down SHIFT and then pressing → twice. Notice the status line says D5:F5.

2. Choose Format/Style.

3. Choose Right alignment from the dialog box.

Now let's add a place for recording the transaction date, something every invoice should have. It can go in the upper left-hand corner.

1. In A1, enter the label **Date:**

2. In A2 type in **11/10/87**.

Works is capable of some interesting date manipulations. Since you've got a date in cell A2, try this.

1. Move to A2. Choose Format/Time/Date. A dialog box appears with lots of buttons for formatting dates and times (see Figure 5-8).

```
   File  Edit  Print  Select  Format  Options  Chart  Window
=SUM(F7:F14)
          A          B         C        D        E        F        G
1                            Uncle Bert's Organic Grocery Store
2
3                                   INVOICE
4
5   ITEM             UNIT PRICE QUANTITY AMOUNT     TAX      SUBTOTAL
6
7   Tofu                $0.89        4    $3.56    $0.18     $3.74
8   Bean Sprouts        $0.39        2    $0.78    $0.04     $0.82
9   Soy Beans           $0.34       10    $3.40    $0.17     $3.57
10  Wheat Berries       $1.10       12   $13.20    $0.66    $13.86
11  Broccoli            $0.69        4    $2.76    $0.14     $2.90
12  Brown Rice          $0.40      3.5    $1.40    $0.07     $1.47
13  Kiwi Fruit          $0.89        2    $1.78    $0.09     $1.87
14  Apples              $0.89       10    $8.90    $0.45     $9.35
15
16                                          TOTAL ---> $37.57
17
18
19
F16                                                      SHEET1.WKS
Press ALT to choose commands.
```

Figure 5-7. The grand total is added and formatted

2. In the Show box, select "Month, Day, Year" and in the Date box, select "Long."

3. The date Cell now changes to Nov 10, 1987. Try typing in any date in the xx/xx/xx format and watch Works translate it to this format.

4. For the final finishing touches, move to F15 and enter

"----------.

(Don't forget the quotation mark. If you do, you will get an error message from Works because it will think you are trying to subtract something instead of drawing a line.)

5. Do the same thing in A6, but make the line long enough to extend across the whole screen. When you're done your screen should look like Figure 5-9.

EDITING YOUR CELLS

Before printing out and/or saving spreadsheets on disk, you may want to alter (edit) the contents of certain cells. In our example grocery store invoice, you probably did most of your cell editing by simply highlighting the cell in question, retyping your data or formula, and pressing ↵ or an arrow key. This is a perfectly acceptable method. You might also have noticed that hitting the Backspace key wipes out the whole line in the formula bar, and, if followed by ↵, then deletes the contents of the cell. (ESC can get you out of this.)

Sometimes though, as with the long formula you first typed into cell F16

(=F7+F8+F9+F10+F11+F12+F13+F14)

or the title at the top of the spreadsheet:

Uncle Bert's Organic Grocery Store

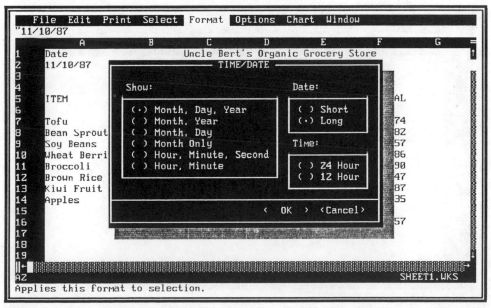

Figure 5-8. *Setting the long date form*

making a change could mean lots of retyping. For this reason, Works has an editing feature that lets you make changes to cell contents easily.

The Edit Key

The easiest way to edit a cell is to highlight the cell in question and press F2. The word *EDIT* shows up on the status line, meaning you are in Edit mode. Try this with cell C1.

Say you decide to drop the "Uncle" part of your store's name in an attempt to modernize the store's image. Here's the easy way to do it.

1. Move to C1. The cell contents appears in the formula bar, as usual.

2. Press F2. The blinking cursor now appears at the end of the line, indicating that you can begin editing. Now you can use the keys listed in Table 5-1 to edit the cell's contents.

```
 File  Edit  Print  Select  Format  Options  Chart  Window
"--------------------------------------------------------------
           A          B        C        D         E       F        G
1  Date                    Uncle Bert's Organic Grocery Store
2   Nov 10, 1987
3                                     INVOICE
4
5  ITEM            UNIT PRICE QUANTITY    AMOUNT      TAX  SUBTOTAL
6  ------------------------------------------------------------
7  Tofu               $0.89        4     $3.56     $0.18     $3.74
8  Bean Sprouts       $0.39        2     $0.78     $0.04     $0.82
9  Soy Beans          $0.34       10     $3.40     $0.17     $3.57
10 Wheat Berries      $1.10       12    $13.20     $0.66    $13.86
11 Broccoli           $0.69        4     $2.76     $0.14     $2.90
12 Brown Rice         $0.40      3.5     $1.40     $0.07     $1.47
13 Kiwi Fruit         $0.89        2     $1.78     $0.09     $1.87
14 Apples             $0.89       10     $8.90     $0.45     $9.35
15                                                       ---------
16                                        TOTAL ---->     $37.57
17
18
19
A6                                                     SHEET1.WKS
Press ALT to choose commands.
```

Figure 5-9. *The finished spreadsheet*

Key	Action
← →	Moves you back and forth
BACKSPACE	Erases letters, moving backwards
DEL	Deletes letter the cursor is on
HOME	Moves cursor to beginning of line
END	Moves cursor to end of line
Typing	Gets inserted where the cursor is

Table 5-1. Keys Active in Spreadsheet Edit Mode

3. Press HOME to get to the beginning of the line.

4. Press DEL seven times to delete the word *Uncle*. (The quotation mark will also be deleted, but Works will insert a new one when you press ↵.)

Now your invoice title is:

Bert's Organic Grocery Store

and it even looks a little more evenly centered now.

SAVING YOUR WORK

Before printing your spreadsheet, it's always a good idea to save it on disk. This way, if something goes wrong with your printer or hookup, and your computer "hangs up" for some reason, you won't lose your data. You save a spreadsheet the same way you saved your letter using the word processor in the last chapter.

1. Choose File/Save. Works now wants to know what file name and drive you want to save your spreadsheet in. We have found that typing in the file name preceded by the drive name and directory (if applicable) is the easiest method. (You could select the drive from the file box if you want to by pressing TAB and then ↓ to highlight the one you want, followed by ↵, but that takes as much work as typing B:, or whatever your data drive is, in front of the file name.)

2. So, in our case you can type in **B:INVOICE** ↵. (Replace the B: with a C: if you're using a hard disk to store your data.) Works does the rest.

USING A SPREADSHEET AS A TEMPLATE

Many spreadsheet layouts are designed to expedite repetitive bookkeeping tasks that may occur on a regular basis. Monthly income or progress reports, invoices, inventory details, and so forth are cases in point. Thus, once you've created a spreadsheet with the correct layout, format, labels and formulas, you'll often want to use that as a form, or template for future use. Here's how.

1. Create a basic layout, complete with formulas, but leave out any particular data that will change from month to month. In other words, make a blank spreadsheet.

2. Save the spreadsheet on disk using a generic name such as BLANKINV for Blank Inventory, or use some other name you'll remember.

3. When you need to create a real spreadsheet from the template, choose File/Open and open BLANKINV, or whatever the name.

4. Modify the spreadsheet template by typing in your data or making any other changes.

5. Choose File/Save As and save the spreadsheet under a new name — not the old one, or you will erase the template! (Well, actually it will be put in the Backup directory until you make the same mistake again, but don't count on it being there.)

PRINTING OUT YOUR SPREADSHEET

Printing your spreadsheet is simple. There are only a few steps to know about basic printing, though printing larger spreadsheets gets a bit more complex. For simple printing there are six steps:

1. Select the range of cells you want to print. This can be done several ways. The easiest is to press F5 and type in the range using a colon between cell names. For example, to print our spreadsheet, enter **A1:F16.**

2. Choose Print/Set Print Area. This tells Works to print only the selected cells. Nothing appears to happen, but it has.

3. Choose Print/Print.

4. Select the applicable printing options from the dialog box. Turn on the Row and Column Labels check box if you want your printout to contain the line numbers and column letters too.

5. Make sure your printer is on, connected, and has paper.

6. Press ↵ to begin printing.

When you print a large spreadsheet, Works divides the printed document into page-sized pieces. The size of these pieces is determined by the dimensions you choose from the Print/Layout dialog box.

In this chapter, you've learned the rudiments of designing, creating, editing, and printing a modest-sized spreadsheet. Of course, many spreadsheets are larger and more complex to create, use, and understand. Bookstores are packed with tomes on the subject. However, even with the skills you have learned here you can probably think of some everyday spreadsheets to build for yourself. Try experimenting on your own, but do save the Invoice spreadsheet as it is now for use in Chapter 9.

Chapter

Using the Database

Six

In this chapter, we'll examine the Works database, how it works, and what it can do for you. You'll probably find that, despite whatever preconceptions you had about databases, they can be pretty interesting, very practical, and even fun. After reading through this chapter, you'll know how to create a database, enter data into it, retrieve desired information from the database, and print out that data.

Recall from Chapter 1 that a database is really nothing more than a list of things—people, addresses, amounts, or anything else that could be put into a list. In other words, it's just a collection of information that has something in common, a bit like an electronic filing cabinet, only you have to type information into the computer instead of just filing pages of paper.

Like any filing system, a database itself isn't very useful unless you have a way of quickly retrieving the information you want and of getting new data into it and old data out of it. You also will want ways of rearranging the database to list out your information in a variety of orders, such as chronological, alphabetical, and so on. For all this, it's necessary to have an intelligent program that maintains the database. This program is typically called, quite logically, a database management system, or DBMS for short.

The Works database tool is just such an item. It has a DBMS built in, and although it's not the most powerful DBMS in town, it does have lots of features and is relatively easy to use. Interestingly enough, the Works database is very similar in appearance and operation to the spreadsheet tool, so some of the operations you learned in the last chapter will carry over to this one.

DATABASE BASICS

Like the spreadsheets we experimented with in the last chapter, databases, too, are comprised of a series of rows and columns. And like a spreadsheet, a database stores its data in cells—the individual pigeonholes created by the intersection of the rows and columns.

In a database, however, the columns are called fields and the rows are called records. To illustrate this, let's consider one of the more common databases we regularly use: a telephone book. A typical entry (record) in a phone book might look something like this:

	Name	*Address*	*Phone*
Record 1	**Martindale, Emily**	**1454 Virginia**	**324-4665**

As you may suspect, the fields in this database would be Name, Address, and Phone. All of Emily Martindale's information (data) is listed in a single record of the database (in this case, record 1). Other people would be listed in subsequent records, one for each person in the phone book.

Each entry in Emily's record is stored in a cell, just as you stored values, labels, and formulas in the spreadsheet. And just as with the spreadsheet, you can copy, move, format, edit, calculate, and print out data stored in the cells. However, the major difference between the Works database and spreadsheet is that the database tool is designed to let you create and maintain lists of things in the same way you would use a filing cabinet or Rolodex file. You can then find what you want in a hurry because Works can keep the items sorted and organized, and can search through heaps of data very quickly to locate just the information you want. The spreadsheet, on the other hand, specializes in performing calculations on a constant number of interrelated values.

List View Versus Form View

An additional difference is that Works lets you enter, view, and edit data in two distinct layouts, so you are not limited to the look of a spreadsheet. These two layouts are called list view and form view. List view displays a whole screenful of records at the same time, one record per row, with cells separated into columns. List view, as seen in Figure 6-1, looks a bit like a spreadsheet.

Form view, on the other hand, shows you one record at a time, displaying data in a customized form that you create to your liking, such as in Figure 6-2.

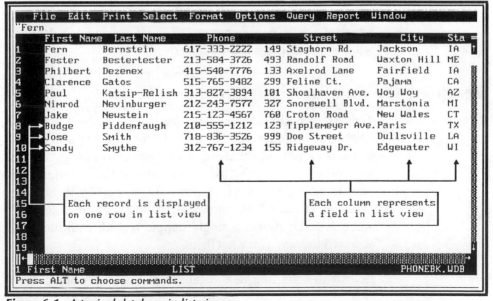

Figure 6-1. *A typical database in list view*

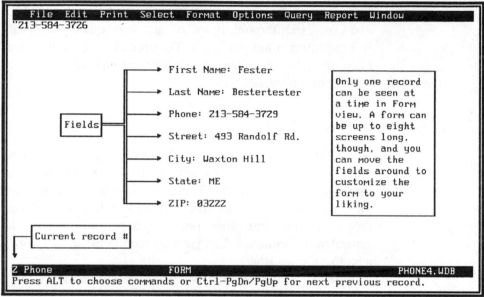

Figure 6-2. A typical database in form view

MAKING A PHONE BOOK DATABASE

Since the telephone book example is a relatively simple and practical one, why not create a personal phone book database with Works that you can use later?

Designing the Database Structure

The first step in creating a new database is to think about the number and arrangement, or order of the fields you'll want in it. Unlike a new spreadsheet, which has cells already created and waiting to be filled in, a database has to be designed by you, in advance of your entering any data. The layout of a database is called its structure. Setting up the structure amounts to laying out a single sample record, with the fields arranged the way you want them.

It pays to put a little advance thought in just how many fields you want in a new database. If you don't break down your data into enough fields, you may find limitations in re-arranging or retrieving records later. For example, you could store each person's street address, city, and state in one field. But should you want to look them up or print them out according to the city later, this could be a problem. So, it's best to separate the street, city, and state data into three distinct fields.

For our personal telephone book we'll use the following fields, at least to start:

First Name   Last Name   Phone   Street   City   State   ZIP

To create the structure:

1. Open a new database document.

2. Your screen will look very blank, with just the menu bar, status line, and message lines showing anything, as in Figure 6-3.

Notice that the status line says

Pg 1   DESIGN   DATA1.WDB

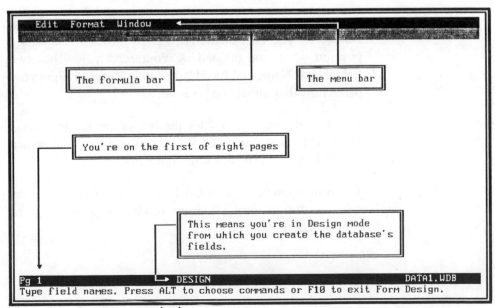

Figure 6-3. *Creating a new database*

This means you're in the form view's Design mode, creating the database named DATA1.WDB. It's in this Design mode that you lay out your database's fields, or structure. Your cursor is in the upper left-hand corner of the work area, waiting for you to type in the name of the first field.

1. Type in **First Name:** (don't forget the colon since this tells Works to create a data field rather than just placing a label on the form). As you type, the letters appear in the formula bar.

2. Press ↵. Now the words *First Name:* appear in the upper left-hand corner of the work area, just below the formula bar, which also says *First Name:*. After First Name:, there is a line, which Works creates. (You may not be able to see this line clearly now, but you will when you move the cursor.) This line indicates the place where your data will eventually go. You've created the first field.

3. Now press ↓ twice so that the highlight is two lines below the First Name field. This is where the next field we place on the form will begin.

4. Now create and place the second field by typing **Last Name:** ↵. The Last Name field pops down to the cursor position when you pressed ↵. Your screen now has two fields, First Name and Last Name, on it. Refer to Figure 6-4 to see how they should be positioned.

5. Now repeat steps 3 and 4 for the rest of the fields: Phone, Street, City, State, and ZIP. When you're done, your screen should look like that shown in Figure 6-4.

For your reference, Table 6-1 lists the keystrokes you can use in the forms view's Design mode for navigating, or moving around the screen.

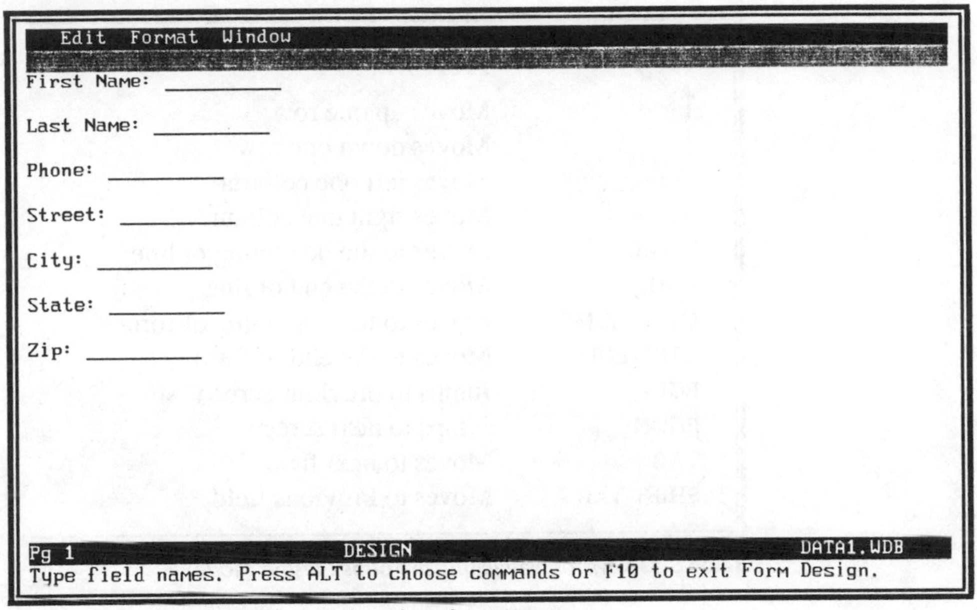

Figure 6-4. *All seven fields are placed on the screen*

Moving the Fields Around

You've now finished creating the basic structure of this database. In fact, you've done more than that. By placing field names onto the design screen, you've also designed the look of the form in which you will view single records later on. In effect, the Design mode creates the database structure and the form view at the same time.

At this point, if you were to enter data (names, addresses, and so on) into the database, your form view wouldn't look very interesting. At the least, it would look off-center since all the fields and field names are sitting along the left margin. Chances are good that you will want to reposition some of your fields on the screen to achieve a more aesthetic or practical layout. The Edit menu's Move command lets you do this. So, before moving on to enter some names and addresses, rearrange the field locations so that they aren't shoved up against the left side of the screen.

Key	Action
↑	Moves up one row
↓	Moves down one row
←	Moves left one column
→	Moves right one column
HOME	Moves to the beginning of line
END	Moves to the end of line
CTRL-HOME	Moves to the beginning of form
CTRL-END	Moves to the end of form
PGUP	Jumps to previous screen
PGDN	Jumps to next screen
TAB	Moves to next field
SHIFT-TAB	Moves to Previous field

Table 6-1. Keys for Navigating in Forms Design Mode

1. Select the First Name field by putting the cursor somewhere on it. As soon as the cursor touches the boundary of the field, the entire field will become highlighted.

2. Choose Edit/Move (or press F3).

3. The status line now says MOVE, meaning that you are now in the Move mode, with Works waiting for you to indicate the field's new location.

4. Using the arrows keys, move the cursor to approximately the center of the screen, two lines down from the formula bar, and press ↵. The First Name: field jumps to the new location.

5. Now, using the same technique, move the remaining fields until your screen looks like that shown in Figure 6-5.

Now the basic design of your database is complete and you can move on to enter some data into it.

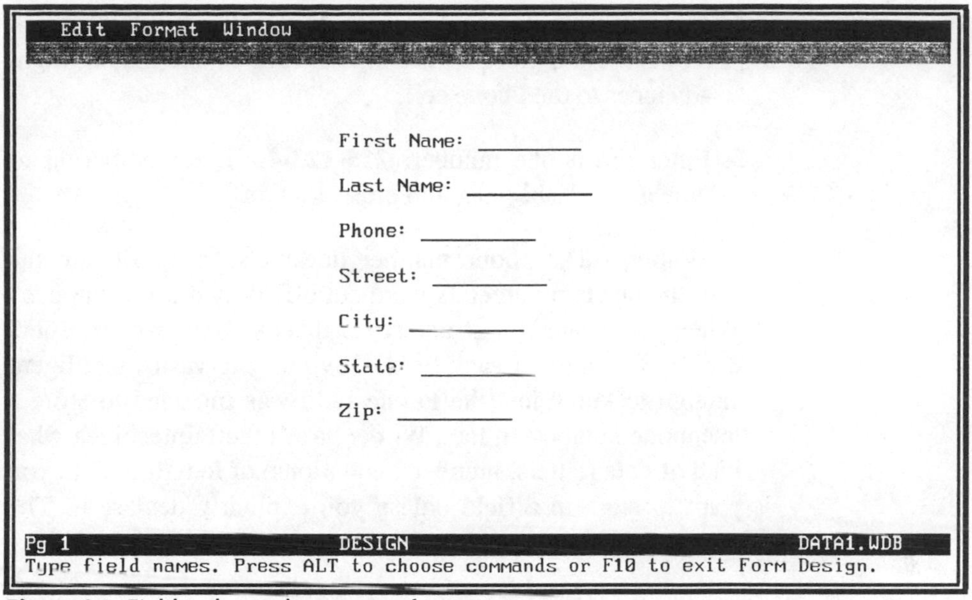

```
  Edit  Format  Window



                      First Name: _____

                      Last Name: _____

                      Phone: _____

                      Street: _____

                      City: _____

                      State: _____

                      Zip: _____




Pg 1                      DESIGN                          DATA1.WDB
Type field names. Press ALT to choose commands or F10 to exit Form Design.
```

Figure 6-5. Fields relocated to center of screen

1. Notice that the message line says you can press F10 to exit the Design mode. Do this now. The screen changes from the Design screen to the form screen, ready for you to start entering your names and addresses. Notice that the menu bar has expanded to nine choices, that the last field you moved is highlighted and that the status line rather than the formula bar now indicates the name of the current field.

2. To enter the first record of the database, first use the arrow keys to position the cursor in the First Name cell. Then type in **Jake**. (The letters appear in the formula bar, not in the highlighted area.)

3. Press ↓. This enters the data into the cell and moves you down to the next cell. (You could also have pressed ↵ followed by the ↓ key, but just pressing ↓ eliminates a step.)

4. Now the highlight is on the Last Name cell. Type in **Newstein** and press ↓. The data is entered and the highlight advances to the Phone cell.

5. Enter the phone number, **215-123-4567**, remembering to type in the dashes too, and press ↓ again.

Whoops! The phone number doesn't seem to fit into the cell; the last two numerals were cut off. Why did this happen? When you created the structure for this database, we let Works decide the length of each field. Obviously it wasn't intelligent enough to know that the Phone field was intended to store a telephone number. In fact, Works hasn't the faintest idea what kind of data (letters, numbers, equations) or length of data you want to store in a field unless you explicitly declare it. The solution to this common problem is to adjust the field's width.

Modifying Field Widths

Before we adjust the field widths, a little background on database field sizes is in order. An advanced feature of Works is that, unlike many other databases, the apparent size of your fields on the screen does not affect the amount of data stored in those fields. So actually, the last two digits of the phone number are in Works' memory. Works remembers whatever you type into a field regardless of how long it is. Likewise, if you type nothing into a field, Works stores nothing, either in RAM or on disk, and therefore does not waste precious space.

In an attempt to simplify the task of designing a database, Works assigns a standard length of 10 spaces for all fields. You will notice that this is what has happened here. Obviously the default 10-space field length may not work for all instances. Clearly we'll have to modify not only the Phone field but also the Street, City, State, and ZIP fields if we want to optimize the form.

Since Works remembers whatever you type into a field, the only reason to alter the widths would be for the convenience of seeing the amount of field data you want, or for making the screen look reasonable. For example, allotting 10 spaces for a two-letter state abbreviation doesn't make much sense, and can even be confusing to data entry people who may not know whether to type in CA or California. Conversely, 10 spaces isn't long enough to display the city name San Francisco.

Field lengths must be altered from the Design mode, and incidentally, unlike some other database programs, altering field length does not cause any loss of data that you may have already typed into your database. Field length can be altered either before or after data is entered into a database with no adverse effects on the data itself.

To practice altering field widths, adjust the fields in the phone book database using these steps.

1. First, get back into the Design mode by choosing Options/Define Form.

2. Select the First Name field just as you did when you moved it. The field now becomes highlighted, which means it's ready for editing or alteration.

3. Choose Format/Width. A dialog box appears, showing the current width, which is 22. Why 22 instead of 10? Because the field's name is included in the total size. The words First Name plus a colon and a space after the colon amount to 12 spaces. Adding that to 10 for the data equals 22.

4. To change the length, just type in the desired new width. Eight spaces is plenty for the First Name field. With the field name, colon, and extra space included, that amounts to 20. Type in **20** and press ↵. The line for this field should now shorten two spaces.

5. Repeat this process for the remainder of the fields, setting the widths as follows:

   Last Name: 26
   Phone: 19
   Street: 28
   City: 19
   State: 9
   ZIP: 10

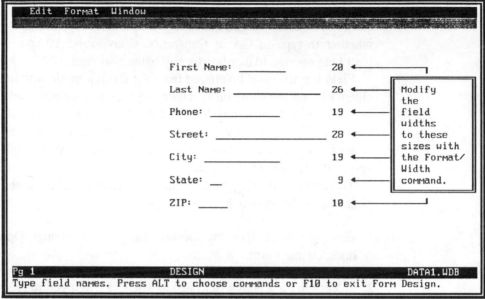

```
  Edit  Format  Window


                    First Name: _____        20 ◄──────────────────┐
                    Last Name: _____      26 ◄────────┌─────────────┐
                                                             │ Modify      │
                                                             │ the         │
                    Phone: _____           19 ◄────────│ field       │
                                                             │ widths      │
                    Street: _____        28 ◄────────│ to these    │
                                                             │ sizes with  │
                    City: _____            19 ◄────────│ the Format/ │
                                                             │ Width       │
                    State: __                     9 ◄────────│ command.    │
                                                             └─────────────┘
                    ZIP: _____                   10 ◄──────────────────┘



Pg 1                         DESIGN                              DATA1.WDB
Type field names. Press ALT to choose commands or F10 to exit Form Design.
```

Figure 6-6. The form with modified field widths

Now your screen should look like Figure 6-6.

6. When you have all the fields sized correctly, press F10 to exit the Design mode and return to form view to continue entering data.

Adding More Records

Now you can continue entering records in the database.

1. Move the highlight to the First Name field of record 1. (If you are not on record 1, press CTRL-HOME.)

2. Press ↓ three times to move down to the Street field.

3. Fill in the rest of the data for the first record until it looks like Figure 6-7. Precede the ZIP code with a quotation mark ("). Without the quotation mark, Works will consider these to be numerical values and will therefore chop off any zeros

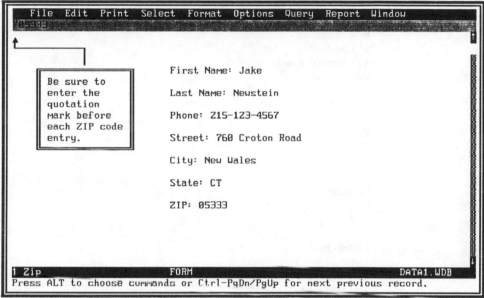

File Edit Print Select Format Options Query Report Window

Be sure to
enter the
quotation
mark before
each ZIP code
entry.

First Name: Jake

Last Name: Newstein

Phone: 215-123-4567

Street: 760 Croton Road

City: New Wales

State: CT

ZIP: 05333

1 Zip   FORM   DATA1.WDB
Press ALT to choose commands or Ctrl-PgDn/PgUp for next previous record.

Figure 6-7. The first record is filled in

at the beginning of the ZIP codes, assuming—ignorantly—
that these leading zeros are not necessary. (You should use
the quotation mark for any other integers that are not used
as numerical values.)

4. When you get to the last field in the first record, press ↓ (or
→) to move ahead to the next record. Now add the following nine records of rather oddly named people to your
database. We'll then use all ten records for experimentation
in this chapter. (If you make mistakes during the process of
entering the data, don't worry. You'll learn how to fix them
later in Edit mode. Of course you can always use the Backspace key to fix errors as you go along too, or simply press
⏎ instead of the ↓ or → key and then retype the data for
whatever field you're on.)

Don't puzzle over the order of the entries here. As we'll see
later in this chapter, sorting the entries in a database is easy
and one of the joys of working with databases.

Fester
Bestertester
213-584-3726
493 Randolf Road
Waxton Hill
ME
" 03222

Philbert
Dezenex
415-540-7776
133 Axelrod Lane
Fairfield
IA
" 52556

Clarence
Gatos
515-765-9482
299 Feline Ct.
Pajama
CA
" 94709

Jose
Smith
718-836-3526
999 Doe Street
Dullsville
LA
" 78263

Budge
Piddenfaugh
201-555-1212
123 Tipplemeyer Ave.
Paris
TX
" 41234

Nimrod
Nevinburger
212-243-7577
327 Snorewell Blvd.
Marstonia
MI
" 65271

```
Sandy
Smythe
312-767-1234
155 Ridgeway Dr.
Edgewater
WI
" 22256

Paul
Relish
313-827-3894
101 Shoalhaven Ave.
Woy Woy
AZ
" 82239

Fern
Bernstein
617-333-2222
149 Staghorn Rd.
Jackson
IA
" 55212
```

Saving Your Work

Before going any further, it's a good idea to save your work on disk to prevent accidentally losing your data if the power goes off or if some other hardware or software error occurs.

1. Choose File/Save. The SAVE dialog box appears.

2. Make sure the correct data disk drive is selected.

3. For the file name, type in **PHONEBK.**

4. Press ↵ or click on <OK>.

MOVING AROUND THE DATABASE

Now that we have semblance of a database entered, we can begin to experiment a bit. For example, thumbing through your records in form view is simple, as we'll see in the the next section.

How to Move Between Records in Form View

1. Try viewing the records you've entered now by pressing CTRL-PGUP and CTRL-PGDN. CTRL-PGUP moves to the previous record; CTRL-PGDN jumps to the next record.

2. Notice that the far left side of the status line indicates the number of the record you are viewing.

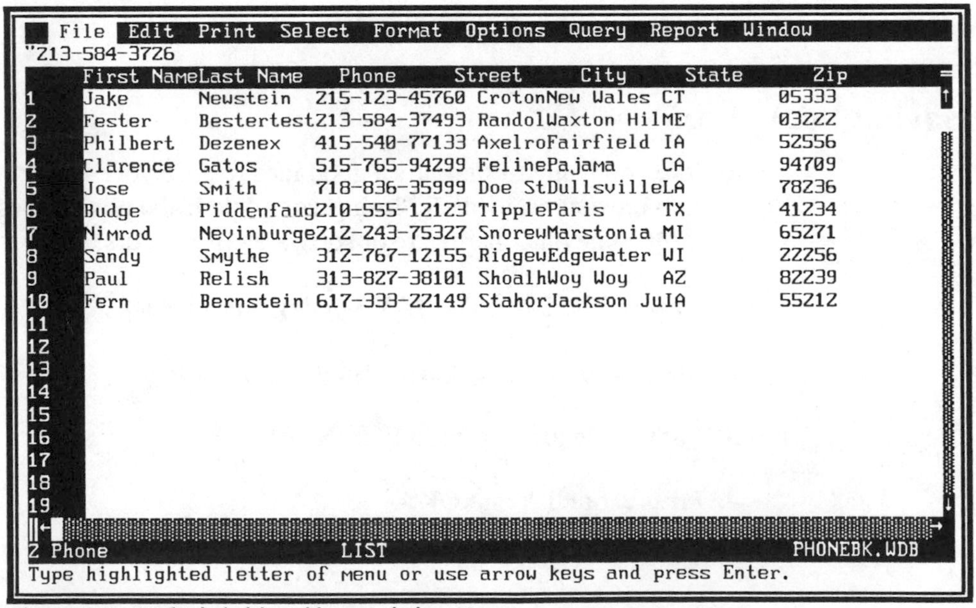

Figure 6-8. *Default field widths need alteration.*

How to Switch to List View

As mentioned earlier, you can view lots of records at once, in a list (in list view), rather than one at a time (form view), as you've been doing. Switching between these views is a simple process.

1. Choose Options/View List. The screen changes to that as shown in Figure 6-8.

2. You could have pressed F9 instead; it switches the screen between form and list views with each press.

(If your fields are in a different order than what is shown in Figure 6-8, you may want to page ahead and read the section on rearranging the fields in list view.)

Notice that each record now occupies a row of the list and that the familiar problem of all fields being displayed in 10 spaces rears its ugly head again. Although we redefined the field length for form view, the settings are not carried over to list view. This allows you more flexibility in designing separate list and form appearances, but it's an extra hassle when first setting up a database.

Actually, for some uses, it's not disastrous that fields run into one another, since (just as with a long number or label in a spreadsheet) the formula bar displays the complete contents of a field anyway. In some cases you may want to leave your screen compressed this way to accommodate a greater number of fields, and just move the highlight around to view specific fields' data in the formula bar when you need to. Otherwise, once you stretch out the field widths, you may have to scroll the screen horizontally to get to certain fields. On the other hand, if it's important to be able to quickly scan a series of fields visually, then you'll probably want to adjust their widths as necessary.

So, to make the fields in list view wider, do the following:

1. Put the highlight anywhere in the Last Name column (it doesn't matter which record), using the → and ← keys.

2. Choose Format/Width.

3. Notice that the width is set to 10. Unlike the form view, the name of the field itself is not added to the total width since the name appears at the top of the column, not adjacent to the field data.

4. Type in **14** and press ⏎.

5. Using this same technique, set the remainder of the field widths to

Phone   14
Street   20
City   12
State   3
ZIP   7

You can leave the First Name field unchanged, since its length is okay. A width of three for the State field is necessary to prevent the State and ZIP fields from running together.

6. Press CTRL ← to pan the screen to the far left, bringing the First Name field back into display.

When you're finished, your screen should look like Figure 6-9. Notice that the ZIP code field is now off the screen.

How to Navigate in List View

You navigate around the screen and scroll vertically and horizontally through a database in list view using the keyboard commands listed in Table 6-2.

How to Rearrange Fields in List View

You may have noticed that the order of the fields, from left to right, in the list view corresponds to the top to bottom order of fields in the form view. This will usually be the case, assuming you create your fields from top to bottom in the forms Design mode. However, there may be times when the fields aren't in the order you want.

Works creates list view fields in same order in which you created them on the form. Thus, it's possible that the list view fields may appear in the wrong order if you inserted new fields to the form after the initial design, if you didn't define fields from top to bottom originally, or if you made some other error while entering the field names.

If you find that your list view columns are in the wrong order, you can rearrange them in list view using the techniques outlined in the following sections.

From the Keyboard

1. Get into list view and move the cursor into the column you want to move.

2. Choose Select/Field.

3. Press F3 or choose Edit/Move.

```
 File  Edit  Print  Select  Format  Options  Query  Report  Window
"Jake
      First Name  Last Name      Phone            Street           City     Sta =
1     Jake        Neustein     215-123-4567  760 Croton Road      New Wales   CT  ↑
2     Fester      Bestertester 213-584-3726  493 Randolf Road     Waxton Hill ME
3     Philbert    Dezenex      415-540-7776  133 Axelrod Lane     Fairfield   IA
4     Clarence    Gatos        515-765-9482  299 Feline Ct.       Pajama      CA
5     Jose        Smith        718-836-3526  999 Doe Street       Dullsville  LA
6     Budge       Piddenfaugh  210-555-1212  123 Tipplemeyer Ave. Paris       TX
7     Nimrod      Nevinburger  212-243-7577  327 Snorewell Blvd.  Marstonia   MI
8     Sandy       Smythe       312-767-1234  155 Ridgeway Dr.     Edgewater   WI
9     Paul        Relish       313-827-3894  101 Shoalhaven Ave.  Woy Woy     AZ
10    Fern        Bernstein    617-333-2222  149 Staghorn Rd.     Jackson     IA
11
12
13
14
15
16
17
18
19
1 First Name                 LIST                           PHONEBK.WDB
Press ALT to choose commands.
```

Figure 6-9. *The list view after adjusting the field widths*

Key	Action
↑	Moves up one record
↓	Moves down one record
TAB or →	Moves right one cell
SHIFT-TAB or ←	Moves left one cell
PGUP	Moves up one screenful of records
PGDN	Moves down one screenful of records
HOME	Moves to the first cell in the current record
END	Moves to the last cell in the current record
CTRL ←	Moves left to the first full-cell/empty-cell boundary
CTRL →	Moves right to the first full-cell/empty-cell boundary
CTRL-HOME	Moves to the beginning of the database
CTRL-END	Moves to the end of the database
F5	Go To a specific record

Table 6-2. Navigation Keys for List View

4. Move the cursor to the field *before* which you want the relocated field to be inserted.

5. Press ↵.

With a Mouse

1. Click on the name of the field you want to move (at the top of the screen). The whole column becomes selected.

2. Press F3 to activate Move mode.

3. Click on the name of the field *before* which you want the relocated field to be inserted. The whole column becomes selected.

4. Press ↵.

EDITING YOUR DATA

There usually comes a time with most databases when you'll want to alter the contents of specific records. For example, since people tend to move from place to place, their addresses and phone numbers (and even names) will occasionally change. Rather than scratching out or erasing the old address and entering a new as you would do with a traditional address book, you can just edit the data in your database.

How to Edit in List View

Let's say you've just received a wedding invitation announcing the imminent marriage of Paul Relish to Linda Katsip, and that they intend to hyphenate their last names. You'll want to change his last name in the database.

1. Move the highlight to the Last Name field in record 9: Relish.

2. Press F2, which is called the edit key. This puts you into Edit mode, just as it did in the spreadsheet. (The status line now says EDIT.)

   As usual, the current cell data (in this case Relish) had appeared in the formula bar. But now the blinking cursor is there too, right after the last character of the name, allowing you to make changes to the existing data.

3. Now you can edit the cell just as if you were altering data in a spreadsheet cell (see the following list). Type in

   -Katsip

   and press ↵. The modified name appears in the database, and Edit mode ceases.

   Of course, you could also have made the change without getting into Edit mode by moving to the cell and typing in the whole new name, Relish-Katsip, and pressing ↵. Using Edit mode just cuts down on retyping, just as in the spreadsheet.

Just as a reminder, the keys you can use in Edit mode are listed in Table 6-3.

Editing in Form View

You could also have edited Paul's record in form view. Editing in form view can be more convenient if you plan to change lots of fields in a given record and would like to see as many as possible on one screen. It's more likely that a form view would display more fields than a list view without scrolling the screen left and right.

There are a couple of ways to make editing data in form view really easy.

♦ The first way is to use list view to move around the database, since you can see more records at once. Position the highlight somewhere on the record you want to alter (preferably the first cell you plan to change). Then press F9 (or choose Options/View Form). The form appears with the highlight already on the cell. Press F2, make your changes, press ↵, ↑, or ↓ for each modified cell and then press F9 to return to list view.

♦ In large databases, moving from one record to another sequentially can take a lot of time, especially if you are jumping large distances. But since each record in a database has a number, you can use the Go To command to jump directly to a specific record very quickly. This can be done from either list or form view.

For example, say you want to edit the Phone cell of record 403. Press F5 (or choose Select/Go To). The GO TO dialog box appears as you see in Figure 6-10.

Key	Effect
$\rightarrow$	Moves you right one space
$\leftarrow$	Moves you left one space
BACKSPACE	Erases letters, moving backwards
DEL	Deletes character the cursor is on, or deletes all characters that you select via SHIFT $\rightarrow$ or SHIFT $\leftarrow$
Typing	Gets inserted where the cursor is
HOME	Moves cursor to beginning of line
END	Moves cursor to end of line
↵	Accepts the changes
ESC	Cancels the changes and leaves the field as it was

Table 6-3. *Keys Active in Edit Mode*

Type in **403** and press ↵. You can even choose the exact field you want to edit by selecting it from the field list in the dialog box. Then the cursor will jump directly to that cell in the desired record.

In large databases, you often won't know the record number you're trying to get to unless you're referring to a printed list that shows the record numbers. Typically you'll know only the name of the person or item whose information you want to retrieve or edit. In such cases, you might use the Select/Search command to find a given record, as explained in the next section.

SEARCHING THE DATABASE

As we've mentioned above, you can quickly land on and display a particular record in a database just based on the information in it. The Select/Search command accomplishes this for you. Search tells Works to look through your database file

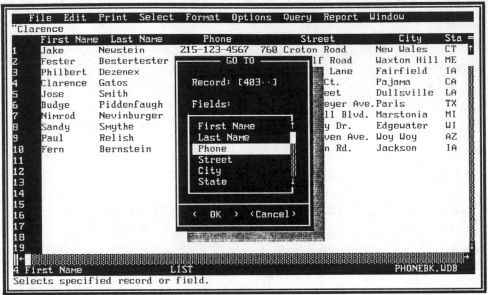

Figure 6-10. *Jumping to a specific record*

until it finds the specific data that you stipulate. When the data is found, the record is displayed.

Searching Order

For technical reasons, you are given the choice of telling Works to conduct the search from left to right (one complete record after another) or top to bottom (one complete column, then another).

Since searching takes time, particularly with large databases, this optimizing of the search pattern can reduce the waiting. If you were looking for John Shuman in a phone book, for example, you would scan only the last-name column rather than waste time analyzing the phone number column. Similarly, you'll more often want Works to perform a column search than a row search.

Row-by-row searches are typically used if you don't remember which field the data you're looking for is in, but you think you may be in the vicinity of the correct record. This way Works doesn't have to search all the way to the end of each column before continuing to the next record.

In any case, you should be aware that seaching begins at the highlighted cell and continues to the end of the database, then loops around to the beginning of it, and stops when the highlighted cell is again reached. Thus, it's wiser to back up a little before beginning a search if you know that you're in the vicinity of the record but are not sure whether it's above or below your current location in the database.

How to Conduct a Search

With this understanding, let's try some experiments.

1. Make sure you are in list view.

2. Choose Select/Search. The SEARCH dialog box appears.

3. Say you want to see who, if anyone, lives in Paris. Type in **paris** ↵ as you see in Figure 6-11.

Now, let's try a search from form view. Say you want to find your friend Clarence's record either to edit or just to view.

1. Switch to form view with F9. (Notice the status line still indicates, by the number in the lower left, that you are on record 6.)

2. Choose Select/Search again. Now type in **clar** ↵. His record appears.

Notice that you didn't have to type in the whole name, just clar. Of course, if there were a Clara in your database, this search would have found that record too. So, the more completely you enter your search information the more exact Works will be in searching for records.

Notice also that you didn't have to use an uppercase C to find Clarence. Works' search command is "case-insensitive," meaning it doesn't care what case you type in. PAUL will find Paul, and even cLaReNcE will find Clarence.

Repeating a Search

The Search command finds only one record at a time. That is, Works finds the first record that has the letters you specify, plops you on the record, and stops. But what if there are several records that meet the search condition? Try these steps to see how you can quickly repeat a search.

1. Get back to list view.

2. Choose Select/Search.

3. Type in **ne** ↵. Works will find the next cell with an *ne* in it.

4. Press F7 (the repeat search key). Works jumps to the next cell with an *ne* in it.

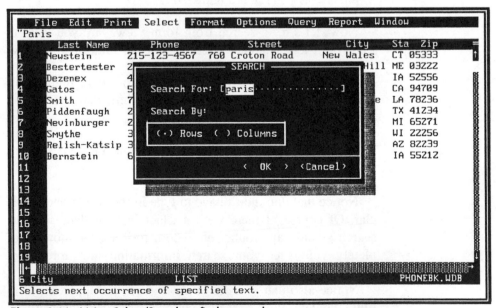

Figure 6-11. *Using Select/Search to find a record*

5. Keep pressing F7 and notice that Works jumps through all the cells with *ne*, and then loops around and repeats the process. There should be five cells that have *ne* in them.

Limiting the Search to a Selected Area

Sometimes you may want to limit a search to a portion of the database, particularly if the database is large and would take a great deal of time to search. Or perhaps you want to search through only one field rather than letting Works lead you through a trail of matching text in other fields that are irrelevant to your search.

Here's an example of how to limit a search (this must be done from list view).

1. Move the cursor into the Phone field.

2. Select the entire Phone field by choosing Select/Field.

3. Choose Select/Search and type in **222** ↵.

Notice that the phone number 617-333-2222 in record 10 was found. Even if you try the search again, the 222 in the ZIP field of records 2 and 8 will not be found. As long as the selection remains active (highlighted), all searches will be restricted to the selected area of your database.

If you want to increase the selected area to include several fields, or just specific records, that can be done too. In fact, knowing how to select a large area of the database is helpful when using other commands such as those from the Format menu. The process is identical to that for manually selecting ranges in the spreadsheet. Try these experiments to see.

1. Move to the Last Name cell of record 2.

2. Depress the SHIFT key and try pressing → and then ↓. Notice that the selection grows with each key press.

3. Pressing the ← and ↑ keys decreases the size of the selection (until you reach the anchor point, after which it increases in the opposite direction).

4. Press ESC and the cells become deselected.

You can easily select multiple records or fields by the following means:

1. Select one cell in each row or column that you want included in the selection.

2. Choose Select/Row or Select/Column.

Using Wildcards to Broaden a Search

Rather than limiting a search, you may occasionally want to broaden it by using *wildcards*. Wildcards are symbols that will match any text during a search and you use them in conjunction with normal search characters. For example, say you wanted to search for all Bernsteins, regardless of whether they are spelled with *e* before *i* or *i* before *e*. You could do this with wildcards. Works recognizes two wildcards: the question mark (?) and the asterisk (*). The ? represents a single character of any value. The * represents any number of characters of any value.

So, for example, Bernst??n would find Bernstein or Bernstien. It would even find Bernstzzn, for that matter.

The ? works fine when you know exactly how many letters are in the word you're looking for. If the number of letters might vary, then use the * sign. For example, say you had a database of words. You want to search for all words that begin with the letter *W* and end with the letter *Y*, regardless of how long they are. You would use this formula as the search attribute:

[W * Y........]

Such a search would find *Woy, Wally, Wy, West Yonkers,* or even *Southwest Yonkers.*

SORTING YOUR DATABASE

It often happens that the order of records in a database is rather haphazard. Records are usually entered in the order they are acquired (chronological order) rather than in the more frequently needed alphabetical or numerical order.

For example, our phone book database was entered in no particular order, so if you were to print it out on paper and thus didn't have the Search command to use, finding a needed record might take you awhile. This would be a real hassle with a database of several thousand names and addresses.

One of the greatest conveniences of computerized databases is their ability to quickly *sort* or rearrange their data records according to your needs. Works is no exception here. You can sort your database in many ways, and fairly rapidly. Once the database is sorted to your liking you can, of course, save it on disk in the new order for future use. For that matter, you could store several copies of a database (assuming you had the disk space for it) sorted in different orders.

In Works, once the database is sorted, all subsequent commands, reports, screen listings, printouts and form viewing you do will occur in the new, sorted order.

The field that the database is sorted on is called the *key field*. Works lets you choose up to three key fields if you wish. Normally, you will use only one, but you may want to use more. The key fields operate in order of precedence. The first key, called the *primary key*, determines the grossest level of sorting. For example, in a city's phone book, this would be last name.

The second and third keys are called *subordinate fields* and determine the order of records that appear identical under the primary key. For example, John Smith should appear after Bob Smith, not before. If you sorted only on Last Name, this would not be assured. You would have to sort on Last Name followed by First Name as the secondary key.

Additionally, Works gives you the option of sorting in ascending (A to Z and 0 to n) or descending (Z to A and n to 0) order. It's rare that you'll want to list the Z's before the A's, but descending order is often useful for numerical sorting. For example, you might want to see your expenses or sales with the largest figures appearing first.

Enough theory. Now let's sort our phone book list according to Last Name.

1. Get back to list view.

2. Choose Query/Sort.

3. The SORT dialog box appears. Notice that there are three spaces you can fill in, indicating the first, second, and third key fields. Also notice that the first field in your database, First Name, is typed into the 1st Field: area. Works does this for you as a convenience, assuming that you would most often want to sort on the first field you created. Actually you want to sort the database by last name, so type in **Last Name** as in Figure 6-12, and press ↵.

4. Almost instantly the database reorders itself in last name order as you see in Figure 6-13.

5. Try the same thing again, only select the Descend button (press TAB then →) to see the names listed in reverse alphabetical order.

6. Now, just to get things back into proper order, re-sort in ascending order.

If you plan to work with large mailing lists, don't forget what a time-saver sorting on the ZIP code field can be, since the U.S. Postal Service requires bulk mail be sorted by ZIP code.

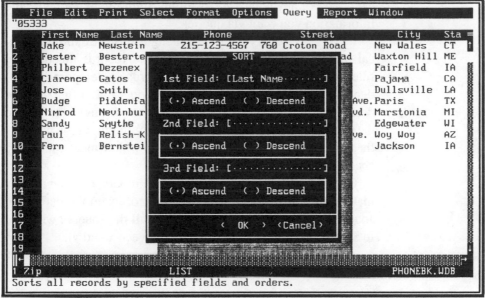

Figure 6-12. Sorting the database by Last Name

CREATING A QUERY

Rather than finding a single record at a time as the Search or Sort commands help you do, you may prefer to ask Works to display a select group of records in a database that meet certain criteria. For example, say you wanted to see

- ♦ All people with ZIP codes falling between 94709 and 95808.

- ♦ People whose last names fall between A and D or Abrahms and Davis.

- ♦ Customers whose accounts are overdue by more than 90 days.

This type of a request is called a query in database lingo, and is achieved in Works via the Query menu. The real and practical power of any database lies in this ability to extract only the information you want via queries.

In Works, a query is created using a series of simple, logical rules. Once a query is created, only records meeting the rules are displayed while the other records are temporarily hidden from view. You can alter your query as often as you desire, with each new query looking through the entire database—even those records hidden by the previous query—then displaying a new list of records which meet the query specifications.

Queries can be based on word(s), numbers, or even mathematical formulas. They can be simple (for example, list all the Joneses) or complex (for example, list all the Joneses who live in Seattle and whose ZIP codes are between x and y).

```
 File  Edit  Print  Select  Format  Options  Query  Report  Window

    First Name  Last Name      Phone            Street            City       Sta
1   Fern        Bernstein    617-333-2222  149 Staghorn Rd.     Jackson      IA
2   Fester      Bestertester 213-584-3726  493 Randolf Road     Waxton Hill  ME
3   Philbert    Dezenex      415-540-7776  133 Axelrod Lane     Fairfield    IA
4   Clarence    Gatos        515-765-9482  299 Feline Ct.       Pajama       CA
5   Nimrod      Nevinburger  212-243-7577  327 Snorewell Blvd.  Marstonia    MI
6   Jake        Newstein     215-123-4567  760 Croton Road      New Wales    CT
7   Budge       Piddenfaugh  210-555-1212  123 Tipplemeyer Ave. Paris        TX
8   Paul        Relish-Katsip 313-827-3894 101 Shoalhaven Ave.  Woy Woy      AZ
9   Jose        Smith        718-836-3526  999 Doe Street       Dullsville   LA
10  Sandy       Smythe       312-767-1234  155 Ridgeway Dr.     Edgewater    WI
11
12
13
14
15
16
17
18
19

11 First Name              LIST                              PHONEBK.WDB
Press ALT to choose commands.
```

Figure 6-13. *The Phonebk file sorted by Last Name*

Query Operators

Works uses a series of logical and mathematical operators to compare the data in the database fields to your criteria. You use these operators in your queries to tell Works how to conduct the comparisons. The operators and what each one does are shown in Table 6 - 4.

Don't worry if you don't understand the meaning of all the operators. They'll become clearer with experimentation.

Let's create a query to display people whose last names begin with letters between *D* and *M*.

1. From list view, choose Query/Define.

2. A screen similar to the Define Form screen appears, as in Figure 6-14.

Notice the status line says QUERY. Though the screen looks like the form view where you would type in data, Works is now waiting for your query formula(s) to be typed into the fields.

Operator	Effect
=	Equal to
< >	Not equal to
<	Less than
>	Greater than
<=	Less than or equal to
>=	Greater than or equal to
*	Wildcard (any length)
?	Wildcard (single character)
|	Or
&	And
~	Not

Table 6-4. Mathematic and Logical Operators

For this query example we want to tell Works to "display last names that begin with any letters between D and M, including D and M." To do this, you have to use the < and > signs for "greater than" and "less than." So what we really want to see is names greater than C and less than N. Thus, the formula would be

C & <N.

Well, almost. Actually, you have to enclose the letters in quotation marks.

1. So, the formula you should type into the Last Name field on the query form is

   "C"&<"N" ⏎

2. Press F10, or choose Query/Apply Query to apply the query to your database, which means to search for records meeting the query criteria. You're returned to the list view.

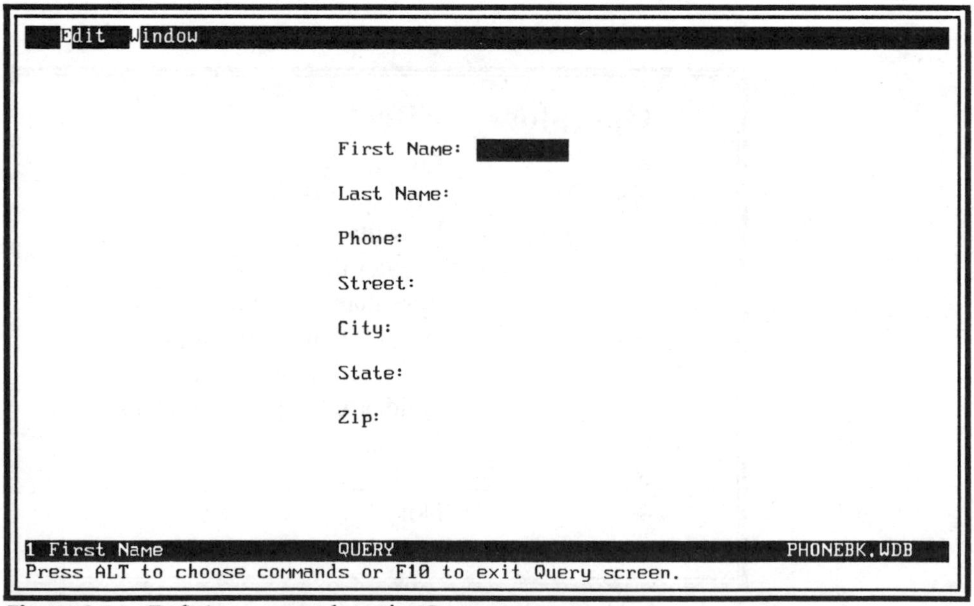

```
 Edit  Window



                    First Name: ████████

                    Last Name:

                    Phone:

                    Street:

                    City:

                    State:

                    Zip:



1 First Name                QUERY                    PHONEBK.WDB
Press ALT to choose commands or F10 to exit Query screen.
```

Figure 6-14. *Defining a query from the Query screen*

3. Notice that now only two records show up: Clarence Gatos and Philbert Dezenex. The query has taken effect, eliminating other records from the display. This applies to form view as well.

4. Want to see all the records again? Choose Query/Show All Records. The formerly excluded records now reappear.

Now try another query, this time on ZIP codes. How would you display only people living in ZIP code areas between 39080 and 79443?

1. Choose Query/Define.

2. Choose Edit/Delete. This deletes the old query information —a necessary step unless you want to combine the effect of the Last Name query with the ZIP code query we're about to define.

3. Move the cursor to the ZIP: field.

4. Type in **>= 39080 &<= 79443** ↵.

   (Recall from the list of operators (in Table 6-4) that the >= and <= signs mean "greater than or equal to" and "less than or equal to.")

5. Press F10 to apply the query. Five records show up.

6. Pan the screen to the right with CTRL → if necessary so you can see the ZIP codes. You should see the following records:

Last Name	Phone	Street	City	Sta	ZIP
Bernstein	617-333-2222	149 Staghorn Rd.	Jackson	IA	55212
Dezenex	415-540-7776	133 Axelrod Lane	Fairfield	IA	52556
Nevinburger	212-243-7577	327 Snorewell Blvd.	Marstonia	MI	65271
Piddenfaugh	210-555-1212	123 Tipplemeyer Ave.	Paris	TX	41234
Smith	718-836-3526	999 Doe Street	Dullsville	LA	78236

If the result of any query you create would be that no records will display, Works will not apply it. Instead you'll see a dialog box that says:

No records matched the query.

These two examples only used four of the eleven possible operators that can be applied to a query. As you may have guessed, queries can be very complex, particularly considering the fact that each field can have its own query formula in it. For example, we could have seven formulas in a single query for the phone book database. The use of more complex queries and of the other operators will be covered in Chapter 10.

PRINTING YOUR PHONE BOOK

Most likely you'll want to print some of your databases on paper. Using a printer or hard copy of your data is often easier than turning on your computer and loading a database just to look up some small tidbit of information.

Works lets you print a database in three ways. You can print from list view which gives you a printout similar to the screen appearance of list view, broken up into separate pages. Second, you can create complex, customized reports, which we'll cover in Chapter 10. Finally, you can print the form view, but this has to be done via the word processor, using a mail merge document.

We'll introduce printing here and show you how to get a simple printout substantial enough for day-to-day use. Later, in Chapter 10, we'll explain more advanced printing techniques.

1. First, deactivate the query you just applied by choosing Query/Show All Records.

2. Turn on your printer and make sure it is on-line and has paper loaded.

3. Choose Print/Select Text Printer.

4. From the dialog box, make sure the correct printer, page feed settings, and printer port are selected. If you are in doubt, chances are that nothing needs to be changed, especially if you have successfully printed from the spreadsheet and word processor; the same printer settings are used here. Then press ↵.

5. Choose Print/Layout. From the LAYOUT dialog box, move to the Header area and type in

   Phone Book Listing ↵

6. Now choose Print/Print.

7. The PRINT dialog box appears. Normally just press ↵ unless you want to change the number of copies or change the other settings.

   Your printer should begin printing in a few seconds. When it's all done, take a look at the product. Most likely what you got was two pages — one that looked like this:

Phone Book Listing

Bernstein	617-333-2222	149 Staghorn Rd.
Bestertester	213-584-3726	493 Randolf Road
Dezenex	415-540-7776	133 Axelrod Lane
Gatos	515-765-9482	299 Feline Ct.
Relish-Katsip	313-827-3894	101 Shoalhaven Ave.
Nevinburger	212-243-7577	327 Snorewell Blvd.
Newstein	215-123-4567	760 Croton Road
Piddenfaugh	210-555-1212	123 Tipplemeyer Ave.
Smith	718-836-3526	999 Doe Street
Smythe	312-767-1234	155 Ridgeway Dr.

followed by a page that looked like this:

Phone Book Listing

Jackson	IA	55212
Waxton Hill	ME	03222
Fairfield	IA	52556
Pajama	CA	94709
Woy Woy	AZ	82239
Marstonia	MI	65271
New Wales	CT	05333
Paris	TX	41234
Dullsville	LA	78236
Edgewater	WI	22256

If this happened to you, it means that just as with the PC's screen, there is more information in each record than will fit on the width of one page. The last three fields—City, State, and ZIP—had to be printed on a second page. This is the same thing that happens with a spreadsheet that's too wide to fit on a single sheet. Once the pages are printed, though, you can separate them and then tape them together (side by side) to visually rejoin the records' data.

Another solution is to *hide* specific fields of a database that you don't really need on your printout. This is done by setting the fields' widths to zero in your list view, and then printing. (Exactly how you do this is covered in Chapter 10.) Finally, depending on which printer you've selected, you may be able to choose a smaller font to print your database with, allowing more characters across the page. You do this via the Print/Font command in form view. Some printers will not allow this, however, leaving you only with the scissors-and-tape solution if you need to print all the fields.

Now that you have some familiarity with the basics of database design and use, try some experimenting on your own. You may want to devise a database or two to keep track of everyday items or tasks — things you normally use paper for, or have never bothered to organize before. In any case, should you put any considerable time into such a project, don't neglect to keep a backup copy of your files in a safe place.

Also, before moving on to the next chapter ("Using Communications"), or to Chapter 10, be sure to save your Phonebk file (now sorted by last name) to disk, because we will use it again later on.

Chapter

Using Communications

Seven

The communications tool of Works lets you and your PC make contact with other computers to exchange or retrieve information. Using the communications tools and the right hookups, you can share data with computers located in the same room as yours, or across the globe.

As discussed in Chapter 1, this information typically consists of electronic mail, instant stock quotes, or complete files (such as word processing or spreadsheet documents) that need to be instantly transmitted between business offices in different locations. However, many people use communications programs to connect to their company's computer so that they can work from home — sometimes called telecommuting.

But there are almost as many types of information available for use with PCs and communications programs as there are interests. Nowadays, many clubs and organizations have their own dial-up *Bulletin Board Systems* (BBSs) where members can leave messages and read notices of interest. Numerous BBSs also provide a wide variety of free software that anyone with a computer, a modem, and a communications program can have just for the taking. A virtually limitless mass of available data lies waiting to be tapped by both home and business computer users, and the size of this data pool is increasing daily. Using your PC, a modem, and Works, you can start to take advantage of the conveniences of computer communications.

SETTING UP YOUR COMMUNICATIONS SYSTEM

In most cases, you'll be using Works to communicate with outside dial up services such as CompuServe, the Source, and MCI Mail, or to call up a friend or colleague's computer to exchange a file or two. The other computer could even be of a different type, such as a Macintosh. This type of communication from a distance (as opposed to communication between computers in the same room) utilizes telephone lines and modems which must be connected to the computers.

As you may recall from Chapter 1, the word *modem* stands for "modulator/demodulator." The modem provides the electrical connection between your computer and the phone line by converting digital information from your computer into an analog signal (a sort of warbling sound) that can be sent over the phone lines to another modem. On the other end of

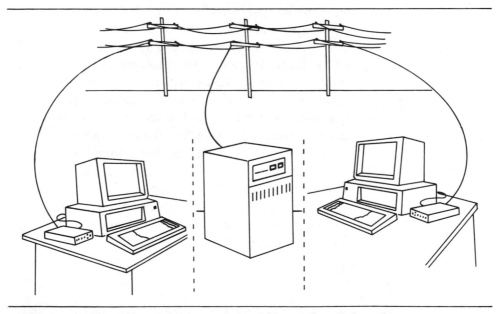

Figure 7-1. *Modems allow PCs to communicate through the telephone lines*

the line, the receiving modem does just the reverse: it reconverts the audio signal into a stream of digital data and sends that to the receiving computer. (See Figure 7-1.)

About Modems

Modems are available in a number of price ranges and styles. Some modems can be installed inside your computer and others sit outside, plugging into your PC's serial port. In either case they work the same way. You install the modem, plug your telephone line into it, and run a communications program (in this case, Works).

The main distinguishing factor among modems is the speed at which they can transfer data over the phone lines. As of this writing, the most popular modems transmit data at 300, 1200, or 2400 baud. The word *baud* refers to the number of bits of data transferred in one second. The larger the number, the faster the transmission. Unfortunately, you pay for increased speed with a higher price tag. You will have to be the judge as to how fast you'll need to send and receive your data, and then buy an appropriate modem.

Since we can't cover all the ins and outs of modem purchasing here, we'll leave the purchase and installation details to you. However, our advice is to purchase a modem that uses Hayes-compatible commands. Hayes compatibility lets you take advantage of some useful features of Works (and most other communications programs) such as the ability to automatically dial the phone for you, redial busy numbers, and so on. If you don't have a Hayes-compatible modem, you can still use Works. You'll just have to type in some of the commands yourself.

Make sure you have installed your modem properly, following instructions in the modem's manual, before continuing. Incorrect modem installation (most often caused by improper switch settings) is the most frequent cause of communications problems.

ABOUT THIS CHAPTER

You'll find that this chapter differs from the others in this book because there are fewer step-by-step exercises to follow. Walking you through a process step-by-step, as the other chapters have done, would involve your calling up a specific electronic mail or other on-line service and then experimenting with Works' commands. Since you may or may not subscribe to or have access to the same services we do, or other readers of this book do, it isn't practical to use specific examples in this chapter. What's more, each service typically has its own way of doing things such as logging on, transmitting and receiving files, and so on, adding another complication. So, instead of demonstrating specific processes, this chapter will introduce you to the Works communications module and suggest more general steps that you can refer to when you begin *telecommunicating*.

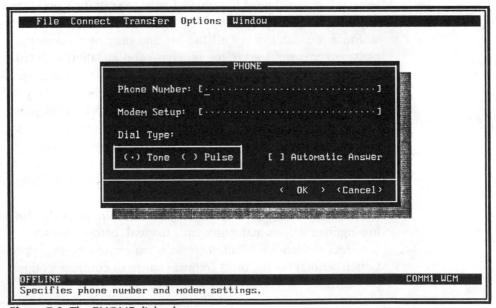

Figure 7-2. The PHONE dialog box

BEGINNING A COMMUNICATIONS SESSION

You begin a session by choosing File/New and opening a communications document. Notice the status line says

OFFLINE

meaning that you aren't currently connected to another computer for communications.

Once you have a new document open, you have to set up various parameters pertaining to your setup before you can begin communicating. There are three groups of parameters that need to be set. They are called Phone, Communications, and Terminal, and each of these settings is made via the Options menu. Here's a description of each one.

- ◆ **Phone**   Used for setting what telephone number you want to dial, and the type of telephone service you have (dial or pulse).

- ◆ **Communications**   Used for setting several details about the speed and format by which data is sent between the two connected computers.

- ◆ **Terminal**   Used for determining how data will be displayed on your screen as it comes into your computer from the modem, and some details about your keyboard.

How to Make the Phone Settings

If you have a Hayes-type modem, Works can dial the phone number of the remote computer for you. But to have your modem do this, you have to fill in the Phone settings using these steps.

1. Choose Options/Phone and you'll see the dialog box as shown in Figure 7-2.

2. Type in the phone number you want your modem to dial. You can type in the number in any of the following forms:

```
(415)-540-1111
415-540-1111
4155401111
540-1111   (if you are calling a local number)
```

The dashes and parentheses won't affect the dialing.

Using Alternative Long Distance Services

If you're using an alternative long distance service such as Sprint, MCI, or others, you can enter all the numbers necessary without limit, unless your numbers exceed approximately 100 digits. You can also insert commas into the phone number to tell your modem to pause before moving ahead to the next digit. On Hayes-compatible modems, each comma results in a two-second pause. At least one comma is usually necessary for alternative services, since it can take several seconds for the second dial tone to come on after the initial connection to the service.

1. Here's an example showing the number you'd use to dial long distance via an alternative service to MCI Mail in Oakland, California from a company phone requiring a 9 to get an outside line. Assume the relevant numbers are as follows:

```
To get an outside line:    9
Your long distance access number:   950-1311
Your private access code:   8273645
The number you're calling:   415-540-1111
```

2. Then the number you'd type into the Phone Number field would be

```
9,950-1311,,8273645,415-540-1111
```

Notice the placement and number of commas. You may have to change the number of commas (particularly of the double set) based on how many rings it takes for your long distance service to answer and then come on with the second dial tone. Hayes-type modems do not acknowledge when the phone on the other end of the line has been answered, so this is compensated for by using the commas.

3. Next, you can fill in the Modem Setup field. This is optional. You can tell Works to send a command to your modem before dialing a phone number. Works will send whatever command you enter here prior to dialing the number. For example, you may want to tell your Hayes-compatible modem how many rings to try before giving up trying to connect with a remote computer. Consult your modem's manual for more details concerning the commands it supports.

4. If you have touch-tone service, leave that option on. If not, set it to Pulse. Sometimes, even if you don't have tone phones, your telephone line will accept tone dialing. You may want to try it and see.

5. Finally, you can set up the modem to answer a call.

You may not always want to be the originator of a communications session. When you want your PC to answer the incoming call from another computer, follow these steps:

1. From the Options/PHONE dialog box, set the Automatic Answer check box on and choose <OK>.

2. Choose Connect/Connect. ANSW appears in the status line, indicating that Works has instructed your modem to "pick up the phone" when a call comes in. Also,

ATS0=1

OK

appears on your screen and the clock on the status line starts to record the passing time. The first line on the screen is the command that Works sent to the modem, instructing it to answer incoming calls. The OK is the modem responding that it got the message. (Your modem may issue a slightly different response.)

Controlling the auto-answer feature from this dialog box only works with Hayes-compatible auto-answer modems, and you'll also have to make sure that your modem's internal switches are set correctly to allow phone answering (see your modem's instruction manual). A non-Hayes-type modem that has an auto-answer feature will still answer the phone; you just won't be able to control that feature from this dialog box.

How to Set the Communications Parameters

Once you've made the phone settings, then you have to set up the Communications parameters. Choosing Options/Communications brings up the even larger dialog box which you see in Figure 7-3.

Let's look at these six option boxes one by one.

Baud Rate

As discussed before, baud rate determines the speed at which data is transferred between your PC and computer at the other end of the line. You'll need to set your baud rate to match that of your modem and that of the remote computer's modem. In other words, all parts of the communications link must be set for the same speed.

Some modems can automatically sense the baud rate and adjust themselves accordingly. Others cannot do this and must be set using switches. You should consult your modem's instruction manual regarding this. If baud rates are mismatched, you will fail to get a connection, or you may see weird letters or punctuation marks on your screen instead of normal text.

Most communications via modem (as opposed to direct connection to another local computer, as explained later in this chapter) take place at 300, 1200, or 2400 baud. It usually makes sense to use as fast a speed as possible to decrease connect time over the phone. However, poor phone connections, not infrequent with long distance calls, can require dropping your speed down a notch (for example, from 1200 to 300) to avoid loss of data. Also most information services, such as

CompuServe, charge twice as much for 1200 baud connect time than for 300 baud.

If you are connecting two computers directly to each other (without using modems), you should read the section later in this chapter entitled "Communicating Without Modems." If you are using a modem, just type in the baud rate you want. Acceptable baud rates range from 50 to 9600.

Data Bits

The Data Bits setting refers to the number of bits (the smallest division of computer information) you want to send out in each byte (the most common division of data). For example, typically each letter is stored in your computer as a byte composed of eight bits. Without going into great detail, suffice it to say that this setting is almost always going to be 8, and must be 8 if you are intending to transfer programs (as opposed to just documents) between computers. If you are specifically told that the other system uses seven bits, change this setting.

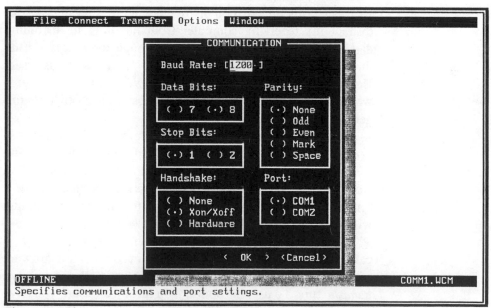

Figure 7-3. The COMMUNICATION dialog box

Stop Bits

Stop bits are used by the computers on both ends to indicate the end of one character and the beginning of the next. Systems vary between using one or two stop bits. More often, one stop bit is used, so you can probably leave this setting as is. If you are specifically told that the other system uses two bits, change this setting.

Parity

Parity is a means by which the communications software can detect if an error has occurred in the transmission of each byte of data. Parity can only be used if you have set the data bits parameter to 7. Otherwise parity should be left at None. If you are specifically told that the other system uses parity checking, find out what kind, and change this setting.

Handshake

In the process of receiving and sending data, the computers on each end of the line often have to attend to other tasks as well, such as storing information on disk. Sometimes these tasks can distract the receiving computer from handling its incoming data. To prevent data from falling through the cracks during these processes, a convention called *handshaking* is used. Handshaking provides a way for the two computers to agree when to stop and start the sending process so that other contingencies can be handled.

Most often, at least when using modems, the *Xon/Xoff convention* (or *protocol*) will be employed. When the receiving computer wants the sending computer to pause, it transmits an Xoff (a CTRL-S) signal. When ready to receive data again, it sends an Xon (CTRL-Q) signal. This is the default setting, and will work for most dial-up information services.

When connecting computers to each other directly via a cable (without a modem), you may want to use the Hardware setting. This tells Works to use something called *hardware handshaking*. To use this option, you must make sure you have a special kind of cable. Please see the section later in this chapter, entitled "Communicating Without Modems" for more details.

If you know that the other computer uses no handshaking, select None from the dialog box. Regardless of which handshaking setup you are using, remember that both computers must use the same type.

Port

The last section of the COMMUNICATIONS dialog box lets you tell Works which *port* your modem or null modem cable (see "How to Set Up a Direct Connection," later in this chapter) is connected to. Most PCs have two serial communications ports, called COM1 and COM2. More often than not, COM1 will be used. Your COM1 port may be tied up for use with a printer or other device though, in which case your modem is probably set up for COM2. Set the port to COM2 if you know that your modem is connected to that port. Otherwise, leave this setting as is.

Note: Remember that all of these parameters, except the port, have to be identical on each end (in each computer) before successful communications can begin. If you are in doubt about how to set one of them, there's a simple solution. Just find out what the settings are for the computer at the other end of the line and set yours accordingly. If you can't find out what those settings are, try the default settings that show up when you open a new document. If those don't work, then start systematically altering the settings one at a time.

If you plan to use the defaults, of course, you can just skip over this entire dialog box altogether. Chances are it will work as is, since the defaults were designed to work with most services.

How to Set the Terminal Parameters

Before PCs were invented, people used computer *terminals* to communicate with one another and with mainframe computers. Terminals are essentially nothing but a screen and keyboard by which data can be entered and displayed. They have no internal computing power or disk storage as does your PC. Since more than one manufacturer made terminals, certain standards had to be established regarding how data was displayed on the terminal screens and how their keyboards worked.

These standards continue today, and apply to communications setups using PCs as well as to terminals. Thus, the dialog box dealing with these settings is named TERMINAL.

This one last group of settings should be at least checked before making a connection to another computer. Normally, you won't have to change the terminal settings, but occasionally you do. To see and/or alter the terminal settings, choose Options/Terminal. The TERMINAL dialog box appears, as in Figure 7-4.

There are four groups of settings in this box.

Terminal Type

Notice that there are two terminal types that Works can make your computer act like. Without going into detail about the

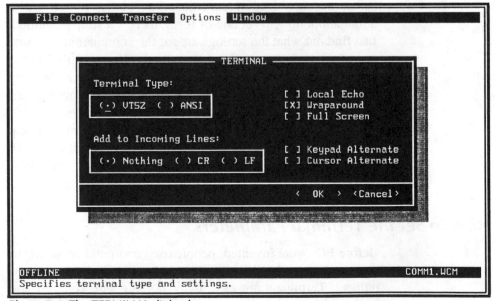

Figure 7-4. The TERMINAL dialog box

differences between these types of terminals, suffice it to say that VT52 tells your PC to emulate (act like) a DEC model VT52 terminal and ANSI makes your PC emulate, or act like, the popular DEC VT100, VT220, and VT240 terminals. The first (and default) setting should work for most purposes. If you find your screen acting unpredictably or displaying bizarre letters, try the ANSI setting. Select the correct terminal type for your communications session.

Option	Effect	Use for
VT52	Emulates the DEC VT52 terminal	Information services such as CompuServe and The Source, BBSs, electronic mail services, and so on.
ANSI	Emulates a standard ANSI terminal.	Communicating with mainframes as though using a DEC VT100, VT220, or VT240 terminal or compatible.

Add to Incoming Lines

The second section, Add to Incoming Lines, is included to deal with some remote (sometimes called host) computers' habit of not moving the cursor down a line and/or moving back to the left side of the screen after sending the previous line of text. If, in the process of receiving text, all the incoming data appears on a single line which gets continually rewritten, or the cursor moves to the right margin and seems to get stuck, try setting the Add CR (carriage return) or Add LF (line feed) options on. For most sessions, however, the Nothing option will do fine.

Option	Effect
Nothing	Adds nothing to end of each incoming line.
Add CR	Adds a carriage return to end of incoming lines.
Add LF	Adds a line feed (moves down a line) to end of incoming lines.

Local Echo, Wraparound, and Full Screen Settings

The next three settings are check boxes that also affect how information will appear on your screen. Local Echo "echoes" what you type on your keyboard to your screen, so you can see what you're typing. It may sound strange, but in some communications sessions — for instance between two PCs using Works — you may find you can't see what you're typing, because the remote computer may not be programmed to echo your transmission back to your screen. Normally this will not be a problem, but if you find you are typing "in the dark," simply set Local Echo on. With two PCs running Works, both should have Local Echo on. On the other hand if you see double characters on the screen (HHEELLLLOO!!), turn local echo off.

Wraparound is a setting that causes incoming text that is longer than the width of your screen to automatically move down a line and jump to the left margin (wrap) to begin the next line. Normally, Wraparound is set on.

Setting the Full Screen option on causes the menu bar and status lines to disappear so you have a full 25 lines available for display of incoming text. Pressing the ALT key will redisplay the menu bar when you need it, but it will disappear again after you use a command. You'll want to turn on the Full Screen option when you're using your PC for terminal emulation, which is to say, when you're connected to a mainframe computer that thinks you are working at a terminal rather than using a PC.

Keyboard and Cursor Settings

Finally, the last two check boxes in the TERMINAL dialog box control the codes that the keypad or cursor keys will send to a mainframe computer if you are using Works for terminal emulation. Usually these options will be of no significance, and you won't have to worry about it. If you are connected to a host computer with which you need to work in Application mode, turn on one of these check boxes.

Option	Effect
Keypad Alternate	Enables Application mode when your PC's keypad is in Num Lock mode (that is, when the keys type numbers because you pressed the NUM LOCK key).
Cursor Alternate	Enables Application mode when your PC's keypad is in cursor mode (that is, when the arrow keys are activated).

SAVING YOUR SETTINGS

Whew! If wrestling with all those settings seemed confusing and time-consuming, don't worry. With some practice you'll see that only a few of the settings need alteration for each new type of communications session. What's more, once you have the details of a particular hookup ironed out, you can save your settings on disk for future use. Your settings are saved as a communications document with the .WCM extension.

To save your settings do the following:

1. Choose File/Save.

2. The familiar SAVE AS dialog box pops up.

3. Give your file a name, preferably a name that will help you remember which information service or computer the settings are for.

MAKING A CONNECTION

Once you've made the settings, the next step in starting a communications session is to make the connection to the remote computer. To initiate the connection, choose the Connect command from the Connect menu.

When you choose Connect/Connect, all the settings made in the Options menu go into effect, including the phone number, which will be dialed. (There are some other options that can be used too, such as automatic sign-on, but you'll learn about those a little further on in this chapter.) While dialing, the status line says DIAL, and the phone number being dialed (along with the command telling the modem how to dial it) shows up in the work area of the screen, like this:

ATDT5401114

If your modem has a speaker in it, you may also hear the number as it is being dialed. When the phone on the other end is picked up, you may hear some high pitched tones indicating that the modems are "talking" to each other.

If connection is successful, the status line will change from OFFLINE to an elapsed time indicator, informing you of the amount of time your computer is connected to the remote machine. Also, everything you type on the keyboard is sent out to the other computer.

If the connection is not successful, after about 15 seconds you will probably see the words

NO CARRIER

just under the phone number. This means the modem gave up trying to make a connection. The typical reasons for failure at this point are

- The other phone was busy.

- The other phone/modem didn't answer.

- The modems are set at different baud rates so they didn't recognize each other.

If the phone number you dialed is busy, your modem may report the word BUSY to the screen, and you may hear the busy signal on the modem's speaker. Usually the modem will hang up and wait for a message from the computer to try again. To dial again, choose Connect/Dial Again. If you want to stop a dialing that is in progress, press any key when DIAL appears in the status line.

If you didn't put a phone number into the Options/PHONE dialog box, then choosing Connect/Connect ties you directly into your modem, not to the computer you are trying to reach. You will then have to type in commands directly from your keyboard which will be sent to the modem. For example to tone dial 555-1212 on a Hayes-compatible modem, you would type

ATDT 555-1212 ↵

If you are interested in using other modem commands directly, consult your modem's instruction manual.

SENDING AND RECEIVING DATA

Assuming the connection proceeds without difficulty, the status line will read ON LINE and you can begin to transfer data between computers. What you do now depends entirely on what the other computer expects from you. If you are calling an information service, BBS, or a mainframe computer, you will typically have to *sign-on* to the remote system by typing your name and possibly a password. For more about sign-ons, see the section later in this chapter, "Using Automatic Sign-ons."

If you are calling a friend's computer or connecting locally, you can probably just begin typing as we describe here. In any case, once the initial connection is made, there are several ways that you can begin to transfer data between the two computers. The next several sections describe these techniques and how to use them.

How to Send and Receive in Interactive Mode

The simplest way to transfer data is directly from your keyboard. As mentioned earlier, once you're connected to the other computer, everything you type is automatically sent out to it. Conversely, letters typed on the other computer will be sent to your computer, showing up on your screen. Sending and receiving data this way is called working in Interactive or Terminal mode. Communication sessions often begin in terminal mode, with each person typing to the other's screen.

Terminal mode is often used, too, when connecting to many of the information services and electronic mail networks that are interactive in nature; that is, in which you type in certain commands to the host computer and it responds by sending you some data. As information comes over the line to your computer, it will appear on the screen as you see in Figure 7-5.

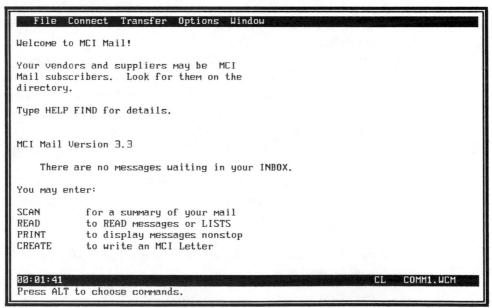

Figure 7-5. An example of incoming data

Capturing Text

You soon notice that when the screen fills up with text, additional text scrolls the old data up and off the top of the screen. Once some text scrolls off the top, you can't get back to it. Obviously, there will be times when you'll want to somehow save this incoming data while you're in Terminal mode, so you can work with it later. You can *capture* incoming text at any time during a communications session and save it in a disk file for later reading, printing, or editing via the Capture Text command from the Transfer window.

Here is the basic procedure for capturing text:

1. Choose Transfer/Capture Text.

2. A dialog box appears, asking you to name the file you want the captured text stored in. Type in the name and press ↵. The status line says CAPTURE.

3. Continue with your session. Whatever you type will be captured too, along with the incoming text.

4. When you want to stop capturing text, choose Transfer/End Capture Text. The CAPTURE message will disappear, and the text will be stored on the disk.

Capturing Selected Portions of Text

During text capturing there may be sections of text you don't want to save, interspersed with portions you do. A case in point would be reading menu choices or sign-on messages from BBSs, MCI Mail, or CompuServe. You can turn text capture on and off at will, to accommodate this situation. Here's how to do it.

1. Assuming Capture is already on, choose Connect/Pause when it looks as though a section of unwanted text is coming across the screen. (If you are using Xon/Xoff protocol, pressing CTRL-S will work, too, and it's easier.)

2. Now with the transmission paused, you have time to turn off Text Capture. Choose Transfer/End Capture Text.

3. Continue receiving data by choosing Connect/Pause again (or pressing CTRL-Q).

4. When you want to start capturing again, choose Connect/Pause again, and set Capture Text on again.

5. Select the same file name for the destination of your text that you previously selected. Works notices that this file already exists and responds with:

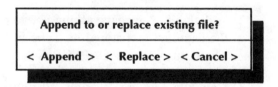

Option	Effect
Append to existing file	Adds text onto end of existing file
Overwrite existing file	Replaces existing file with new text

6. Choose Append to existing file. The incoming data will be added to the tail end of the existing data in the file.

7. Choose Connect/Pause again to turn Pause off and begin capturing data.

Using this method, you can keep capturing data, even from session to session, into the same file.

Incidentally, even if you aren't capturing text, but just reading it, you can momentarily stop and start the scrolling using CTRL-S and CTRL-Q, respectively (with most information services).

Sending and Receiving Files

Obviously just sending text to another computer by typing it in from your keyboard isn't very efficient. Works gives you an alternative to this approach by letting you send documents that are already prepared by a word processor or other programs. This is a much more efficient method of data transfer.

There are two ways to do this. One method uses error correction to insure that your file is received by the other computer without any loss of data. The other technique does not use error correction, but can be used with a wider variety of host computers.

Send Text

The Send Text command from the Transfer menu is the method that doesn't use error correction. Use this command to send letters via electronic mail services, BBSs, and information services. By composing your messages first, using the word processor, you minimize connection time (and resultant cost).

Note, however, that the Send Text command can only be used with ASCII files (plain text files without control codes in them), so make sure the file you want to send was created or at least saved as an ASCII file from whatever program you created it in. You cannot send PC programs (files with the extensions .EXE or .COM) with this command. Captured text files are ASCII files, as are Works word processing, database, or spreadsheet files saved using the Text or Plain options from the SAVE AS dialog box. So, if you intend to send a file you've created with Works to another computer that doesn't use Works, you'll have to save the file with one of these two options before sending it. You will definitely have to do this when preparing to send a document over an electronic mail service such as MCI mail, since these services typically accept only ASCII data. (See the end of Chapter 8 for more details about using the Text and Plain options.)

To send a file using the Send Text command,

1. Make a connection to the other computer.

2. Choose Transfer/Send Text.

3. A dialog box appears as you see in Figure 7-6.

   There are two things you have to indicate: the name of the file you want to send and the End-of-Line Delay.

4. Type in the file name, or select it from the file box. For the time being, leave the End-of-Line Delay at 0.

5. Press ↵, and the file will be sent.

   SEND appears on the status line while the sending is in progress, and the contents of the file will appear on your screen as the file is sent so that you can monitor the progress of the transfer. Occasionally you may hear your disk drive whir as Works reads more data from the file on disk in order to send it.

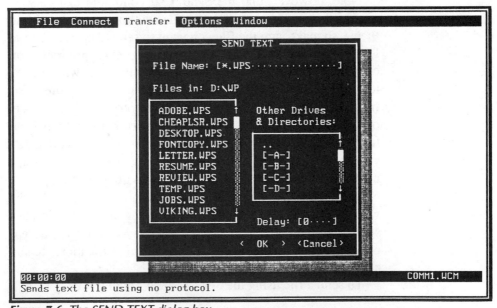

Figure 7-6. *The SEND TEXT dialog box*

If you notice that letters are missing at the beginning of each new line of text on your screen, you will have to stop the transfer (press any key) and alter the Delay setting in the SEND TEXT dialog box before sending the file again. This setting controls how long Works will pause at the end of each line before beginning the transmission of the next line. If the host computer is having trouble keeping up with your computer, this may have to be increased from the default of zero to some higher number. The number you enter represents 1/10th of a second, so 5 would equal 5/10ths or 1/2-of-a-second delay. Normally no delay is needed, and typically a few tenths of a second will solve most problems.

If you find that all the sent text is being typed on a single line of your screen, you can fix this by selecting the add LF option on the Options/TERMINAL dialog box. Wordstar and SideKick files will have this appearance. However, you can't get to this or any other dialog boxes while in the process of sending. If you try to, you'll just hear a beep. You either have to do it before you begin sending or after you terminate sending. On the other hand, if the single line display doesn't bother you, don't worry. Your text is still being sent properly.

Finally, remember that you have to be on-line before you can send a file. If you try to send before actually connecting to the remote computer, Works will display an error message when you try to choose Transfer/Send Text.

When Works reaches the end of the file, SEND disappears from the status line.

Send Protocol

It's not uncommon for data to be lost or corrupted during the transmission process over telephone lines, particularly when long distances are involved. As we all know, long distance lines often suffer from noise, static, or even other people's conversations accidentally being crossed with ours. Usually we just put up with the noise, asking the other party to repeat their last sentence, or one of the parties redials the call.

Computers are less tolerant of such maladies. Noise on the line between two computers can cause a plethora of erratic data alterations during a file transfer. In response to this, computer scientists have devised numerous error detection and error correction schemes to determine if errors have occurred in transmission, and methods to correct them. Works uses one of these schemes with its Receive Protocol and Send Protocol commands.

Called the XMODEM protocol, this error correction scheme was devised by Ward Christensen and given to the public in 1977 for use on microcomputers, which were just then becoming available. XMODEM is now widely used and supported by many communications programs as well as some information services such as CompuServe. XMODEM divides a file into a series of small sections, called blocks. The blocks are then sent sequentially, along with a mathematically calculated code (a checksum) that tells the receiving computer what should be in the block.

After getting the block, the receiving computer looks to see if the block matches this calculated code. If it does, the sending computer is advised to send the next block. If there was a detected error in the block, the receiving computer asks the sending computer to retransmit the block until it's received properly. This process continues until the entire file is received error free.

Another advantage to using XMODEM is that you can transmit all types of files, be they programs, worksheets, graphics, or what have you. The Send Protocol command doesn't care what's in the file, nor does it display the file on screen as it is sent. The only catch is that both computers *must* be using the XMODEM protocol. If the other computer is not using it, the transfer will not even begin. Nothing will happen. If the other computer isn't using Works, then you must also make sure the receiving computer is using the XMODEM Checksum mode, not the XMODEM CRC mode.

To send a file using XMODEM protocol, follow these steps.

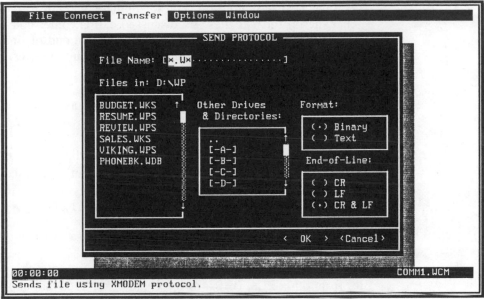

Figure 7-7. The SEND PROTOCOL dialog box

1. Make sure you're on-line (connected).

2. Make sure the receiving computer is ready to receive an XMODEM file. How you do this depends on the computer system, BBS, or information service to which you are connected. If sending to another PC, you may want to type a message in Terminal mode telling the operator to do what is necessary to prepare for receiving a file.

3. Choose Transfer/Send Protocol. A dialog box appears, asking for the name and type of the file, as you see in Figure 7-7.

4. Type in the file name and format. Use the Binary setting if you want to send the file exactly as is. Use this setting for programs or for documents with formatting that you want to keep intact.

Use the Text setting if you want to stipulate the end-of-line character(s) for text files. As discussed earlier, other computers or word processors may require different end-of-line characters. This option lets you handle those contingencies.

5. Press ↵. This will begin the file transfer. The progress of the transfer will be reported in a dialog box, as shown in Figure 7-8.

If errors are detected, these are reported in the dialog box. If more than 10 consecutive errors are detected during transmission, Works will abort the sending process. If you want to abort the sending process in midstream, press the ↵ key.

Receive Protocol

You'll want to use the Receive Protocol command to receive files from other PCs, BBSs, or information services that support XMODEM protocol. Receiving an XMODEM file is essentially the reverse of the sending process.

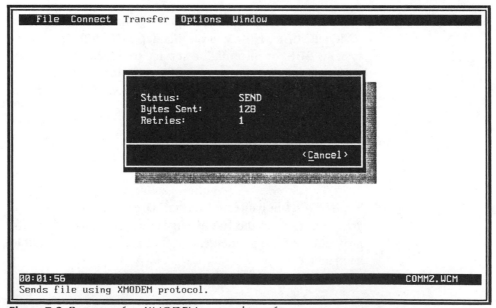

Figure 7-8. Progress of an XMODEM protocol transfer

1. Tell the sending computer to get ready to send via XMODEM. How you do this varies depending on the computer and program(s) involved. With some systems, you control the sending from your computer. In other cases a person at the other end will issue the command. BBSs typically will say something like:

   Ready to receive Y/N?

   or

   Press ↵ to start download

2. Choose Transfer/Receive Protocol. The SAVE AS dialog box appears, as you see in Figure 7-9, because you are telling Works to save the incoming data as a file.

3. Enter the file name.

4. Enter the file type. Use the Binary type to receive a program or formatted material, such as a Word, Works (except

Figure 7-9. *Receiving an XMODEM protocol transmission*

files saved as Text), Wordstar, or Lotus 1-2-3 file. Use the Text type when the file being sent to you is an ASCII text file or other file that has no special characters in it. In this mode, all incoming lines of text will be converted by Works to have a CR (carriage return) and a LF (line feed) at the end, making the file a valid DOS file.

5. Press ↵ and the transmission should begin. A dialog box appears, indicating the progress. If errors are detected, these are reported in the dialog box. If more than 10 consecutive errors are detected during transmission, Works will abort the receiving process. If you want to abort the transmission for some other reason, press ESC.

Often you will not know the size of the file you're about to receive. Thus, it's likely that you'll occasionally run out of disk space while receiving a file. This is a real hassle, particularly if you've spent half an hour receiving most of a large file only to get an error message from Works saying there isn't enough room on your disk for the rest of it. Works will abort the receiving process if there isn't enough room, so *make sure* the disk you choose to store the file on has enough free space on it before you begin the transfer. If you forget to do this, you'll have to change disks and/or drives and choose Receive Protocol again.

USING AUTOMATIC SIGN-ONS

Signing-on is the process of typing in some identification information such as your name, a password, and so forth, when connecting to a remote computer system. Many systems have sign-on requirements of this nature, and it's inconvenient to type this data in each time you connect. Works has a way of watching you sign-on to each system once, recording what you do, and storing the procedure in your communications document (along with any other settings) for future use.

By opening the correct document the next time you want to call a given system, you can have Works do the sign-on for you by playing back the "script" you created. In fact, since Works also remembers all the terminal, phone, and communications settings too, the whole process of dialing the number, setting the various parameters and signing on can be automated, saving you time and possibly money. However, only one script can be saved in each communications document.

To record a sign-on interaction, you first should decide at what point you want the script to begin. Do you want Works to record all of the sign-on procedure or only part of it? Should it start immediately after dialing the phone number or wait for you to type in some commands first? Your decision will probably vary from system to system. The best approach is to

1. Sign-on to a given system several times manually until you have understood the procedure.

2. Then figure out which part could be automated. Works can record the following interactions:

   ♦ The Connect command

   ♦ Keyboard input

   ♦ Incoming data from the host

   ♦ The Disconnect command

How to Record a Script

In this example, we'll have the script include the Connect command.

1. Open a new document, and make the correct settings from the Options menu, including phone number, baud rate, and so on.

2. Try logging on to the remote computer system once yourself just to see that all the settings are correct. Then disconnect.

3. Choose Connect/Record Sign-On. RECORD appears on the status line. Works begins recording the session.

4. Choose Connect/Connect to dial the phone.

5. Enter all the sign-on names, codes, or whatever is necessary to get to the point after which your interaction with the host normally would alter from session to session.

6. Choose Connect/Record Sign-On again. This stops the recording.

7. Save your script file for future use by choosing File/Save and giving the file a name (unless you've already saved and named it before). The script will be saved along with all the other settings.

How to Play Back a Script

To play back the script, simply follow these steps:

1. Open the desired communications document from the File menu if it isn't already open.

2. Make sure your modem is connected and turned on.

3. Choose Connect/Sign-On. This dials the number, makes the connection, and performs the sign-on, unattended. When it is completed, you can begin your interactive typing, file transfers, and so forth.

Some Tips About Automatic Sign-ons

There are some important things to know about scripts. First, if the host computer issues variable responses from session to session, such as the date, this will disorient Works, and confuse the playback of the script. Thus, your script should only interact with stable, non-changing sections of the communications session.

Second, if your password, name, log-in code, or other data changes, you must re-record your script. When you choose Connect/Record Sign-on again, the old script is erased and the new one takes its place. You may do this as many times as you like within each communications document, but only one script is stored per document. If you need more than one script per information service, make several and name them accordingly.

After you dial up a system, it's very important to start playing back the script at the right time or else it won't work. For example, if you started recording when the remote system displayed the prompt

ENTER YOUR LAST NAME:

you'll have to start playing back the script at the same place, otherwise things will get out of synch.

One final note on scripts: If you want to abort the playing of a sign-on script, press any key. You may want to do this if a script isn't working. For example, if Works just sits there for an extended time apparently doing nothing, you should probably abort. Chances are that something is wrong with the script or the connection. Works will wait for up to one hour before terminating the script itself, so don't expect to be informed of an error for some time.

MULTIPLE COMMUNICATIONS SESSIONS

There probably aren't too many times that you'd want to do this, but it is possible to have two communications sessions connected at the same time. To do this, open a new communications document while you already have another one open. Set the parameters and connect as usual. You must not use the same communications port as that being used by the first session. From the COMMUNICATIONS dialog box you'll have to select the unused COM channel (1 or 2) as the port for the second session. Of course, you'll need another modem (or cable in the case of direct connection) connected to the second port, too.

Since Works is not a multitasking program, data coming into the document not currently activated (and on your screen) will be lost. It will not be captured, stored on disk, or even put on the screen. Only the active window's session will send and receive data. But, using the Pause command and Window menus, you can hop between the two communications sessions, pausing in one while jumping to the next.

SENDING A BREAK SIGNAL

Some host computers respond to a special command, called Break, to interrupt or abort the execution of a program or to pay attention to a remote user. On other systems, the Break signal disconnects you or logs you off. In any case, Works will send this signal for a period of four seconds when you choose Connect/Break. How the host computer will respond to the Break signal depends on the system.

COMMUNICATING WITHOUT MODEMS

As mentioned earlier, communications between computers doesn't have to involve the use of modems. Modems are only necessary when using the telephone or similar communications networks over long distances. When computers are closer to one another (preferably in the same room) you can connect them directly. There usually isn't much sense in doing this unless the computers are of dissimilar types. After all, you can transfer text and files more quickly by simply passing someone a floppy disk than by sending the files over a wire. Similarly, if you want several PCs in the same locale to share information such as databases and local electronic mail, you should install a *local area network (LAN)* rather than using Works.

Direct connection between computers is very useful for sending files between PCs and other types of computers, such as Apple Macintoshes, Apple IIs, older style CP/M computers, various laptop computers, minicomputers or mainframes (if they happen to be in proximity). This is because these computers typically can't work with floppy disks from an IBM PC or IBM-compatible. So, the only way to exchange data between your PC and these other machines is via a direct connection.

How to Set Up a Direct Connection

First a warning. Generally speaking, getting computers to talk to one another via a direct connection is problematic. It may take several tries, a great deal of knowledge, lots of wire, and a good soldering iron to pull the whole stunt off successfully. On the other hand, you may have beginner's luck.

If you're only trying to send text files between dissimilar machines, both of which have working modems and can successfully log onto an electronic service such as MCI Mail, use that avenue instead of trying to wire the machines together directly. Here's how to transfer data between two computers without having to connect them directly together.

1. The sending computer logs onto the mail service.

2. Using some communications program, it then sends (uploads) the text file(s) (no protocol) to a person who has a "mail box" on the system. (Actually with MCI Mail, you can send to your own mail box, making the next step easier.)

3. The sending computer then logs off of the mail system.

4. The receiving computer then logs onto the mail service over the modem, receives (*downloads*) the file, and then logs off.

However, if you intend to transfer lots of files between the computers, using an electronic mail service can take lots of time, even at 1200 or 2400 baud. (Direct connections with Works can transfer at speeds up to 9600 baud.) And if you intend to transfer program files (binary files), most electronic mail services won't work at all. In either of these two cases, it's better to rig up a direct connection between the machines.

Unfortunately, the ins and outs of direct connections are too vast to cover in this book. In fact, there are entire books devoted to this subject. Also, you may want to refer to the Works manual, Appendix C for more information on cables. However, here are the basic steps you'd go through.

1. You will need to connect a special cable, called a *null modem,* between the two computers in place of the modems and the telephone lines. Null modem cables reverse certain wire pairs within the cable and are designed specifically for this purpose. Depending on the computers, the ends of the cables will have different genders. The IBM PC and compatibles require a nonstandard connector (female instead of male) compared to most other types. For many situations, particularly among microcomputers, acceptable null modem cables can be purchased at a local computer store. However, for the technically inclined or strong of heart, a cable constructed with connections as listed in the table on the next page will usually do the job.

Another solution is to purchase one of the intelligent cables now available from computer dealers that figures all this out for you. Or you can use a *breakout box* wired to the given configuration and use a standard cable (no wire reversals) with it.

2. Load up Works on the PC, and some other communications program on the other computer.

Computer 1   *Computer 2*

Pin Number—connect to—Pin Number

1...............chassis ground 1

2 ....data 3

3.. ....data 2

4 ....handshaking (RQS).............5

5 ....handshaking (CTS) 4

6 ....handshaking (DSR).............20

7 ....signal-ground................7

3. Next, set both computers to the same baud rate. You learned how to do this with Works, in the beginning of this chapter. How you set the other computer's baud rate will vary. Use the highest baud rate available. (Works' highest is 9600.)

4. Get into terminal mode on both computers. (With Works, this just means choosing Connect/Connect.) Make sure there's no script attempting to play back. Then see if typing on one keyboard shows the corresponding characters on the other computer's screen. If it does, then you're more than halfway home. If it doesn't, there's something wrong with the wiring, one or both computers, the software, or how you're using the software.

5. Now try typing on the other keyboard. Letters should show up on the other screen.

If everything worked so far, you can try sending the files. Otherwise, don't move ahead until you've fixed whatever is wrong.

6. If the other computer's program supports XMODEM protocol (in the Checksum mode, not the CRC mode), you can send files using XMODEM. Otherwise use simple text sending and receiving commands. In Works, you'd use Capture Text to receive a file and Send Text to send a text file. (If you use Capture Text and Send Text, you will probably have to increase the delay factor if transmitting at 9600 baud.)

If you are using XMODEM and having no success even though things work all right in Terminal mode, you may be having synchronization problems. Try telling the receiving computer to receive the file before you tell the sending computer to send. That way the receiving computer is ready for the data when it begins coming in. See the other troubleshooting tips later in this chapter.

ENDING A COMMUNICATIONS SESSION

Once you've finished your work (or play) during a session, you should end it by following some simple rules.

1. If you are logged onto an information service, electronic mail, or BBS, follow the system's instructions for signing off. This may be important to free up a connection for other users, or to cease billing you for connect time.

2. Choose Connect/Connect again. Works will ask

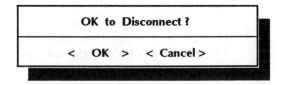

3. Choose OK. Then save your communications document if you have made any changes to scripts or settings that you'll want to use later.

TROUBLESHOOTING

Despite great strides in the field of communications, mostly due to conveniences spurred by the personal computer market, communications is still a bit of a black art. Chances are that you'll run into some problem or another while transferring files, sending mail, or whatever it is you end up doing with the Works communications tool. The fault will not necessarily lie with Works, but much more likely will be the result of improper wiring, faulty modems, noisy telephone lines, incorrect log-on procedures, or incompatible software on the other end of the line.

Here's a small list of tips and possible cures in the event of trouble.

General Problems

♦ If you keep getting beeps when you try to type, it's because you have to choose Connect/Connect first.

Possible Modem Problems

♦ Is the modem on?

♦ If using an external modem, is it connected to the computer's serial port?

♦ Did you select the correct port from the Options/COMMUNICATIONS dialog box?

♦ If using an internal-type modem, did you select the correct port assignment (COM1: or COM2:)? Make sure there are no conflicts with other equipment such as printer ports, a serial mouse, or others. Only one device can be assigned to a port. You may have to switch to COM2: if COM1: is being used by another device.

♦ If you are using a Hayes-type modem, choose Connect/Connect. Type **AT** (uppercase) and press ↵. The modem should respond with OK on your screen. If it doesn't, there may be something wrong with the wiring, the modem, or the port selection.

♦ If you and the person on the other end of the line see garbage on the screen, such as

!!!!!!12#())))@(#^&**(&@#%^,

when you type in terminal mode, most likely you are transmitting at different baud rates. Hang up, call the other person, agree on a baud rate, and try again.

♦ If your Hayes modem (external type) answers the phone even when you don't want it to, open the modem and set switch 5 to the down position. That disables automatic answering.

Log-on Problems

♦ Did you type the log-on, password, and so on exactly as they are supposed to be typed? Uppercase and lowercase letters are often considered as different by remote systems.

♦ Try pressing ↵ or CTRL-C first thing upon seeing a prompt from the host computer.

♦ If using a script, and it hangs, make sure you didn't record part of an interaction that changes from day to day, such as the date, or some news bulletin. See the earlier section entitled "How to Record a Script."

File Transfer Problems

- If transferring via XMODEM, you will have to start both computers (sending and receiving) at roughly the same time; otherwise they will time-out. Timing out occurs when two computers fail to successfully exchange data within a given time period. Typically XMODEM programs will completely abort the transmission process after a time out. Works only waits 100 seconds before aborting an XMODEM sending or receiving attempt, after which you will have to begin the process again.

- If transferring in Send Text or Capture Text and characters at the beginning of each line are lost in the process, increase the end-of-line delay of the sending computer. If the sending computer is the PC running Works, this is done from the Transfer/SEND TEXT dialog box.

- If you need to perform lots of file conversions between the Apple Macintosh and your PC, you may want to consider other alternatives, such as hardware/software products devised specifically for that purpose. TOPS from Centram Systems in Berkeley, California, or products such as MacCharlie from Dayna Communications in Salt Lake City, Utah, are two good examples.

File Compatibility Problems

When exchanging files with people not using Works, there are a few things to remember. Works uses its own proprietary codes to store formatting information such as paragraph settings, font, typesize, special characters, headers, footers and so on. This is true for all four Works tools. For another program to use a Works file, or for Works to use another program's files, some common format must be used. In most cases, this is the ASCII or Text format, though there are exceptions, since Works can use Microsoft Word files and Lotus 1-2-3 files (with certain limitations) directly. In any case, be sure to coordinate the data format of your file transfers with the other party involved in your communications effort before sending lots of files. Transfer a short text file first to test for compatibility, and then proceed with others. Refer to Chapter 12 for more information about integrating communications files into other types of Works documents. Refer to Appendix B for more information about transferring files between Works and other programs.

Chapter

Expanding Your Word Processing Skills

Eight

In Chapter 4 you learned the basics of using the Works word processor. In this chapter you will expand on those skills by learning:

- How to format paragraphs and copy formats between paragraphs

- How to format individual characters

- How to set the tab stops

- More about the Undo command

- Automatic search and replace of words

- Inserting the date, time, and other special characters

- How to use Works' built-in spelling checker

- How to split the window to see two portions of a document at once

- How to copy text between two documents

- How to add headers, footers, and page numbers

- More about printing

Since we will use the LETTER1.WPS file we created in Chapter 4, you'll first have to make sure that file is open and on your screen in the active window.

FORMATTING PARAGRAPHS

Paragraphs are the most essential division of your text when it comes to formatting or controlling the looks of your text. A paragraph is defined by Works as any text terminated by a carriage return (that is, the ↵ key). So even a single letter, line, or word will be treated as a paragraph if you press ↵ after it.

Works handles each paragraph as a separate entity, each with its own formatting information. You may have noticed in Chapter 4 that the LETTER1.WPS file used a standard block paragraph format typical of many business letters. The first line is not indented, and paragraphs are separated from one another by blank lines. Also notice that the right margin is ragged, rather than straight, or justified.

These and other qualities affecting the looks of your paragraphs can be altered while you are entering text or any time thereafter, and although you don't normally see the formatting information directly, it is stored in the document along with each paragraph.

For most documents, for example our letter, you may find you are happy with the default format that Works is set up with. In the example letter, Works applied the default format for you, carrying it from one paragraph to the next as you typed. If you decide you'd rather use a different format for a new document, you just alter some settings from a dialog box and begin typing away. Then everything you type into the new document will be formatted accordingly until you change the settings.

Viewing and Altering the Paragraph Formats

To display and/or modify the settings for a given paragraph, you put the cursor anywhere on it and then choose the Paragraph command from the Format menu. As an example, let's look at the settings for the first paragraph in the document.

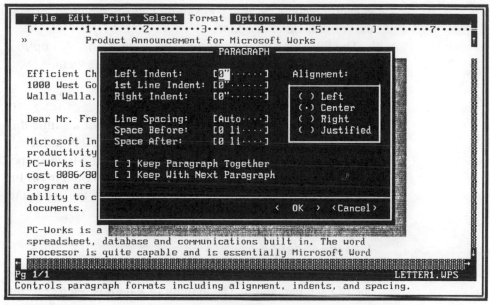

Figure 8-1. The dialog box used to format paragraphs

1. Move the cursor to the top line of the document. This is the line we utimately centered in Chapter 4.

2. Choose Format/Paragraph. Your screen now looks like Figure 8-1.

Figure 8-1 shows the dialog box used to display and set a paragraph's format. This box will always show the settings for the paragraph on which the cursor is currently positioned. Thus, since the cursor was on the first line of the document, the Center option in the Alignment option box is selected.

Paragraph Formatting Options

There are eight format settings you can alter from the Format/PARAGRAPH dialog box. As you can see from Figure 8-1, some of these settings require that you type in numbers. Unless otherwise noted, the examples here use inches as the basic unit of measure. If your dialog box indicates other units, such as centimeters or points, you should choose Window/Settings and select the Inches option.

The following sections provide descriptions of each option, followed by some exercises that will demonstrate them.

Left Indent

In typewriter terms, this means left margin. But it's a little different from a typewriter's left margin setting in that it doesn't apply to the the first line of the paragraph (that's treated specially). The number typed in here determines how far (in inches, centimeters, or points) from the left side of the page your paragraph will print.

1st Line Indent

This setting controls the amount of the left indent for the first line of each paragraph. The amount of indent is relative to the Left Indent setting. On a typewriter, if you want the first line indented, you have to type a tab or press the spacebar several times. You can achieve an indent with Works the same way if you want, but the method is imprecise and doesn't give you the option of easily resetting the indents from the dialog box later on. A setting of .5 will indent the first line half an inch (if you've chosen inches from Windows/Settings) from the left indent. Incidentally, setting the 1st Line Indent to a negative number, such as -.3, will cause the first line to hang out (outdent) that amount, relative to the left indent. (See the section entitled "Hanging and Unhanging Paragraphs.")

Right Indent

Basically, this means the right margin. Right Indent determines how far from the right side of the paper your text will print.

Line Spacing

The amount of space between lines within the paragraph is called *line spacing*. Normally you'll want to indicate single, double, or triple spacing. Thus, the number you type in here will be an integer (1, 2, 3, or higher) followed by the word *li* meaning line. However, some printers are capable of spacing your lines in smaller or more exact increments. Works supports this feature in many of the popular printers, including laser printers. You can declare your spacing value in lines, inches, centimeters, points, 10 pitch, or 12 pitch. Points are measurements used by typesetters, equal to 1/72 inch. Pitch refers to the numbers of characters per inch. Most typewriters and printers print in 10 or 12 pitch (10 or 12 characters per inch, respectively). Note that you can also enter 0 here for auto spacing. Then each line will be as tall as necessary to accommodate the largest font in a line.

Space Before and Space After

These two parameters set the amount of space (typically in lines, but could also be in the units just mentioned) before and/or after a paragraph. For example, upon pressing ↵ to end a paragraph, you may want Works to automatically enter 1-1/2 lines before the next paragraph begins. Space After has the same effect only it adds the space at the end of the paragraph.

Alignment

This section of four buttons selects how the text is lined up between the right and left margins. Left is the default, causing text to be flush (straight) against the left margin. Center centers the entire paragraph. Notice that in Figure 8-1, this button is selected. The reason is that the line the cursor is on was set to center alignment. Right performs a similar function as left, just for the right margin. Justified causes both the right and left margins to be flush by adding space between words and letters to fill out the line. Incidentally, alignments can also be selected directly from the Format menu or via CTRL-key combinations (see the section entitled "CTRL-key Shortcuts for Paragraph Formatting").

Keep Paragraph Together

This controls line breaks within a paragraph rather than breaks between separate paragraphs. If you want to keep a whole paragraph intact rather than breaking it between pages, you should set this option on for the paragraph in question. If you know that the paragraph will not occur at the end of the page, then this will not be necessary.

Keep with Next Paragraph

If checked, this option will keep the selected paragraphs from being separated by a page break. You must select the paragraphs to be "glued" together, then set this formatting option on. A good example of instances in which you'd use this would be tables or lists of items.

Experimenting with Paragraph Formats

Works is enough of a WYSIWYG (remember: what you see is what you get) word processor to show you at least the basic

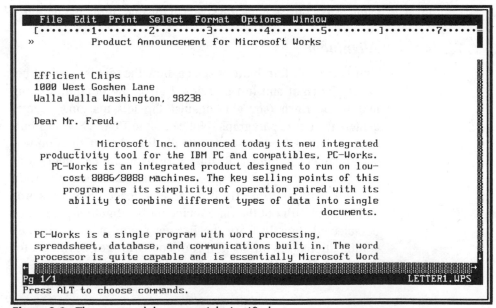

Figure 8-2. *The paragraph becomes right-justified*

effects of these formatting settings on the screen. Try the following exercises to familiarize yourself with some of them:

1. Move the cursor to the first paragraph of the letter body.

2. Choose Format/Paragraph.

3. Press ALT-R followed by ↵ to set the alignment to Right. The paragraph becomes right-justified, looking like that shown in Figure 8-2.

Now let's try some other changes. This time we'll use a shortcut by choosing the alignment from the menu rather than the PARAGRAPH dialog box. For the most common settings, this is simpler.

1. With the cursor on the same paragraph, choose Format/Justified. Now you get flush left and right margins, as in Figure 8-3.

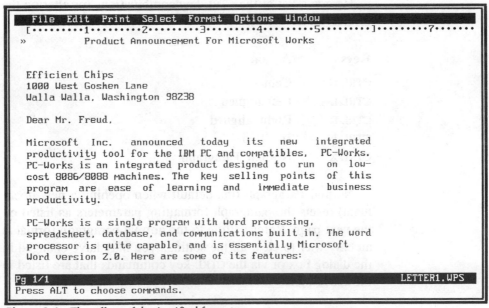

```
 File  Edit  Print  Select  Format  Options  Window
[•••••••1•••••••2•••••••3•••••••4•••••••5•••••••]•••••••7•••••••
»          Product Announcement For Microsoft Works


Efficient Chips
1000 West Goshen Lane
Walla Walla, Washington 98238

Dear Mr. Freud,

Microsoft  Inc.  announced  today  its  new  integrated
productivity tool for the IBM PC and compatibles,  PC-Works.
PC-Works is an integrated product designed to  run  on  low-
cost 8086/8088 machines. The  key  selling  points  of  this
program  are  ease  of  learning  and  immediate  business
productivity.

PC-Works is a single program with word processing,
spreadsheet, database, and communications built in. The word
processor is quite capable, and is essentially Microsoft
Word version 2.0. Here are some of its features:

Pg 1/1                                             LETTER1.WPS
Press ALT to choose commands.
```

Figure 8-3. *The effect of the justified format*

2. Notice the extra spaces between certain words. In most cases, this is only an approximation of what the printed copy will actually look like. Many printers can do what's called *microspaced justification,* a technique for spreading out the words and letters so that justified text looks more evenly spaced. Yours may be able to, but you should probably try printing out a justified document before deciding whether to use this format.

CTRL-key Shortcuts for Paragraph Formatting

Now here's a super shortcut. You can use CTRL-key combinations to do some of this, too.

1. With the cursor still somewhere on the paragraph, press CTRL-C. The paragraph becomes centered.

2. Press CTRL-R. The paragraph moves flush right.

3. Press CTRL-L. The paragraph moves flush left.

Here is a list of the CTRL-key combinations for altering the format:

Keys	Action
CTRL-C	Centered
CTRL-L	Left aligned
CTRL-R	Right aligned
CTRL-J	Justified
CTRL-X	Normal Paragraph

Normal Paragraph (the default when opening a new document) resets the paragraph formatting parameters as listed on the next page. Reformatting to the normal paragraph format is an easy way to clear all the settings you may have changed in the dialog box or via the CTRL-key commands that are listed in the above table.

Parameter	Setting
Left Indent	0
1st Line Indent	0
Right Indent	0
Line Spacing	0
Space Before	0
Space After	0
Alignment	Left
Keep With Next Paragraph	Off
TAB stops	Every .5 inch

You can also use these keys to alter the appearance of text as you are entering it. Try pressing CTRL-C and then typing in some text. It will automatically center as you type. The format will continue in the selected style until you alter it again, even when you begin new paragraphs. (Don't forget to press CTRL-X to return to normal mode after experimenting.)

Changing the Line Spacing

You may have noticed the two line spacing commands on the Format menu, Single Space and Double Space. Try these line spacing exercises to see their effect.

1. First get the paragraph back to left aligned by typing CTRL-L or choosing Left from the Format menu.

2. Choose Format/Double Space. Works inserts extra blank lines between each text line. Your screen looks like Figure 8-4.

3. Choose Format/Single Space to return to single spacing.

4. CTRL-key combinations will do the same thing, a little more easily. Press CTRL-2 (use the 2 key above the W key) to double space.

5. Press CTRL-1 to single space the paragraph.

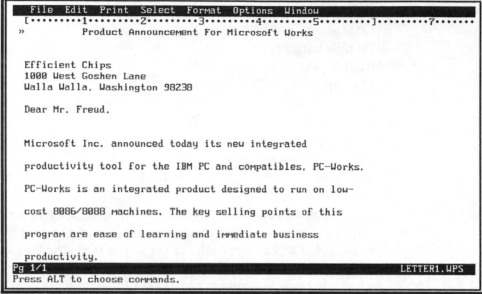

Figure 8-4. Double spacing the first paragraph

6. Press CTRL-5 to set 1-1/2 spaces between lines. (This will look the same as double spacing on some systems, but will print differently if your printer is capable of fractional line spacing.)

7. Reset the paragraph to single spacing again by pressing CTRL-1.

For more precise line-spacing alteration, use the Format choices in the PARAGRAPH dialog box. You can enter fractional values there (such as 2.74) and Works will convert them to points the next time you look at the dialog box.

As you can gather by now, the conceivable combinations for formatting are enormous. You can mix and match any of the parameters with the PARAGRAPH dialog box or Format menu (including character formatting, which we'll get to soon) to achieve numerous effects. But for most documents short of the collected works of Ezra Pound, the variation needed isn't that great.

As mentioned earlier, probably the most popular format is what's already set up as the default (normal) paragraph. In lieu of that, another traditional setting would be single spaced, with a first line indent of 1/2 inch. To try out this setting on the first two paragraphs and as a preparation for the next section, in which we discuss paragraph marks, do the following:

1. Select the first two paragraphs of the letter. (Actually, you only have to select a portion of each paragraph in order to change their format.)

2. Choose Format/Paragraph and set 1st Line Indent to .5 inches, and Line Spacing to 0.

3. Now your paragraphs reformat.

4. Deselect the paragraphs (by pressing an arrow key or clicking elsewhere with the mouse) and your screen will look like that shown in Figure 8-5. Notice that the first line of each paragraph is indented.

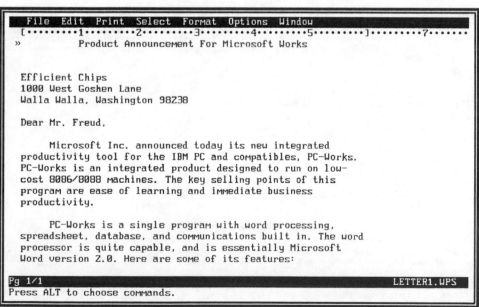

Figure 8-5. *Half-inch indents*

Even though you set the line spacing between paragraphs to 0, there is still a blank line between them. This happened because of the extra ↵ you keyed in when originally entering the text. You did that as a means of skipping a line between paragraphs. As you can see, extra ↵ key presses can cause some difficulty later on if you want to reformat, because each ↵ creates a paragraph mark. Works treats the text before each paragraph mark as a separate paragraph, even if there is nothing in the paragraph except the mark itself. The next section will clarify this and show you how to better control the space between paragraphs without using extra ↵ key presses.

Displaying the Invisible Characters

Normally, paragraph marks are invisible, making it difficult to see whether a blank line is caused by setting the Space Before or Space After to 1, or it's there because you pressed another ↵. The Show All Characters command lets you see invisible characters (such as paragraph marks) so you can tell what's causing what, and add or delete them as necessary.

```
 File  Edit  Print  Select  Format  Options  Window
[••••••••1••••••••2••••••••3••••••••4••••••••5••••••••]••••••••7••••••
 »          Product·Announcement·For·Microsoft·Works¶
 ¶
 ¶
 Efficient·Chips¶
 1000·West·Goshen·Lane¶
 Walla·Walla,·Washington·98238¶
 ¶
 Dear·Mr.·Freud,¶
 ¶
      Microsoft·Inc.··announced·today·its·new·integrated·
 productivity·tool·for·the·IBM·PC·and·compatibles,·PC-Works.·
 PC-Works·is·an·integrated·product·designed·to·run·on·low-
 cost·8086/8088·machines.·The·key·selling·points·of·this·
 program·are·ease·of·learning·and·immediate·business·
 productivity.¶
      ¶
      PC-Works·is·a·single·program·with·word·processing,·
 spreadsheet,·database,·and·communications·built·in.·The·word·
 processor·is·quite·capable,·and·is·essentially·Microsoft·
 Word·version·2.0.·Here·are·some·of·its·features:¶
 ¶
 Pg 1/1                                              LETTER1.WPS
 Press ALT to choose commands.
```

Figure 8-6. Invisible characters displayed

1. Choose Options/Show All Characters. Lots of weird marks appear on your screen now, particularly the ¶ (paragraph) indicators. Also, tabs are shown as little arrows and spaces are represented by dots. Your screen should look like that shown in Figure 8-6.

2. Notice the extra paragraph mark between the two main paragraphs, along the left margin. We'll now delete this extra paragraph mark, just as you would delete a single letter. Move the cursor onto it, then press DEL. The extra line disappears, leaving the paragraphs formatted in normal letter style.

3. Choose Options/Show All Characters again to hide the invisible characters.

Altering the Space Before and Space After

Now if you later decided that you wanted to add a blank line in between each paragraph, you could do it easily using the PARAGRAPH dialog box's Space Before or Space After parameters. When working with large documents, this approach can be a real time saver, as opposed to moving to the beginning of each paragraph and pressing an extra ↵. In other words, the rule of thumb is this: Let the word processor do your paragraph formatting for you. This way it's easily alterable later.

To demonstrate, let's now add a line between paragraphs using the format commands.

1. Select both paragraphs again.

2. Choose Format/Paragraph.

3. Move to the Space After field, type in 1, and press ↵. A blank line is added between the paragraphs.

4. Now to show that this type of extra line is easily removable, repeat steps 2 and 3, typing in 0 instead. The line is deleted.

As discussed earlier, you use Space Before to set whether a blank line is automatically inserted before each new paragraph, as opposed to after. Normally this is set from the PARAGRAPH dialog box, but there is a shortcut for altering the Space Before setting. CTRL-O sets the space before each new or selected paragraph to one line. Pressing CTRL-E sets it to zero lines.

Space Before and Space After spacing can be set in units of inches, points, or centimeters as well. However, the default units are lines.

Nesting and Unnesting Paragraphs

Okay. Here's another neat trick. First, select just the first main paragraph.

1. Press CTRL-N. The left margin of the paragraph jumps to the next default tab stop, which in this case is to the right five

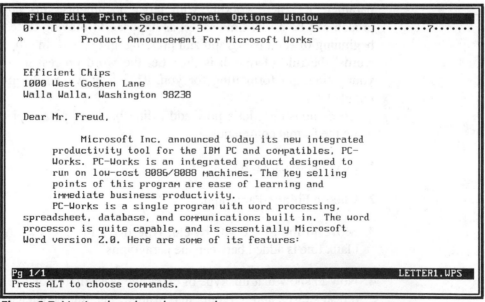

Figure 8-7. Nesting the selected paragraphs

spaces. The paragraph then reformats itself to fit into the narrower margins, as in Figure 8-7.

2. Press CTRL-N again. The left margin moves in five spaces again.

3. Press CTRL-M. This reverses the process, moving the margin five spaces left each time you press CTRL-M.

4. Press CTRL-M again to return the paragraph to its original left margin.

This process is called *nesting* paragraphs. It's useful for formatting such things as quotes within a body of text. Notice also that the square bracket in the ruler moves to indicate the location of the nesting point.

Hanging Paragraphs

Hanging indents occur when the first line of each paragraph is "outdented" rather than "indented." That is, it hangs out farther to the left than the rest of the paragraph does. This accents the first line more. It's also an easy way to format numbered paragraphs to make the numbers stand off to the left.

There are two ways to format outdents. As mentioned earlier, you can set the 1st Line Indent to a negative number (it doesn't matter what the number is, as long as it is negative). An easier method, though, is to use CTRL-H.

1. Put the cursor on the first main paragraph.

2. Press CTRL-H. The first line stays as it was, but all other lines in the paragraph step in five spaces as you see in Figure 8-8. Each press increases this by five spaces.

3. Now press CTRL-G. This unhangs the indent with each press.

Summary of Paragraph Formatting Shortcuts

Before moving on to the next section, review this complete listing of the CTRL-key combinations that affect paragraph formatting:

Key	Effect
CTRL-C	Centered
CTRL-L	Left
CTRL-R	Right
CTRL-J	Justified
CTRL-X	Normal
CTRL-O	Set Space Before to 1
CTRL-E	Set Space Before to 0
CTRL-N	Nest one tab stop right
CTRL-M	Unnest one tab stop left
CTRL-H	Hang or outdent
CTRL-G	Unhang
CTRL-1	Single space
CTRL-2	Double space
CTRL-5	1-1/2 space

SETTING CHARACTER FORMATS

In addition to paragraph formatting, the Format menu includes commands for altering the look of the individual letters on the printed page. This is called *character formatting*. You can use character formatting to emphasize a section of text by having it print out in bold, underline, or italic letters. Or you may want to change the size of certain letters or even the type style (font) of the letters.

You might use optional character formats for these purposes:

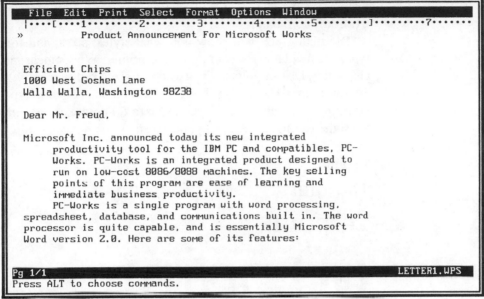

```
 File  Edit  Print  Select  Format  Options  Window
|····[····1·········2·········3·········4·········5·········]·········7·······
 »          Product Announcement For Microsoft Works


Efficient Chips
1000 West Goshen Lane
Walla Walla, Washington 98238

Dear Mr. Freud,

Microsoft Inc. announced today its new integrated
      productivity tool for the IBM PC and compatibles, PC-
      Works. PC-Works is an integrated product designed to
      run on low-cost 8086/8088 machines. The key selling
      points of this program are ease of learning and
      immediate business productivity.
      PC-Works is a single program with word processing,
spreadsheet, database, and communications built in. The word
processor is quite capable, and is essentially Microsoft
Word version 2.0. Here are some of its features:


Pg 1/1                                                   LETTER1.WPS
Press ALT to choose commands.
```

Figure 8-8. *Creating a hanging indent with* CTRL-H

Format	Typical Uses
Bold, *Italic*, <u>Underline</u>	As emphasis for key words, warnings, or headlines
^{Super}script Subscript	For chemical, mathematical, or scientific formulas; trademarks; and footnotes
~~Strikethrough~~	To indicate obsolete or non-applicable wording, such as for text to be stricken from a contract

On many printers, various character formats can be combined. For example, bold and italic could be combined on Epson MX printers (or compatibles).

You can change the formatting of individual letters, selected blocks of text, or the whole document whenever you want. You can even change formats as you type. Just as with paragraph formatting, Works formats the characters to standard font, style, and line position until you specifically alter them from the CHARACTER dialog box and/or by pressing CTRL-key commands.

The dialog box will show you what styles, sizes, and font types are available for your particular printer. Works measures character sizes in points. Typical point sizes range from 9 to 14 for normal text. This book is printed in 12-point type. Headlines may appear in anything up to 60 points or so. Here are some examples of actual point sizes:

12 point

18 point

24 point

60 point

How to Change the Character Formats

Just as with paragraph formatting, character formatting can be achieved in three ways:

- ♦ from the Format menu

- ♦ from the CHARACTER dialog box

- ♦ using shortcut CTRL-key combinations

Character formatting is applied to existing text just as paragraph formatting is — you select the text to alter, then choose the style. In addition, though, if you set the style without having selected any text, subsequently typed letters will be formatted in that style and remain in that style until set back to normal.

You can choose the most-often-used formats from the For-mat menu or by using shortcut keys. Use the CHARACTER dialog box when you need to choose a new font, type size, or make multiple changes to the character formatting.

Here are the CTRL keys that affect character formatting:

Keys	Effect
CTRL-B	Bold
CTRL-U	Underline
CTRL-I	Italic
CTRL-S	Strikethrough
CTRL-SHIFT-=	Superscript
CTRL-=	Subscript
CTRL-SPACE	Normal

Seeing What Format Is Set

Unfortunately, Works doesn't show you the final effects of character formatting on the screen. You will have to wait until you print out your document for that. However, there are a couple of ways that Works informs you of the settings you've selected for areas of text.

Just as with paragraph formats, you can put the cursor on a letter in question (it must be directly on the letter), open the CHARACTER dialog box, and look at the settings. This will give you the complete list of settings, including font and size.

A quick way to see the state of the most common settings is to look at the status line. The status line will indicate the setting for the letter the cursor is on, using the following codes:

Symbol	Meaning
B	Bold
U	Underline
I	Italic
S	Strikethrough
+	Superscript
=	Subscript
(blank)	Normal

If the status line says BUIS, then you know the current setting is bold, underline, italic, and strikethrough (a rather unlikely combination, but possible nonetheless).

Finally, you can easily tell at a glance which text has some special character format set because Works will display the affected text in another video attribute (such as bold letters or slightly dimmer letters) on your screen.

Trying Some Formatting Changes

Now, using our letter, let's practice changing some character formats.

1. Select the top line of the letter.

2. Choose Format/Bold or press CTRL-B. The look of the letters changes on screen.

3. Select the top line of the table (the words *Feature, Notes*).

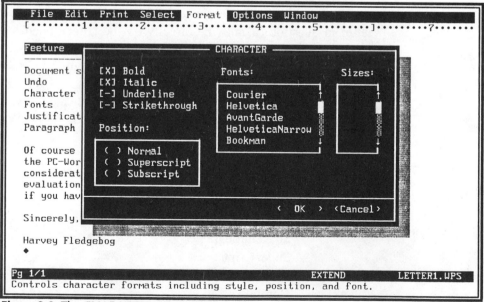

Figure 8-9. The CHARACTER FORMAT dialog box

4. Choose Format/Character. The dialog box appears as in Figure 8-9. (Yours may look a little different.)

5. Press ALT-B then ALT-I to turn on the Bold and Italic check boxes. (Notice that the Normal, Superscript, and Subscript boxes are option-type choices, and only one of these can be on at a time.)

6. If your printer accommodates different fonts and sizes, you may want to try choosing a different setting in the boxes on the right. You can view the list of font names or sizes by moving to the appropriate box and using the arrow keys. Once you highlight a specific font, the size numbers appear.

That's all there is to altering the character formats. There are a couple of things you might want to remember, though. You can alter the look of an entire document by selecting it all and changing the character format. This is an easy way to change the font, for example. Also, if you forget how a particular section is formatted, put the cursor on one character in the section in question and choose Format/Character. The settings in the dialog box will indicate the current format.

COPYING PARAGRAPH AND CHARACTER FORMATS USING COPY SPECIAL

It's possible that a document may have one or more special character or paragraph formats recurring sporadically throughout it. For example, in addition to the main body text, a document could have several additional types of paragraphs such as indented quotations, tabular columns, or paragraphs that use specific character formats. Rather than making you stipulate the formats each time you enter a new one of these paragraphs into your document, or having you reformat each paragraph individually after the fact, you can copy an existing paragraph's format to the new one.

The process of Format copying is almost identical to actual text copying and moving. You simply place the cursor on the text containing the formatting specifications that you want to copy. Then you choose Edit/Copy Special. Next you move to the paragraph or word you want to format, press ↵ and fill in a dialog box. Let's try an example that will copy the hanging indent format we assigned to the first paragraph down to the last paragraph.

1. Place the cursor anywhere in the first paragraph. It should still have a hanging indent of one half inch. If it doesn't, follow the instructions in the section on hanging indents to achieve it.

2. Choose Edit/Copy Special. Nothing appears to happen, except that COPY is displayed on the status line. Actually, the formatting characteristics of the paragraph (or selection, if you had made one) are copied, waiting to be copied elsewhere.

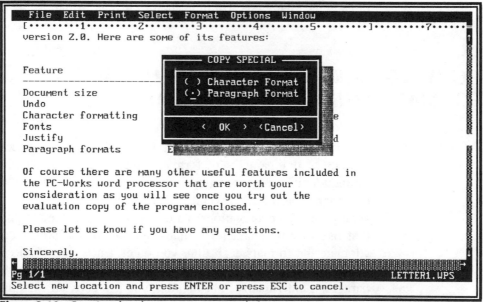

Figure 8-10. *Copying the character or paragraph format*

3. Move the cursor onto any part of the last paragraph.

4. Press ↵. A dialog box appears, as in Figure 8-10.

5. The dialog box asks which characteristic of the format you want to copy to the new cursor location. Notice there are two choices here.

   ♦ **Character Format**: Copies the character format to the target text.

   ♦ **Paragraph Format:** Copies the paragraph format (including tab settings) to the target text. (More about tabs later in this chapter.)

6. Since we want to copy only the paragraph formatting, select the Paragraph Format option and press ↵. The paragraph changes to a hanging indent.

Remember that you can use this command to copy character formats too.

Using Copy Special to Create Makeshift Style Sheets

Since you can use Copy Special to copy formats around, this can be a real time saver for complex layouts such as multi-column tabular formats. It'll also help you keep your documents internally consistent. Just make up a series of example formats, one for each element in your document, and copy them around.

This can be done in a couple of ways. To prevent hopping around too much in the document to find a paragraph of the right format to copy from, you can wait until you're through entering your text. Then, there are two ways to format it.

   ♦ Move through it from beginning to end setting up one format at a time. Repeat the process for each special type of paragraph format, pulling the format through the document with you. For example, say you wanted to format paragraphs 1, 4, 7, 10, and 15 of a manuscript identically. Copy the format of 1 down to 4. Your cursor is now on paragraph 4 which has the new format in it. So rather than going back up to paragraph 1 to copy the format, copy it from paragraph 4 instead.

♦ The second approach is to use a second word processing document to hold nothing but sample paragraphs, each formatted in a desired format (actually all you need are single words separated by paragraph breaks, one for each format). The sample paragraphs can even have words to help you remember what each one is, for example:

Body
Quotes
Lists
Main headings
Sublevel headings

Keep this other document available (open) so you can switch to it via the Window menu. Put the cursor on a paragraph that contains the format you want, select Edit/Copy Special, switch windows and press ↵. Check the dialog box appropriately, and press ↵ again. (For more about copying between documents in different windows, see "Copying Between Two Documents," later in this chapter.)

You can use the same approaches for character formatting, of course, but in most cases the CTRL-key combinations are faster for character formatting unless you're changing fonts and sizes a lot.

WORKING WITH TABS

As with a typewriter, you can vary the tab settings to suit your needs. When you entered the table in our example, you had to press the TAB key several times to get to the second column.

But we could have eliminated the need for extra presses by setting the tabs exactly where we wanted them. For more complex multicolumn tables, you'd probably want to set up your own tab stops.

In addition to being placed where you want, tabs can also be formatted in a variety of useful ways:

- **Right** Text within the tab column lines up on the right (as defined by the beginning point of the next tab column to the right).

- **Left** Text within the tab column lines up on the left, beginning at the tab.

- **Centered** Text in this type of column is centered between the beginning of the tab and the beginning of the next tab to the right.

- **Decimal** Text flanks the decimal point as in monetary figures.

In addition to these options, you can select a leader character to fill in the extra blank spaces in a tab column. The leader character will be inserted into your text each time you move to that tab stop. Leaders are useful for lines such as

Setting Tabs...............................pages 24-25

How to Set Tab Stops

You create tab stops one at a time using the Format/TABS dialog box. Let's create a small table at the end of the current document.

1. Move to the end of the document with CTRL-END.

2. Choose Format/Tabs. The dialog box appears as in Figure 8-11.

Notice that current default tab stop is indicated in the position field, set at 0.5 inch. (The units of measurement may be

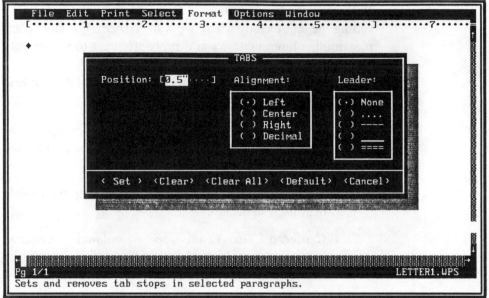

Figure 8-11. The TABS dialog box

different on your screen if you have altered this setting from the Windows/Settings box. If you have, then reset it now to inches.)

3. Let's set tabs at 1.5, 2.5, and 3.5 inches. To set the first tab, type in **1.5** ↵. Notice that the letter *L* appears between the 1 and 2 on the ruler line at the top of the screen.

   [·········1···L····2·········3·········4·········5·········]

   This indicates the location and format (Left) of the first tab stop. Works assumes you want to set a left-formatted tab unless you indicate otherwise.

4. Let's make the second tab stop right formatted. Open the dialog box again.

5. Type in **2.5** (don't press ↵ yet).

6. Set the alignment to Right.

7. Now press ↵. An R appears on the ruler between the 2 and 3 markers, indicating a right-formatted tab stop at that location.

[·········1····L····2····R····3·········4·········5·········]

8. Repeat the procedure now, setting the third stop at 3.5 inches. Format it Decimal, and choose . as the Leader. Then press ↵. A *.D* shows up on the ruler, giving the finished ruler the following appearance:

[·········1····L····2····R····3····.D····4·········5·········]

Okay. Now we can begin entering some text into the columns.

1. Press ↵ to start a new paragraph.

2. Press TAB once to move to the first tab location.

3. Type in **Pistons.**

4. Press TAB to move to the second tab.

5. Type in **26**. Notice that the letters appear to slide sideways to the left as you type. This is because this tab is right-aligned.

6. Press TAB again to get to the next column. A line of periods fills the gap to the next tab.

7. Press BACKSPACE. Suddenly all the periods disappear. Why? Remember that they are just filler for the tab, and a tab is only one character wide even though it looks like it is longer. Backspacing over the tab you just pressed erases it along with the automatic leader characters.

8. Press TAB again. The periods appear. Now enter **24.90** as the price of the Pistons.

9. Go ahead and enter the rest of the table as you see here:

```
Pistons  26 ....................24.90
Rings    45 ......................3.50
Filters  10 ......................5.85
Plugs    45 ......................1.98
```

How to Change Existing TAB Stops

Changing existing tabs for a table or list is easy enough to let you play with the look and size of your layout without ever having to retype or add and delete spaces between columns. You just select all the lines you want to reformat, bring up the TABS dialog box, and make the changes. Try these steps to alter our four-line table.

1. Select the whole table.

2. Choose Format/Tabs.

3. Let's move the second tab a bit to the right. The first step is to clear the current position. Type in **2.5**.

4. Type ALT-C or click on < Clear > with the mouse.

   The tabs reform as you see here. What happened? Since the second tab stop is now gone, our second column used the third tab's original location, along with its leading characters. This makes sense, since that's now the second tab location on the line. The third column moved to the next available tab position to the right (.5 inch over) which Works had there already by default.

```
Pistons   ......................26      24.90
Rings     ......................45       3.50
Filters   ......................10       5.85
Plugs     ......................45       1.98
```

   But this isn't what we really wanted. Let's move the second column left a bit and remove the periods.

5. Open the TABS dialog box and set a new tab at 3 inches, left-aligned, no leader.

6. Open the dialog box again and Clear the tab at 3.5 inches.

7. Open it again and set a new tab at 4.0 inches, decimal, no leader. Now your columns are evenly spaced.

Pistons	26	24.90
Rings	45	3.50
Filters	10	5.85
Plugs	45	1.98

A Few Other Points About Tabs

There are a few other points concerning tabs that you may want to be aware of. These are listed below.

- You can clear all the tabs (restoring the defaults) by choosing <Clear All>.

- The <Default> button can be used to set the position, alignment, or leader of the default tabs. Be careful. They change the default tabs for the entire document.

- You can copy tab formats from one place to another using Copy Special.

- You can see where the actual tabs in your document are by turning on Options/Display All. The little arrows indicate tabs.

- Finally, when you set a tab manually, all default tab stops to the left of that stop are eliminated automatically by Works. All remaining stops to the right will contain whatever characteristics have been ascribed to the default.

MORE ABOUT UNDO

Though mentioned in Chapter 3 briefly, the Undo command didn't get a lot of explanation there. You didn't actually get a chance to undo a possibly catastrophic mistake while editing. So before going any further, let's take a closer look at Undo.

Undo is a selection from the Edit menu that is only available in the word processor tool of Works, not in any of the other three tools. It is most heartily appreciated when called upon to salvage portions of text that you accidentally delete without prudent forethought. Undo is capable of reversing these actions:

♦ Block deletes, using the Delete command from the Edit menu or the DEL key on the keyboard. This kind of block delete is usually the kind you regret the most. Choosing Undo jumps back to the place in your text where the deletion occurred and replaces it.

♦ Individual or multiple letters that you erased using the DEL or BACKSPACE keys. Undo will return only the last letter or series of letters erased. That is, once you move the cursor to another location using any of the navigation keys and delete again, that text is lost. However, Undo does remember the last place you deleted letters, jumps back to that location, and retypes the letters in their original places.

♦ Selected blocks directly deleted and replaced by typing new text on the keyboard. As mentioned in Chapter 4, a simple way of replacing a selected block of words with new words or letters is simply to type in the new text after selecting the part you want to replace. Undo will reverse this type of deletion.

♦ New text that you typed in. This can be undone (erased) up until the point that you issue some other command.

- ◆ Undo is also capable of reversing character and paragraph formatting changes.

Here are some exercises to try with Undo.

Undoing Deleted Blocks

1. Select the entire first paragraph of the body.

2. Press DEL or choose Edit/Delete. The paragraph disappears.

3. Now move the cursor to some new location in the text using the navigation keys.

4. Choose Edit/Undo. The paragraph returns, appearing in its original location, along with the cursor.

Undoing Backspacing

1. Position the cursor on the colon at the end of the second paragraph, after the word *features*.

2. Now press the BACKSPACE key eight times. This erases the word.

3. Choose Edit/Undo. The word returns.

Undoing Text Deleted by Replacement

1. Select the first paragraph again.

2. Type the word **Testing**. The paragraph disappears and is replaced by *Testing*.

3. Choose Edit/Undo. The paragraph returns, and the word *Testing* is deleted.

Undoing New Typing

1. Move the cursor to the beginning of the first paragraph of the text body, on the *M* of *Microsoft*. Enter

A software design company known as

2. Choose Edit/Undo. The new phrase should disappear. This technique will always work unless you back up to insert letters or fix typos.

Remember that the Undo command can only recall the last action. If you decide you have made a mistake, whether entering or deleting, you must undo the damage before using any other editing commands.

Another salient point: Not all commands can be undone. For example, Undo will not return a section of text to its original location once it has been moved. After you've moved a block of text, you'd have to reverse the procedure step by step if you decide it was better off where it was. That's just one example. There are lots of others. But rather than listing all the irreversible actions Undo can't reverse, here's an easy way to determine it for yourself. Just open the Edit menu after using a command and try to select Undo. If you get a beep, then your last action can't be reversed.

COPYING BLOCKS OF TEXT

In Chapter 4 you learned how to move text from one section to another. You can also copy text within a document or from one document to another. Copying works the same way as moving, only the original text is left intact rather than deleted by Works. Copying can be a real blessing for documents using repeated elements.

To illustrate copying, let's copy the table you just created. Since the Copy command copies not only text but also character, paragraph, and tab formats, the tab settings you just made should be copied along with the text.

1. Select the entire table.

2. Choose Edit/Copy.

3. Move the cursor to a blank line, preferably directly above the table.

4. Press ↵. The table is copied. Now you have two tables.

Pistons	26	24.90
Rings	45	3.50
Filters	10	5.85
Plugs	45	1.98
Pistons	26	24.90
Rings	45	3.50
Filters	10	5.85
Plugs	45	1.98

Bear in mind when copying that you have to complete the copy before the ↵ key returns to its normal mode. Also, you cannot Undo a copy. You have to select the text and delete it.

SEARCHING AND REPLACING TEXT

Works offers Search and Replace commands to look for specific letters, words, or series of words in your text. Once the word processor finds the text, you can have it automatically replace that text with other text.

Searching can also be used to quickly get to a particular place in your document. If you put unique markers (for example, ##1, aaa) in your text, you can search for them, in effect moving you from one part of a document to another using them as tags or place markers.

Using Search and Replace together, you can replace abbreviated words with the full word after you're done typing. For example, in preparing the manuscript for this book, we replaced *MW* with *Microsoft Works* and *wp* with *Works word processor.* This eliminated lots of repetitive typing.

Here's how to use Search and Replace to find the word *data:*

1. Choose Select/Search... The dialog box in Figure 8-12 appears.

2. Type in **data** and press ↵.

3. The cursor moves to the word *data*.

4. To find out if there are any other occurrences of the word, choose Select/Search again. The dialog box appears again, with the word *data* already typed in. Works always remembers the last word you searched for, so you can repeat the

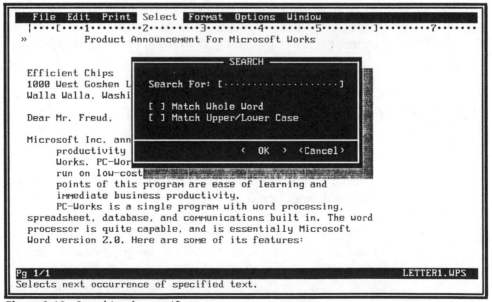

Figure 8-12. *Searching for specific text*

action more easily. Just press ↵ and the next occurrence is found.

5. Do the search again and a dialog box appears saying:

Search for text not found.

This means there were no other occurrences of the word in your text. Just press ↵ or click on <OK>.

There are two other options when searching: whole-word matching and case matching. Sometimes you'll want to search for a word that could also be embedded in other words. For example the word *me* would be found in the word *time*. If you don't want the search to stop at *time* set the Match Whole Word check box on before doing the search.

If you set the Match Upper/Lower Case check box on, the search will respond to the case (uppercase and lowercase) of the word you type in the Search For: field. For example, if you had typed in the word *Data*, it would not have found data.

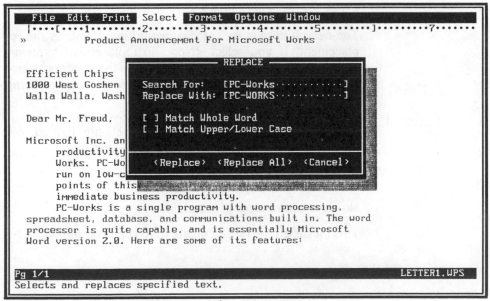

Figure 8-13. *Replacing specific text in a document*

The search command always starts at the current cursor location and searches to the end of the document. Then it wraps around to the beginning and continues until it reaches the cursor.

Here's how to replace a word. Say we want to replace the words *PC-Works* with *PC-WORKS*.

1. Choose Select/Replace. A slightly larger dialog box appears. Notice that the settings from the last search show up in this box too. But we're going to change the settings. See Figure 8-13.

2. Type in the information as you see in the figure. It doesn't matter if the Whole Word check box is on or not, but the Match Upper/Lower Case should be set on.

3. Now select <Replace> or press ↵.

4. The first occurrence of Works is highlighted on the top line of the screen and a dialog box appears saying:

   Replace this occurrence?
   < Yes > < No > <Cancel>

   The default answer is Yes. So just hitting ↵ causes the replacement. If you select <No>, no replacement happens, and the search continues. Cancel stops the process. Since you want to replace it, press ↵. You see the change being made.

5. The second occurrence of Works now gets highlighted, and the dialog box reappears. Press ↵ for a replacement.

6. Now a box appears saying:

   No more occurrences of search for text

   This means all the replacements have been completed.

Tips for Using Search and Replace

If you want the word processor to make replacements without asking your permission each time, select <Replace All> from the dialog box. Also, the search and replace can be limited to a selected text block. Just highlight the selection before doing the search and replace. This will not work for just searching.

Search and Replace and Search have a number of other options that you may want to use from time to time. When searching, you can use a wildcard character to broaden the possible matching words that Works will find. Say you wanted to find all words that started with t, had four letters, and ended in l. For the search word, type in **t??l**. The question marks are wildcards that will match with any letter. Thus, both *tool* and *teal* would be found. Or you could search for all five-letter words, say, by using *?????* as the search criteria.

Some other special characters that Works will search for and replace are shown in the following table:

Type This	To Find or Replace
^W	White space
^s	Non-breaking space
^d	Page break
^t	Tab
^p	Paragraph mark
^n	End-of-line-mark
^~	Non-breaking hyphen
^-	Optional hyphen
^?	Question mark
^^	Caret
^#	Any ASCII character
?	Any character

White space is any combination of non-breaking spaces, tabs, spaces, new lines, paragraph marks, and hard page breaks. This cannot be used as a Replace item.

A non-breaking space is a space such as the one in "Microsoft Works" when you don't want the words to separate during line wraps.

To enter one of these special characters as the search or replace character, type SHIFT-6 to get the ^ mark, followed by the character in the list that represents the special item to be searched for or replaced.

INSERTING SPECIAL CHARACTERS INTO YOUR TEXT

You can insert a number of special characters and control codes into a document via the Edit/INSERT SPECIAL dialog box. For example, you can use a CTRL code to insert a blank page into the middle of a letter, or press a key to insert the current date or time rather than typing it automatically. Some of the options apply only to printing form letters (which we'll cover in Chapter 12).

There are 11 options from the dialog box, only one of which can be selected at a time. The item will be inserted into your text at the cursor position.

Let's put the current date into our letter.

1. Insert two new lines just above the address, using ⏎.

2. Press ↑ twice to position the cursor on the top line. Then choose Format/Left. This moves the cursor to the left margin, two lines above the address.

3. Choose Edit/Insert Special. The large dialog box appears, as in Figure 8-14.

4. Press ALT-C to choose the Current Date option.

5. Today's date appears against the left margin of the top line.

Name	Code	Effect
End-of-Line Mark	SHIFT ↵	Lets you decide where a line breaks.
Manual Page Break	CTRL ↵	Lets you decide where a page breaks.
Optional Hyphen	CTRL -	Lets you designate where a word will split.
Non-Breaking Hyphen	CTRL - SHIFT -	Holds hyphenated words together at line breaks.
Non-Breaking Space	CTRL - SHIFT-SPACE	Holds words together at line break.
Print Page	CTRL - P	Causes a blank page to print.
Print File	CTRL - F	Prints the name of the word processing file.
Print Date	CTRL - D	Prints the date the document is printed.
Print Time	CTRL - T	Prints the time the document is printed.
Current Date	CTRL - ;	Inserts today's date.
Current Time	CTRL - SHIFT - ;	Inserts the current time in hh:mm: am/pm format.

Table 8-1. Special Word Processing Characters

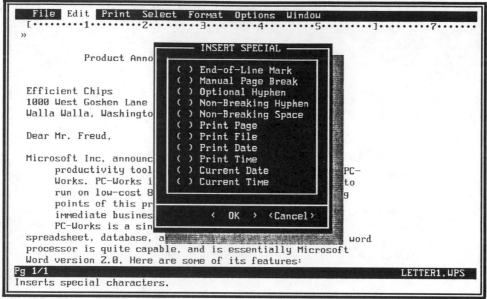

Figure 8-14. *Inserting special characters into text*

All the other special characters work the same way. Table 8-1 provides a list of special characters and their meanings, as well as the CTRL-key combinations you can use to insert them in lieu of selecting from the dialog box.

CHECKING YOUR SPELLING

Before printing your documents, it's a good idea to check your spelling. Works can give you a substantial hand here, using its built-in spelling checker. The spelling checker uses an 80,000 word dictionary stored in the disk file called MAIN.DIC. Every word in your document is methodically compared against the entries in the dictionary to determine whether they are spelled correctly or incorrectly. Of course your documents may regularly use words not found in the supplied dictionary. It can get pretty tedious telling the program that these words are really not misspellings. To accommodate such situations, you can create, update, and call upon custom dictionaries when using the spelling checker. Custom dictionaries are always named PERSONAL.DIC.

In addition to simple spell checking, Works also looks for incorrect capitalization, incorrect hyphenation, and accidentally repeated words (such as *the the*), and alerts you to these errors.

When the spell checker encounters an error, you may ask the program to make suggestions for alterations to the word in question. Suggestions are displayed in a list box from which you can select the replacement word. The word is dropped into your text automatically, in place of the misspelled one.

To use the spell checker:

1. While in the LETTER1.WPS document, move to the top of the file, and retype the word *for* in the title as *frr*. (You'll have to delete a few letters after inserting the two *rs*.)

2. Make sure the cursor is on the word *frr*.

3. Choose Options/Check Spelling. (At this point, Works may prompt you to insert the Spell disk, which contains the dictionary. You must do this before continuing.) The dialog box and screen then appear as in Figure 8-15.

   The dialog box reports it has found a misspelled word. The word is always seen highlighted in context on the second line of the screen, just above the dialog box. Also, the word appears in the dialog box, waiting for you to retype it if you wish and press ↵. The suggestion box is empty unless you select Suggestions.

4. This word is obviously just a simple typo, and it's easier to retype than look up, so just type **for** and press ↵. (Pressing ↵ from this box always amounts to selecting < Change > from the dialog box, thus inserting your changed word into the document.

The spelling checker pops *for* into the right place, and actually checks its spelling before moving on. If you were to type in a misspelling again, this would be caught and reported, just as *frr* was.

5. Now the next suspect word, *Microsoft*, appears in the dialog box. As will be the case with most proper names, the dictionary does not know about Microsoft (even though they created it). This is a good candidate for addition to the personal dictionary. Press ALT-A and press ↵. The word is left as is, but added to the file PERSONAL.DIC, your personal dictionary of words.

6. The next misspelling is Randolf. It doesn't make much sense to add this to the dictionary, so press ALT-I to ignore it.

7. Try typing in some other errors, such as repeated words (its its), or slight misspellings, and running the spelling checker. If the problem is a misspelling, press ALT-S to see the Sug-

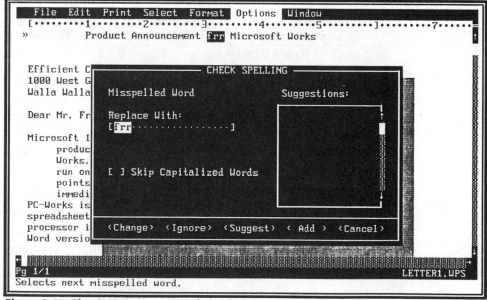

Figure 8-15. *The CHECK SPELLING dialog box*

gestions. Then select the correct spelling and press ↵ to drop it into your text.

8. When you're through experimenting, return any altered words to their original spellings. We'll be using the letter in Chapter 12.

Spelling Checker Tips

The checker remembers the correction you make for each word. If it encounters the same misspelling again, your correction is proposed in the Replace With: field.

If you start to change a word, but then decide to leave it as it was, you can leave the misspelling intact by typing ESC or selecting < Ignore >.

If you want to check a single word for accuracy as you're typing along, just select the word and run the checker. Whenever a selection is active, the checker looks only at words in the selection, not the entire document.

You can bail out of the checking process at any time by pressing ESC. You don't have to select < Cancel >

You can tell Works to skip the checking of capitalized words by setting the Skip Capitalized Words check box on.

When you choose < Add > , the word is stored in your personal dictionary. It's conceivable that you'll want to have more than one personal dictionary on hand for different types of documents. This is possible, but since Works always looks for a file called PERSONAL.DIC, you will have to do some file renaming and/or copying from the DOS prompt outside of Works if you want to use multiple dictionaries. When you are not using a dictionary, just name it something else, preferably a name that will jog your memory about its contents.

```
COMPUTER.DIC
MUSIC.DIC
BOOK.DIC
PARENTS.DIC
```

Then use the DOS RENAME command to change the name when you need to use a given dictionary.

C> rename music.dic personal.dic ↵.

Caution: Don't forget to rename it back again after you're done using it, otherwise you could overwrite it next time you rename another dictionary.

An easy way to build new specialized dictionaries is to create a new word processing document containing nothing but your special words. You can use either a column or paragraph layout. Then run the spelling checker on that document. You can then add all unrecognized words to the dictionary of your choice.

SPLITTING THE WINDOW

A rather interesting feature of the Works word processor allows you to divide the screen into two separate horizontal sections, each acting as an independently scrollable window. This way you can view and edit, say, the first and last pages of a large document almost simultaneously. The real advantage of this scheme becomes evident when you want to move or copy portions of one segment into the other, or to keep a particular segment of your document on-screen as reference for other paragraphs as you type them.

There are two ways to split the screen, depending on whether you have a mouse or not. Before beginning this exercise, move the cursor to the top of the LETTER1.WPS file by pressing CTRL - HOME.

1. Choose Options/Split. Then press the ↓ 11 times to move the horizontal line that spans the screen. Then press ↵.

If you're using a mouse, move to the upper right-hand corner of the screen. You'll notice an = sign there. Hold down the left button and drag the = down about halfway

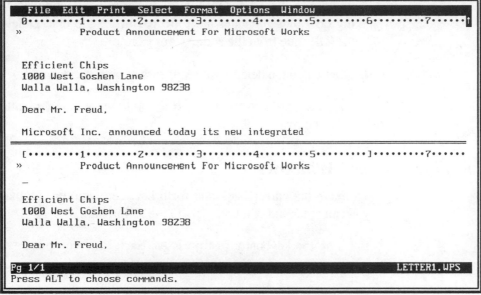

Figure 8-16. *Splitting the screen to see two sections*

down the screen. It becomes a horizontal line spanning the screen from left to right. Release the button.

2. A second ruler appears in the bottom window, and the first part of the letter is visible in both windows, as in Figure 8-16.

At first, what you see is a little confusing and you may wonder what's going on. Just think of the split screen as a way to scroll through the document with two separate windows. You're still only editing a single document, not two documents. You can scroll the windows independently and edit in either window. Any changes made in one window will show up in the other one when you scroll to the section involved.

Note that the cursor is now in the lower window. This window will work normally, complete with scrolling, editing, menu commands, and so forth.

3. Try making some changes in the lower window and watching how those changes are reflected in the top one. Delete the ZIP code from the address, for example.

4. Now Undo the deletion. It reappears in both windows.

5. Press PGUP and PGDN. The text in the lower window scrolls up and down.

Jumping Between Windows

To move the cursor back and forth between windows so that you can enter and edit text, you do the following.

1. Using the keyboard, just press F6. Each time you press F6, you are moved to the other window.

2. With a mouse, just position the pointer anywhere inside the other window and click the left button. Now you can scroll, edit, use commands, or whatever else you'd like.

Works remembers the cursor positions in each window so that you don't lose your place when jumping between them. Also, you can tell which window is the active one by looking at the ruler. The inactive window's ruler has a 0 on its far left end. The active window's ruler has the usual square brackets and other ruler indicators, such as tab markers, displayed.

Once you become comfortable with working with a split screen, you may want to experiment more with various editing commands. You can delete, copy, and move from one window to the other, as you normally would. For example, to move some text from the lower to the upper window, use the following steps:

1. Jump into the lower window.

2. Select the block and select Edit/Move.

3. Jump to the other window by pressing F6.

4. Place the cursor where you want the text copied to and press ↵.

Of course you can do this with only one window. However, if you're copying lots of items from one section of a document to another, it's tedious to jump back and forth within the document when you can use two windows.

To return to normal (unsplit) mode, or to resize the windows, simply reverse the process you used to create the split. Move the horizontal bar all the way to the top of the screen to eliminate the split totally.

COPYING BETWEEN TWO DOCUMENTS

Even more common than the need for a split is the need to copy portions of text between two or more separate documents. Many professionals use word processors because they enable them to use "boilerplates" to piece together new documents from existing ones. This is particularly useful for constructing legal documents or contracts that regularly include standard clauses or paragraphs. A more domestic example is creating a series of somewhat similar letters to a number of friends.

Since Works lets you have up to eight documents open at once, you have a fair amount of flexibility here. Most people only use two or three documents at a time, at the most, so eight is pretty liberal. Once your documents are open, you can select text from one, copy it, then open another window, position the cursor and press ↵. That places the copy of the original text in the new location. Of course the Move command will work too, assuming you want to move the original text rather than leaving a copy of it in the original document.

Let's try an example. Say you want to copy the address in the LETTER1 document to a new document in preparation for sending Mr. Freud a follow-up letter about Microsoft Works.

1. Select the text you want to copy.

2. Press SHIFT-F3 (or choose Edit/Copy).

3. Choose File/New and open a new word processor document. (If you wanted to copy to an existing document, you'd use File/Open instead, and open the other file.)

4. Position the cursor where you want the copied text to go.

5. Press ↲. The text is copied.

This technique can be a real time saver when you are working with several documents. If you are used to the limitations of most PC-based word processing programs that let you have only one or two files open at once, you'll really learn to love this feature. The way Works lets you jump between them, scroll up and down, copy and move text, as well as copy paragraph and character formatting, is very slick.

HEADERS AND FOOTERS, PAGE BREAKS, AND PAGINATION

Once you've successfully entered and edited a document, you may want to fine-tune it prior to printing. One of the changes you'll probably want to make is the addition of headers and footers that will print on each page. You'll probably also want to have some control over page numbering, and just how your text is divided into specific pages.

Headers and Footers

A header is a line of text that appears at the top of every printed page, such as a page number or chapter title. Footers, which print at the bottom of the page, typically contain similar text. Works lets you include headers, footers, or both in each document.

There are two ways to create headers and footers. The first is via the Print/LAYOUT dialog box, which has the following fields for you to enter your header and footer text:

```
Header: [........................................]
Footer: [Page - &p ...............................]
```

Notice that as a default, Works inserts the code necessary to print a page number on the bottom of each page, preceded by the word *page*. Thus, you will always see something like:

```
Page - 3
```

at the bottom of each printed page unless you specify otherwise. The details of creating headers and footers with this dialog box, along with the list of &-codes that can be used for inserting variables such as the date, time, and file name are found in Chapter 3 of this book, and apply to all four Works tools. In addition to the standard headers and footers, the word processor lets you declare headers from within your document, making it easier to enter, edit, and select character and paragraph formats for them. Once created this way, you can turn these footers and headers on and off so that they will print only when you want, by choosing the Options/Headers and Footers command. When turned off, the headers and footers declared in the Print/LAYOUT dialog box take over, if there's anything in these fields. Otherwise the headers and footers in your document take precedence.

Use these steps to put headers and footers into your documents with the Options/Headers and Footers command.

1. First, move to the top of the LETTER1.WPS file with CTRL-HOME.

2. Choose Options/Headers and Footers.

3. Two new lines appear at the top of the screen.

```
H
F                    Page - *page*
```

Notice the two letters, H and F, in the selection bar at the left. The H indicates the line you'll type your header on. The F indicates the line you'll type the footer on, if you want one.

To type in your header or footer, just move to the appropriate line and type it in. Don't forget that since headers and footers can include anything that normal text can, you can change the alignment, font, and size, and you can insert special characters such as date and time using the Edit/Insert Special commands. Notice that the default is for the page number to appear on the footer line.

You can also create multiple-line headers or footers by ending each line with a SHIFT ↵ instead of ↵. Works will then create an additional footer or header line.

```
H
H
F                    Page - *page*
```

However, you'll have to increase the Header Margin and/or Footer Margin settings in the LAYOUT dialog box to adjust your pages accordingly. There is no easy way to calculate how much extra space will be needed per page since the font size and number of lines will affect this. You may have to experiment a bit to finalize the settings.

The following boxes in the Print/LAYOUT dialog box determine whether your headers and footers appear on the first page of your printer document, regardless of how you created them:

```
[ ] No Header on 1st Page
[ ] No Footer on 1st Page
```

Pagination, Page Breaks, and Page Size

Pagination refers to the numbering of pages, whether pages in a three-page letter or in a book. If we were still printing on continuous, long rolls of paper as the Egyptians did with their papyrus scrolls, pagination could be dispensed with. Current tradition requires breaking text into separate pages, so Works lets you preview the pages on your document as best it can. This way you can see just where the page breaks occur, and thus where your text will divide into pages when printed.

Works shows page breaks as a double arrow >> in the left margin of the screen. Also, the status line indicates which page the cursor is on, and the number of pages in the document. For example, the notation 2/7 means "page 2 of 7."

Like any good word processor, Works automatically minds the page breaks for you. Works even prevents against widow and orphan lines: short, single lines that might otherwise be left hanging alone at the beginning or end of a page.

Despite all this built-in intelligence, there are a number of situations begging for human control and customization of the pagination process. First, Works calculates pagination and display of page breaks on-screen based on information in the Print/LAYOUT dialog box.

The margin and paper sizes are particularly important in this respect. The 1st Page Number does not affect the on-screen page numbering, unfortunately, so if you plan to edit from pages with numbers starting from something other than 1, you may have to mentally compensate for the difference.

In any case, if you plan to print paper other than 8.5 inch by 11 inch, or print with larger margins, you should inform Works of it so that page numbers will be calculated accordingly.

Automatic Versus Manual Pagination

Two commands on the Option menu (Manual Pagination and Paginate Now) offer a useful feature to those who will prefer to edit their text on paper rather than on the computer. This is not an uncommon need after all, since many business letters, reports, and other types of documents pass through numerous hands and are marked up with comments before being finalized.

The problem arises that as insertions and deletions are made with the word processor, the original page references are thrown off, making it difficult for the word processor operator to find the mistakes and enter the changes. The Manual Pagination command compensates for this.

When set on, Works will not bother figuring out where the page breaks are; as a result, it maintains the page breaks established as of the last automatic pagination, even while you are adding or deleting text. When you are ready to paginate again, choose Paginate Now. In a few seconds (or maybe longer if the document is long), Works will update the page breaks and page numbering.

Incidentally, if you want to suppress the printing of page numbers, you have to delete any references to the symbols &p or *page* in the Print/LAYOUT dialog box or your header/footer lines at the top of your document, respectively.

PRINTING IT OUT — OTHER POINTS OF INTEREST

When you are about ready to print, don't forget to save your file first, just in case the computer or the printer goes berserk in the process and you lose your file. The rest you already know from previous chapters. Just choose Print/Print, fill in the applicable blanks, turn on the printer, and press ⏎.

As you may have surmised from other commands on the menus, you can insert spreadsheet charts into your word processor documents when you print, creating documents that combine text and graphics. You can also create and print customized forms, mailing labels, and form letters using the word processor tool in conjunction with data files in the database tool. These techniques, since they involve the use of two or more tools at once, will be covered in Chapter 12, "Pulling It All Together." Please refer to that chapter for details.

You may want to exchange files with people using different word processors, such as WordStar, WordPerfect, Microsoft Word, or others. Works comes with a program called WPTOWP that facilitates exchange of word processing files between such programs. Please refer to Appendix B for instructions on importing and exporting files between Works and other programs.

Chapter

Expanding Your Spreadsheet Skills

Nine

In Chapter 5 you created, edited, and printed a relatively simple spreadsheet — an invoice. But certainly the most popular use for spreadsheets is budgeting, so in this chapter we'll create a budget for a fictitious company, Bob's House of Gadgets. The budget will help us assess the cost of adding a new store to this already successful chain. In the process of building the spreadsheet, we'll use some new features of the Works spreadsheet tool. You'll learn more about entering and copying formulas, how to view separate *windows* of your spreadsheet at the same time, how to *freeze* certain row and column headings, how to set standard values, how to protect certain cells, and how to control recalculation of your data. You'll also glean some pointers for setting up a typical budget.

Suppose your retail chain, Bob's House of Gadgets, is doing so well that you've considered adding a new store in another part of the city. Obviously, you'll want to carefully consider a lot of variables before committing to such a business venture. What will your new monthly expenses be? How much income can the new location be expected to generate? What are your start-up costs? A spreadsheet model can help you efficiently budget your venture, experiment with variables, and keep track of your store's finances if you decide to go ahead with the expansion.

```
                        BOB'S HOUSE OF GADGETS
                         Budget for New Store


=========================ASSUMPTIONS=================================
EMPLOYEES             NUMBER  SALARIES 1ST GRTH   8.0%   RENT     2000
STORE MANAGER             1    2,500  2ND GRTH  12.0%   UTIL      400
ASST. MANAGER             1    2,000  3RD GRTH  12.0%   MAINT     500
SENIOR CLERK              1    1,600  4TH GRTH  15.0%  DEPREC     750
JUNIOR CLERK              4    1,200  RETURNS    2.0%   INSUR     250
                                     C O S     63.0%   PHONE     150
TOTAL SALARIES       10,900          P/R TAX   15.0%   MISC      150
                                     FRINGE     7.0%
                                     POST/FGT   1.0%
                                     EXC. TAX   0.5%



==========================BUDGET====================================
BUDGET CATEGORY      QTR 1    QTR 2    QTR 3    QTR 4    TOTAL  % SALES
-------------------------------------------------------------------

REVENUE
  SALES             113,400  127,008  142,249  163,586  546,243  102.0%
  RETURNS             2,268    2,540    2,845    3,272   10,925    2.0%
    NET SALES       111,132  124,468  139,404  160,315  535,318  100.0%

  COST OF SALES      70,013   78,415   87,825  100,998  337,251   63.0%

GROSS PROFIT         41,119   54,455   69,391   90,301  255,266   47.7%

EXPENSES
  SALARIES           32,700   32,700   32,700   32,700  130,800   24.4%
  PAYROLL TAXES       4,905    4,905    4,905    4,905   19,620    3.7%
  FRINGE BENEFITS     2,289    2,289    2,289    2,289    9,156    1.7%
    SUBTOTAL LABOR   39,894   39,894   39,894   39,894  159,576   29.8%

STORE RENT            6,000    6,000    6,000    6,000   24,000    4.5%
UTILITIES             1,200    1,200    1,200    1,200    4,800    0.9%
MAINTENANCE           1,500    1,500    1,500    1,500    6,000    1.1%
DEPRECIATION          2,250    2,250    2,250    2,250    9,000    1.7%
ADVERTISING           4,500    2,000    1,750    1,500    9,750    1.8%
POSTAGE AND FREIGHT   1,111    1,245    1,394    1,603    5,353    1.0%
INSURANCE               750      750      750      750    3,000    0.6%
TELEPHONE               450      450      450      450    1,800    0.3%
EXCISE TAXES            556      622      697      802    2,677    0.5%
MISCELLANEOUS           450      450      450      450    1,800    0.3%
  SUBTOTAL NONLAB     18,767   16,467   16,441   16,505   68,180   12.7%

TOTAL EXPENSE        58,661   56,361   56,335   56,399  227,756   42.5%

NET PROFIT          (17,542)  (1,906)  13,056   33,903   27,510    5.1%
```

Figure 9-1. *The completed budget for Bob's House of Gadgets*

Figure 9-1 shows the budget as it will look when you are finished building it. Notice that it is divided into two main sections, labeled "Assumptions" and "Budget." The assumptions section contains all the facts upon which to base your budget. Such factors as the number of employees and their salaries, the expected growth per quarter, and your fixed expenses, including rent and utilities, are contained in this section.

Of course, all these figures could be stored in the body of the spreadsheet, just as we included the TAX multiplier (5 percent) in the formula for each cell of the TAX column of our invoice spreadsheet from Chapter 5. Imagine, though, if the tax rate changed from 5 percent to, say, 6 percent. Updating the spreadsheet would require altering the formulas in eight cells. Of course you wouldn't have to change each cell individually, since you could use the Fill Down command to copy the edited formula from cell E7 and adjust it accordingly.

However, in a complex spreadsheet, making a single change to an assumption that is widely referenced elsewhere could end up being a very time-consuming task. Moreover, you could easily overlook one of the references and fail to update it. The result would be an inaccurate bottom line somewhere. It's much easier to use *references* to a small group of assumption cells to derive your formulas. This allows you to easily see what your assumptions are, and to change them later at will.

For example, in our TAX column, rather than using the formula D7*0.05 for cell E7 and D8*0.05 for cell E8, we could have used the formulas D7*E4 and D8*E4. The "E4" in each formula is the referenced cell. By entering the value of the current tax rate into E4 (which was previously empty), the spreadsheet would calculate the tax as before, only it'd be a snap to alter the rate of tax if it were to change. You'd simply change the value in E4 and all cells containing references to it would recalculate automatically.

Assumption Details

The assumptions section of the budget spreadsheet can be divided into three parts:

- Employees
- Percentages
- Fixed expenses

Employees' Salaries

We'll assume that the number of employees will stay constant, and that their salaries will, too. The spreadsheet shows the number of employees in each category type, along with the monthly salaries for each type. By multiplying the number of employees in each salary type by the salary and then summing the results, the total salary outlay per month can be calculated.

The Percentage Assumptions

Percentage assumptions break down as follows: the first four entries indicate what you expect the store's income growth percentages to be, per quarter. Next we have a 2 percent allowance for customer returns of goods sold. This will be calculated against the store's revenues. The cost of sales (COS) we'll assume to be 63 percent. Cost of sales is essentially your gross sales minus your inventory costs and selling expenses. Payroll tax (P/R TAX), fringe benefits (FRINGE), postage and freight (POST/FGT), and excise tax (EXC.TAX) are assumed to be 15, 7, 1, and .5 percent, respectively.

The Fixed Expenses

Fixed expenses are expenses that are not expected to change each month. Actually, salaries could fit into this category, but it's easier to break those out as we have, for clearer reference. Our fixed expenses include rent, utilities, maintenance, depreciation, insurance and telephone costs, and miscellaneous odds and ends. All of these are rounded to the nearest dollar, which makes sense, since budgets are usually only approximations anyway.

Budget Details

The budget section of the spreadsheet uses the numbers from the assumptions section to calculate detail and total reports for the first year's operation of your new store. Each quarter of the year is broken out separately, to show the numbers resulting from the estimated quarterly growth rates. Additionally, each category down the left side of the sheet is totaled for the year in the TOTAL column, and the percentage of net sales that each category accounts for is displayed in the % SALES column.

SETTING UP THE FORMATTING IN ADVANCE

Much of what's necessary to enter the spreadsheet you already know about from Chapter 5, so we won't go into all the details this time. What won't be immediately obvious, though, are the formulas for each cell in the budget section.

In Chapter 5 we postponed formatting the cells to look a particular way until most of the data had been entered. Actually, it's just as easy, and a little clearer, to do it beforehand since numbers will then appear in the correct form as you enter them. The following steps will set up most of the formatting for the chapter, though we'll have to do a little more later on.

Altering the Column Widths

1. Open a new spreadsheet document with File/New.

Notice that, in Figure 9-1, all the columns except one will probably fit into an eight-character space. To get as many columns on screen as possible at once, we'll want to cut them down to 8 from the default of 10. Column A is going to require more space, though.

2. Press the GO TO key, F5. A dialog box appears.

3. Type

B1:G1 ↵

in the reference area of the dialog box. The range becomes selected. (We'll discuss referencing a little more later, but in the meantime, just remember that you can use the GO TO key, F5, to select a range of cells.)

4. Choose Format/Width. Type in **8** as the width and press ↵.

5. Press ← to select cell A1. Set column A's width to 20 to accommodate the large labels in that column by choosing Format/Width and typing in

20 ↵

Notice that in both cases, the entire column changed even though only one cell in each column was selected. You only have to select one cell in a column to alter the column's width. Now columns A through G fit on the screen.

Formatting with Commas

Now we want to set up a large section of the spreadsheet (cells B19 to E48) to display numbers with commas, and with no decimal places (since we're rounding off to the nearest dollar).

1. Using the GO TO dialog box, select cells B19 to F48.

2. Choose Format/Comma and set Number of Decimals to 0.

Formatting the Percentage Cells

Finally, you'll need to set two ranges to display their contents in percent format. We'll use the EXTEND key, F8, to select the range this time, just to practice using another technique of selecting. (Recall that you can select cells using the shifted arrow keys, using the GO TO key, or using the EXTEND key. All have the same effect. Depending on how many cells you need to select, one technique will be easier than another.)

1. Move the cursor to cell E5.

2. Press the EXTEND key, F8.

3. Press ↓ nine times, or until the status line reads E5:E14.

4. Press ESC to exit the Extend mode.

5. Choose Format/Percent and set one decimal place.

6. Now set the same percent formatting (with one decimal place) for range G19:G48.

7. Choose File/Save and save the file under the name BUDGET.

ENTERING THE DATA

Since most of the assumptions section consists only of labels and numbers (not formulas), let's start entering data into those cells first.

1. Referring to Figure 9-1, start by entering the title and main heading, BOB'S HOUSE OF GADGETS, into cell B1.

2. Just below it, in cell B2, enter a single space (using the spacebar) followed by the words *Budget for New Store*. The extra space helps center this heading below the store name.

3. Now move the cursor to A4 and type

```
"=====================
```

That's 20 equal (=) signs. You must begin the row with double quotation marks or Works will think you are trying to create a formula.

Entering Data into Multiple Cells with CTRL ↵

Well, that puts a bunch of equal signs into cell A4, but it doesn't create a line all the way across the screen. You could hold down the equal sign key until it repeats, and enter one long line into cell A4, but then the word *ASSUMPTIONS*, when entered into cell B4, would overwrite the right half of the line. There are a couple of solutions to this problem. You could select each adjacent cell one at a time and enter equal signs into them. There is an easier way, though. You can use CTRL ↵ to enter identical data into multiple cells.

1. Move the cursor to B4.

2. Select B4 to G4 by pressing SHIFT and → five times (or any other way you like).

3. Now type in

   "========

   That's 8 equal signs.

4. Press CTRL ↵ to enter the equal signs into all the selected cells.

Incidentally, this technique can be used to copy formulas into a range of cells. Works will automatically adjust any formulas in the process. This is a slightly faster technique than the one we used in Chapter 5 (Edit/Fill Right and Edit/Fill Down) to copy formula cells.

Now your spreadsheet should look like that shown in Figure 9-2.

Oops. What about the word *ASSUMPTIONS*, which we want in the middle of the line of equal signs?

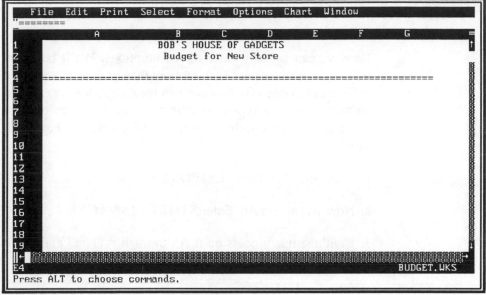

Figure 9-2. The first four lines are entered

1. Move to B4 and type

   "=====ASSUMPTIONS======== ↵

   That's 5 equal signs before and 8 after.

   Now you see

   ====ASS=====

   That's a start, but the equal signs in cells C4 and D4 are preventing the rest of the word from being seen.

2. Move to C4, and clear out its contents by pressing

   BACKSPACE ↵

3. Do the same for cell C5. Now the line reads

=================================ASSUMPTIONS=================================

ENTERING THE ASSUMPTIONS

Now we can actually enter the assumptions. We'll begin by telling you how to enter each section; then you're on your own to finish each one off. You can use the CAPSLOCK key so that all the letters you type appear in uppercase. Notice that the status line says CL to indicate when the CAPSLOCK key is activated.

1. Move to A5 and type **EMPLOYEES** ↓.

2. Now you are on A6. Enter **STORE MANAGER** ↓.

3. Continue this process until A5 through A11 are entered as indicated.

A5	EMPLOYEES
A6	STORE MANAGER
A7	ASST. MANAGER
A8	SENIOR CLERK
A9	JUNIOR CLERK
A10	
A11	TOTAL SALARIES

   Don't forget to skip a line before entering **TOTAL SALARIES**.

4. Move to cell B5 and type in the heading, **NUMBER** ↓.

5. Enter the four numbers 1, 1, 1, and 4 in the next four rows. (Look back to Figure 9-1 and you'll see why.)

6. Move down to B11, but don't type in the number 10,900 as you see it in Figure 9-1. This is a calculated number which reflects the sum of the salaries in column C. Instead, enter the formula

   =(B6*C6)+(B7*C7)+(B8*C8)+(B9*C9) ↵

   Don't forget the equal sign at the beginning, or Works will think you're creating a label instead of a formula. If this happens to you, get into Edit mode via F2, press HOME to get to the beginning of the formula, and then press DEL to delete the quotation mark. Then enter an equal sign and press ↵.

Notice that a zero appears in cell B11. This is because there is currently nothing in the cells referenced by the formula you just entered.

7. Now move to C5 and type **SALARIES** ↓.

8. Enter the salaries as shown (without any commas) in the cells indicated:

   C6   2500
   C7   2000
   C8   1600
   C9   1200

   Notice that the number in cell B11 is recalculated with each entry you make in the column, and should now read 10900.

9. Now select C6 to C9 and use Format/Comma to set the format to commas. Set Number of Decimals to 0.

10. Do the same for cell B11.

11. Move to D5 and enter the 10 labels in that column:

    D5   1ST GRTH
    D6   2ND GRTH
    D7   3RD GRTH
    D8   4TH GRTH
    D9   RETURNS
    D10   COS
    D11   P/R TAX
    D12   FRINGE
    D13   POST/FGT
    D14   EXC.TAX

    Notice that the words *SALARIES* and *1ST GRTH* run together as

    SALARIES1ST GRTH

Let's widen column C to fix this. First, move to any cell in C. Then choose Format/Width and set it to 9. This fixes the problem of words running together, but adds a blank space to the ASSUMPTIONS title line. Fix this by moving to cell B4 and pressing F2 to edit the cell. Type in a single equal sign and press ↵. Now your screen should look like that shown in Figure 9-3.

13. Move to E5 and begin entering the percentages now, using the following form:

E5	8%
E6	12%
E7	12%
E8	15%
E9	2%
E10	63%
E11	15%
E12	7%
E13	1%
E14	.5%

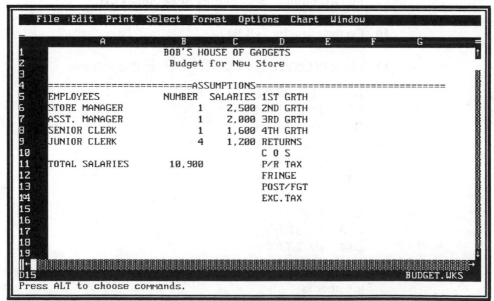

Figure 9-3. *The first four columns are entered*

If you don't include the percent (%) sign, the values will be multiplied by 100. As an alternative to using the % sign, you could enter .08, .12, and so on. However, since we formatted these cells for percentage, Works will convert such data entries to 8%, 12%, and so on.

14. Move to F5 and enter the fixed expenses row:

F5   RENT
F6   UTIL
F7   MAINT
F8   DEPREC
F9   INSUR
F10 PHONE
F11 MISC

15. Oops! Looks like these labels are running up against the neighboring column again. Here's a way to fix it. Select F5 through F11.

16. Choose Format/Style and set their alignment to Right. This cleans things up a bit.

17. Move to G5 and enter the fixed expenses amounts:

G5   2000
G6   400
G7   500
G8   750
G9   250
G10 150
G11 150

Good. That completes the assumptions section. Now your screen should look like Figure 9-4.

18. Choose Edit/Save to save your work so far and continue.

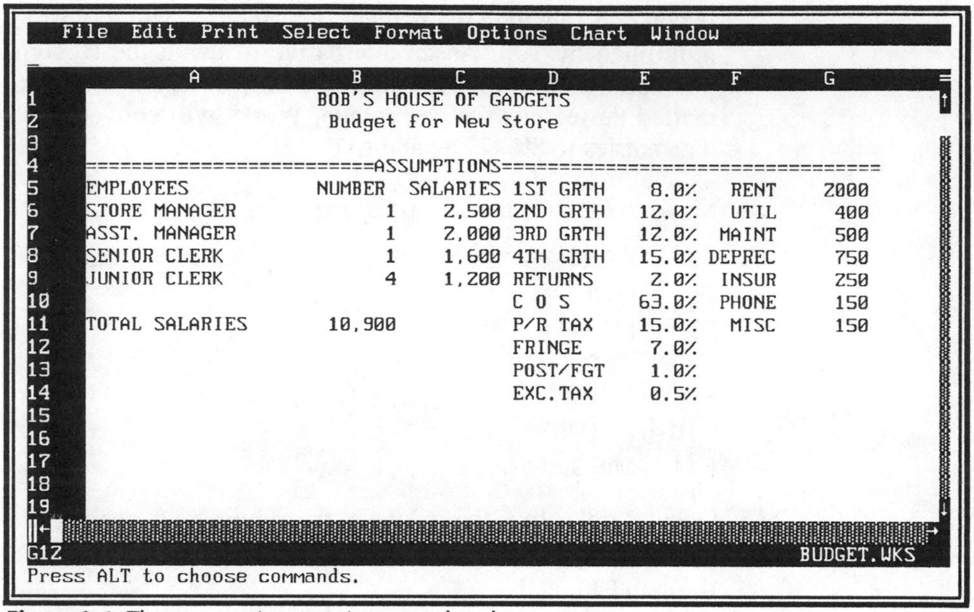

Figure 9-4. *The assumptions section completed*

ENTERING THE BUDGET

Now you can move ahead to enter the budget itself, along with the formulas. During this process, you'll learn several new techniques, mostly pertaining to how you use a spreadsheet that's larger than your screen.

First we'll enter the heading line, the column names, and the line of single dashes to separate the budget section from the assumptions section. Refer to Figure 9-1 to refresh your memory during the following steps.

1. Select A15 and enter 20 equal signs into it. (Don't forget the quotation mark at the beginning.)

2. Select B15 and enter "======BUDGET=====

   That's 6 equal signs before BUDGET and 5 after.

3. Select D15 to G15.

4. Enter

"======== CTRL ↵

That's 8 equal signs.

This looks pretty good — or does it? Actually, it looks as though the dividing line was supposed to be one row lower, in row 16, not 15, at least according to Figure 9-1. Besides, it's a little too close to the assumptions where it is now, so let's move it all down a row.

Inserting Rows in a Spreadsheet

Inserting a row in your spreadsheet is simple, which is good since it's something you'll often need to do, usually because of incomplete planning when sketching out a spreadsheet on paper, or just moving things around on screen to see how they look.

1. Move to any cell on row 15.

2. Choose Select/Row.

3. Choose Edit/Insert.

A new row is inserted just above the row you had selected. Incidentally, to insert more than one row, simply select more rows before choosing the Insert command. Selecting two rows inserts two rows, selecting three rows inserts three rows, and so on.

4. Continue now, entering the seven column headings across row 17. Use → to move to the next column after each entry. After you've entered the final column heading, press ↵.

A17   BUDGET CATEGORY
B17   QTR 1
C17   QTR 2
D17   QTR 3
E17   QTR 4

```
F17   TOTAL
G17   % SALES
```

5. Center the headings except the first one by selecting B17 through G17, choosing Format/Style, and choosing the Center option.

6. Now enter the row of single dashes in row 18 to set off the headings from the body of the budget. This can be done in one fell swoop by typing

```
"-----------------------------------------------------------
```

(Don't forget the quotation mark.)

Entering the Row Labels

Now you can type in the row labels, or headings. Note that there are 24 headings to be typed in and that some of them are indented. There are also six blank rows. Don't forget the blank rows, or put them in the wrong places. If you do, things won't line up correctly.

Here is the list, with the rows listed to make the job a little easier. You indent some of the labels, as indicated, by pressing the spacebar a couple of times before typing the label.

```
19 REVENUE
20    SALES
21    RETURNS
22      NET SALES
23
24      COST OF SALES
25
26 GROSS PROFIT
27
28 EXPENSES
29    SALARIES
30    PAYROLL TAXES
31    FRINGE BENEFITS
32      SUBTOTAL LABOR
33
34    STORE RENT
35    UTILITIES
36    MAINTENANCE
37    DEPRECIATION
```

```
38   ADVERTISING
39   POSTAGE AND FREIGHT
40   INSURANCE
41   TELEPHONE
42   EXCISE TAXES
43   MISCELLANEOUS
44      SUBTOTAL NON LAB
45
46 TOTAL EXPENSE
47
48 NET PROFIT
```

Dividing the Screen into Panes Using the Split Command

You probably noticed that as soon as you reached row 20 or 21, your spreadsheet scrolled upwards to let you continue adding rows. There are times, however, when you'll want to keep certain parts of a spreadsheet on screen while other parts move around. Just as with the word processor and database, Works lets you divide your screen into separate panes, each displaying a different part of your document. You use the Split command from the Options menu to achieve this.

Splits in the spreadsheet tool can be horizontal, vertical, or both. Thus, you can have up to four separate panes defined at one time, and hop between them.

Dividing the screen into panes is especially helpful when you need to repeatedly refer to a set of values, such as a list of assumptions, while entering formulas or checking your work. To ease the process of entering formulas, let's create two panes: one for the budget and one for the assumptions, using the following steps:

1. Move to the top of the spreadsheet by typing CTRL-HOME.

2. Press the ↓ key enough times to scroll the screen up until row 5 is the first you can see.

3. Move the cursor to A5.

4. Choose Options/Split. A line appears across the top of the spreadsheet, and a vertical line appears just under the word

File in the menu bar. These are the split lines. SPLIT appears on the status line to inform you that you are in the Split mode, and Works is waiting for you to move the split line. At this point, the → and ← keys move the vertical split, and the ↓ and ↑ keys move the horizontal split.

(If you are using a mouse, click on the equal sign in the upper right-hand corner, and drag it down the screen. It will turn into a horizontal line. Drag it down as far as you want and then release the mouse button.)

5. Since we only want a horizontal split, press ↓ until the split is on row 15, and press ↵. This sets the split and exits Split mode.

6. Now, since we want to work with the budget section only, jump the cursor down into that pane by pressing the PANE key, F6. (Incidentally, if you have four panes, F6 moves you through them in sequence.) Position your panes so that your screen looks like that in Figure 9-5.

Entering the Formulas

Working in a pane is really no different than what you've done so far, other than the fact that you can't see as much of your work at one time. But first, a few words about the growth factors may be useful here. Each quarter's growth is composed of the prior quarter's sales multiplied by the intended growth factor. That figure must then be added to the normal revenues for the period to arrive at a meaningful projection of actual sales. (Just figuring 12 percent of the previous quarter's sales, for example, won't result in the number we want to see under SALES.) To arrive at this number, the formula has to increase the percentages listed in the assumptions (1ST-4TH GRTH) by 100 percent, since, for example, we want the 2nd quarter's revenues to be 112 percent of the first quarter's, not 12 percent.

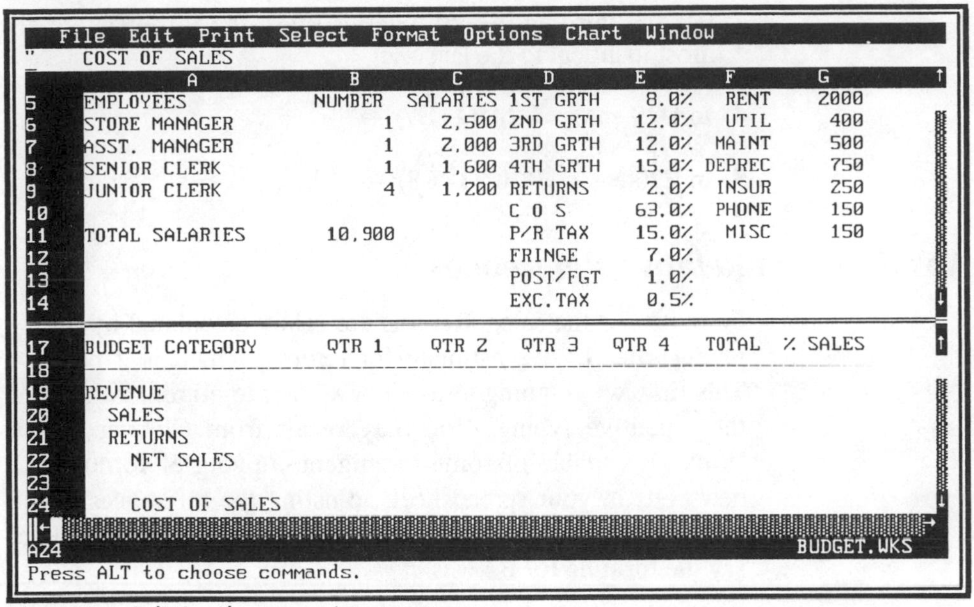

```
   File  Edit  Print  Select  Format  Options  Chart  Window
"      COST OF SALES
          A           B         C       D         E        F        G      ↑
5   EMPLOYEES       NUMBER   SALARIES 1ST GRTH   8.0%    RENT     2000
6   STORE MANAGER        1    2,500  2ND GRTH   12.0%    UTIL      400
7   ASST. MANAGER        1    2,000  3RD GRTH   12.0%    MAINT     500
8   SENIOR CLERK         1    1,600  4TH GRTH   15.0%   DEPREC     750
9   JUNIOR CLERK         4    1,200  RETURNS     2.0%    INSUR     250
10                                   C O S      63.0%    PHONE     150
11  TOTAL SALARIES   10,900          P/R TAX    15.0%    MISC      150
12                                   FRINGE      7.0%
13                                   POST/FGT    1.0%
14                                   EXC.TAX     0.5%

17  BUDGET CATEGORY    QTR 1    QTR 2    QTR 3   QTR 4    TOTAL  % SALES  ↑
18  -------------------------------------------------------------------
19  REVENUE
20    SALES
21    RETURNS
22      NET SALES
23
24     COST OF SALES
A24                                                          BUDGET.WKS
Press ALT to choose commands.
```

Figure 9-5. *Splitting the screen into two panes*

Remember that all the navigation keys and commands will work identically to what you're already used to. With that in mind, follow these steps to begin entering the formulas:

1. Move to cell B20, sales for the first quarter.

2. Let's assume the sales will be about 113,400 during the first quarter. Enter the value

   113400 →

   (Remember: don't use commas.)

3. Now you're on C20, where things get more complex. The formula for this cell should multiply the previous quarter's sales times the growth factor for the second quarter (12 percent, or actually 112 percent, as just explained). Enter the formula

   =B20*(1+E6) →

For the third and fourth quarter sales, the formulas are almost identical to the last one.

4. In D20 enter =**C20*(1+E7)** →

5. In E20 enter =**D20*(1+E8)** →

Absolute and Relative References

So much for the sales. Returns are easily calculated by multiplying sales by the estimate for returns, which is 2 percent. This time we're going to use a new trick to eliminate some of the repetitive typing. You may recall from Chapter 5 that Works is capable of some intelligent copying of formulas to new cells in your spreadsheet, adjusting the references in the formulas as necessary for their new locations. For example, say the formula for B4 was

=B1+B2+B3

and you copied it (using the Edit/Copy command) to cell C4. Works would adjust the formula to

=C1+C2+C3

unless you instructed it not to. What Works does is assume that the cell names in the formula are relative references, meaning that they should change when moved. Relative references are the most common type of references used in electronic spreadsheets because, more often than not, the formulas in a row or column refer to other cells in the same row or column — not in other rows or columns. So, unless otherwise informed, Works assumes you want relative references and adjusts the pointers in formulas it copies.

However, there is another type of reference, called an *absolute reference*. You use absolute references to tell Works *not* to adjust the pointers in formulas when copying cells, but rather to leave them as they are. This way you can "borrow" key values from specific cells elsewhere in the spreadsheet. You indicate an absolute reference in a formula by placing a dollar ($) sign before each part of the referenced cell's address, such as $B$3. For example, when the formula

=B1+B2+$B$3

is copied to cell C4, Works adjusts the first two cell references, but leaves the last one absolute, resulting in the following formula in C4:

=C1+C2+$B$3

Actually there is a third type of reference, the *mixed reference,* that incorporates both absolute and relative references into a single cell address. For example, the pointers B$3 and $B3 are both mixed references. B$3 means the column is relative and the row is absolute. $B3 means the reverse. However, this type of reference is rarely used in spreadsheets and will not be covered here.

Most of the remaining formulas in the budget example will use absolute references, so you'll get lots of exercise in learning to use them. Here's an example: consider the quarterly calculations for returned merchandise. This figure is always calculated using the value in cell E9 (2%). Similarly, the quarterly Cost of Sales calculation repeatedly calls upon cell E10 (63%).

To get the Copy command to duplicate the absolute reference, you'll manually enter the formula for the first quarter. Then you'll copy it to the remaining quarters. Let's fill in the RETURNS row using this method.

1. Enter the formula

   =B20*$E$9

   into cell B21.

2. Make sure the cursor is on B21.

3. Press SHIFT and press the → key three times. This selects B21:E21.

4. Choose Edit/Fill Right. The formulas are copied into the remaining columns, and the cells' values are calculated and displayed. That was a bit easier than last time.

The figure for net sales is nothing more than the sales minus returns. Calculating that should be even easier, since there are no absolute references here, only relative ones. Follow these steps to fill in B22 through E22.

1. Move to B22 and enter

=B20 - B21 ↵

2. Now select B22:E22 and choose Edit/Fill Right. That's it for net sales.

Cost of sales for each quarter is calculated using the formula Net Sales * COS.

1. Move to B24 and enter

=B22*$E$10 ↵

2. Now select B24:E24 and choose Edit/Fill Right.

Move to B26 to begin filling in the gross profits. This is calculated by subtracting the cost of sales from the net sales.

1. In B26 enter

=B22 - $B$24 ↵

2. Select B26:E26 and choose Edit/Fill Right.

3. Save your work now, before moving on.

The revenues section isn't quite finished, since we haven't filled in the columns for totals and percent of sales. The Totals column is nothing more than the sum of the columns to its left, and can be calculated in a similar fashion to the subtotals and totals you entered into the invoice example in Chapter 5.

1. In F20 enter the formula

   =SUM(B20:E20)

   The value 546,243 should appear.

   Since net sales and gross profit totals are calculated the same way, we can use Fill Down to enter these formulas. In fact, since the Totals column will use the same formula all the way down to the last row, 48, why not complete it all in one move? And since all the references are relative, no dollar signs are required in the source cell.

2. With the cursor on F20, press F5 and select F20:F48.

3. Choose Edit/Fill Down.

   All the totals we wanted (and more) are calculated. For rows we haven't completed yet, the totals show up as zero, for obvious reasons. In addition, there are some rows we didn't want anything in that got zeros too. Don't worry about them now. The zeros will change as we add more data, and we'll use the Clear command to erase cells that should be blank later on.

   If you were to print your spreadsheet now or scroll through the entire document, it would look like Figure 9-6.

Entering the Sales Percentages

To enter the sales percentages, we have to calculate the percentage of total net sales that each budget category accounts for. Thus, sales divided by net sales will yield the proper answer for the Sales column.

1. Move to G20 and enter

   =F20/$F$22

   (The net sales figure is an absolute reference, remember.) Now, "102.0%" appears, which makes sense since we expected returns of 2%.

```
                        BOB'S HOUSE OF GADGETS
                         Budget for New Store


==============================ASSUMPTIONS===================================
EMPLOYEES            NUMBER  SALARIES 1ST GRTH    8.0%    RENT   2000
STORE MANAGER             1   2,500 2ND GRTH    12.0%    UTIL    400
ASST. MANAGER             1   2,000 3RD GRTH    12.0%   MAINT    500
SENIOR CLERK              1   1,600 4TH GRTH    15.0% DEPREC     750
JUNIOR CLERK              4   1,200 RETURNS      2.0%   INSUR    250
                                    C O S       63.0%   PHONE    150
TOTAL SALARIES       10,900         P/R TAX     15.0%    MISC    150
                                                       FRINGE    7.0%
                                                      POST/FGT   1.0%
                                                      EXC. TAX   0.5%



============================BUDGET========================================
BUDGET CATEGORY       QTR 1    QTR 2    QTR 3    QTR 4    TOTAL  % SALES
-------------------------------------------------------------------------

REVENUE
  SALES             113,400  127,008  142,249  163,586  546,243
  RETURNS             2,268    2,540    2,845    3,272   10,925
    NET SALES       111,132  124,468  139,404  160,315  535,318
                                                              0
    COST OF SALES    70,013   78,415   87,825  100,998  337,251
                                                              0
GROSS PROFIT         41,119   54,455   69,391   90,301  255,266
                                                              0
EXPENSES                                                      0
  SALARIES                                                    0
  PAYROLL TAXES                                               0
  FRINGE BENEFITS                                             0
    SUBTOTAL LABOR                                            0
                                                             0
STORE RENT                                                   0
UTILITIES                                                    0
MAINTENANCE                                                  0
DEPRECIATION                                                 0
ADVERTISING                                                  0
POSTAGE AND FREIGHT                                          0
INSURANCE                                                    0
TELEPHONE                                                    0
EXCISE TAXES                                                 0
MISCELLANEOUS                                                0
  SUBTOTAL NONLAB                                            0
                                                            0
TOTAL EXPENSE                                               0
                                                           0
NET PROFIT                                                 0
```

Figure 9-6. *Assumptions, row headings, and revenue formulas in place*

2. Now select G20:G48 and copy this formula all the way down to G48 using Fill Down.

As expected, lots of zeros followed by percent signs (0%) appear. Most of these will be recalculated as we add data. The rest you can remove later.

Freezing Titles

It's probably getting a little complicated to see where you are in your bottom pane, since the headings are out of view. You've probably been counting left to right to figure out which quarter you're in or where the columns are for totals and sales percentages. There's an easier way, however, called "freezing the titles" (get out your mittens). The Freeze Title command lets you lock selected rows or columns from moving when you scroll through your spreadsheet. This is particularly useful for accounting work, which typically incorporates 14 columns (headings, 12 months, and totals). You can lock either column(s), rows(s), or both.

Lock the Titles column in the bottom pane (rows 17 and 18) by doing the following:

1. Bring row 17 to the top of the pane, just below the split line.

2. Move to cell A19.

3. Choose Options/Freeze Titles to freeze all the rows above A19.

Now as you scroll down to enter the remaining budget, the titles stay in view. Try it now to see the effect:

1. Press ↓ and hold it down for several seconds to scroll down.

2. Press ↑ and scroll up.

Notice that you can't see any rows above 19 now. This is due to the way the Freeze Titles command works. For your future reference, the rules to freeze by are shown here:

Command	Action
Freeze Rows	Move the cursor to column A on the row *just below* the one(s) you want to freeze. Then select Options/Freeze Titles. All rows above the cursor will freeze.
Freeze Columns	Move the cursor to row 1 and in the column *just to the right of* the column(s) you want to freeze. Then select Options/Freeze Titles. All columns to the left of cursor will freeze.
Freeze Rows and Columns	Move the cursor to any row except 1 and any column other than A. Then select Options/Freeze Titles to freeze all rows above cursor and all columns to the left of cursor.

If you accidentally freeze the wrong rows or columns, you must select Options/Unfreeze Titles before you can try it again. You'll also have to use the Unfreeze command to turn off any freezing after you're done with it.

ENTERING THE EXPENSES

With the revenues section finished, you can begin entering the expenses formulas. There are three types of formulas: those mainly using constants, those with variables, and those using functions (such as SUM).

This first section, constants, is relatively uncomplicated, since for the most part these cells just involve multiplying numbers in the assumption section by 3 (because there are three months in a quarter).

1. Move to B29 and enter

   =3*$B$11 ↵

   (B11 is the Total Salaries cell, visible in the upper pane.)

2. Select B29:E29 and Fill Right.

   Repeat this process for the other cells using constants listed in the assumptions:

   STORE RENT,
   UTILITIES,
   MAINTENANCE,
   DEPRECIATION,
   INSURANCE,
   TELEPHONE, and
   MISCELLANEOUS.

Make sure the cell you're pointing to (for example, B11 in the last example) is the right one and that you precede it with a dollar sign (to indicate the absolute reference) before copying to the last three quarters. You won't have to worry about the Total or % Sales columns since these cells have already been entered and will recalculate as you progress.

When you have finished this section, your spreadsheet looks like that shown in Figure 9-7.

Fluctuating Expenses

Actually there's only one fluctuating expense in the budget: advertising. Since it fluctuates from month to month, it's not included in the assumptions section. Enter the following values for advertising for each quarter:

QTR 1 4500
QTR 2 2000
QTR 3 1750
QTR 4 1500

```
                     BOB'S HOUSE OF GADGETS
                      Budget for New Store

=========================ASSUMPTIONS==============================
EMPLOYEES            NUMBER  SALARIES 1ST GRTH    8.0%   RENT     2000
STORE MANAGER            1    2,500 2ND GRTH    12.0%   UTIL      400
ASST. MANAGER            1    2,000 3RD GRTH    12.0%   MAINT     500
SENIOR CLERK             1    1,600 4TH GRTH    15.0% DEPREC      750
JUNIOR CLERK             4    1,200 RETURNS      2.0%   INSUR     250
C O S        63.0%  PHONE      150
TOTAL SALARIES        10,900          P/R TAX   15.0%   MISC      150
FRINGE        7.0%
POST/FGT      1.0%
EXC. TAX      0.5%


=========================BUDGET===================================
BUDGET CATEGORY      QTR 1    QTR 2    QTR 3    QTR 4    TOTAL  % SALES
------------------------------------------------------------------
REVENUE
  SALES            113,400  127,008  142,249  163,586  546,243  102.0%
  RETURNS            2,268    2,540    2,845    3,272   10,925    2.0%
     NET SALES     111,132  124,468  139,404  160,315  535,318  100.0%
                                                            0    0.0%
     COST OF SALES  70,013   78,415   87,825  100,998  337,251   63.0%
                                                            0    0.0%
GROSS PROFIT        41,119   54,455   69,391   90,301  255,266   47.7%
                                                            0    0.0%
EXPENSES                                                     0    0.0%
  SALARIES          32,700   32,700   32,700   32,700  130,800   24.4%
  PAYROLL TAXES                                              0    0.0%
  FRINGE BENEFITS                                            0    0.0%
    SUBTOTAL LABOR                                           0    0.0%
                                                            0    0.0%
STORE RENT           6,000    6,000    6,000    6,000   24,000    4.5%
UTILITIES            1,200    1,200    1,200    1,200    4,800    0.9%
MAINTENANCE          1,500    1,500    1,500    1,500    6,000    1.1%
DEPRECIATION         2,250    2,250    2,250    2,250    9,000    1.7%
ADVERTISING                                                 0    0.0%
POSTAGE AND FREIGHT                                         0    0.0%
INSURANCE              750      750      750      750    3,000    0.6%
TELEPHONE             450      450      450      450    1,800    0.3%
EXCISE TAXES                                                0    0.0%
MISCELLANEOUS         450      450      450      450    1,800    0.3%
  SUBTOTAL NONLAB                                           0    0.0%
                                                           0    0.0%
TOTAL EXPENSE                                               0    0.0%
                                                           0    0.0%
NET PROFIT                                                  0    0.0%
```

Figure 9-7. Most of the formulas are now entered into the budget

Formulas Using Functions

The remaining cells use functions in their calculations, and draw upon values in other budget categories.

1. In B30, the row for payroll taxes, enter

   =B29*$E$11

   (This is total salaries per quarter times the payroll tax rate).

2. Copy this formula to the rest of the quarters using Fill Right.

3. In B31 enter

   =B29*$E$12

   to calculate the fringe benefits for the first quarter. This is simply the total salaries for the quarter multiplied by the fringe percentage in the assumptions.

4. Copy the formula to the rest of the quarters using Fill Right.

5. The labor subtotal is the sum of salaries, payroll taxes, and fringe benefits. Enter

   =SUM(B29:B31)

   into cell B32.

6. Copy the formula to the rest of the quarters with Fill Right.

7. Postage and freight are calculated by multiplying the net sales by the percentage in the Post/Fgt cell. Move down to row 39 and type in

   =B22*$E$13 ↵

8. Copy the formula to the rest of the quarters with Fill Right.

9. Calculate excise taxes the same way, only multiply by the value in D14 (.5%). The formula for B42 (don't forget to skip down three rows) is then

=B22*$E$14

10. Copy the formula to the rest of the quarters.

11. The nonlabor subtotal is the sum of rows B34 to B43 — in other words, all the expenses in this section. Simply enter

=SUM(B34:B43) ⏎

12. Copy the formula to the rest of the quarters.

This time, you're going to learn how to do the copying operating for several rows all at the same time. We'll go ahead and enter the first quarter formulas for total expense and net profit, then copy all the formulas across at once.

13. In cell B46, enter

=B32+B44

This is the sum of the two subtotals (labor and nonlabor).

14. In cell B48, enter

=B26 - B46.

(gross profits minus total expenses).

Copying Several Formulas at Once

Though you've been copying formulas across columns on a line-by-line basis, there's actually a much faster way to perform this type of fill. Works is smart enough to allow a block fill from left to right, adjusting formulas for the whole block. To copy the remaining formulas to the rest of the quarters on each row, do the following:

1. Select B44:E48 (the source cells are in the leftmost column of this selection).

2. Choose Edit/Fill Right.

You may want to make a point of remembering this trick. It's a real time saver. Remember though, that the source formulas must be in the leftmost column for a block fill to work.

The spreadsheet now looks like Figure 9-8.

Well, your bottom line should make it sufficiently clear to the bank loan officer that, assuming operations proceed as planned, your new retail store will be turning a tidy profit by the end of its second quarter. Also, by the first year's end, it will have cleared $27,510. Incidentally, the numbers in parentheses indicate negative values. Thus, it appears your new store will lose money in the first two quarters after opening.

CLEANING UP

With all the data now entered, you can go ahead and do a little cleaning up. There are a number of rows with extra zeros in them which should be removed. The first thing to do is to remove the split so you have only one large pane to work in.

1. Choose Options/Split.

2. Press the ↑ key until the split line is all the way at the top and will go no farther.

3. Press ↵.

Notice that unsplitting also unfreezes the headings we had frozen earlier. This is because we obliterated the pane that contained the freeze. If we had frozen some titles in the upper pane, they would still be frozen and could have been unfrozen using the Unfreeze Titles command in the Options menu.

4. To delete the extra zeros in unwanted cells, you can use two methods. If there are a number of zeros on one row, select the whole row using Select/Row and then choose Edit/Clear. The other technique is to just move to the of-

```
                      BOB'S HOUSE OF GADGETS
                      Budget for New Store


===========================ASSUMPTIONS===================================
EMPLOYEES            NUMBER  SALARIES 1ST GRTH   8.0%  RENT    2000
STORE MANAGER          1     2,500 2ND GRTH    12.0%  UTIL     400
ASST. MANAGER          1     2,000 3RD GRTH    12.0%  MAINT    500
SENIOR CLERK           1     1,600 4TH GRTH    15.0%  DEPREC   750
JUNIOR CLERK           4     1,200 RETURNS      2.0%  INSUR    250
                                   C O S       63.0%  PHONE    150
TOTAL SALARIES       10,900        P/R TAX     15.0%  MISC     150
                                   FRINGE       7.0%
                                   POST/FGT     1.0%
                                   EXC. TAX     0.5%


===========================BUDGET=======================================
BUDGET CATEGORY       QTR 1    QTR 2    QTR 3    QTR 4   TOTAL   % SALES
-----------------------------------------------------------------------

REVENUE
   SALES            113,400  127,008 142,249 163,586 546,243   102.0%
   RETURNS            2,268    2,540   2,845   3,272  10,925     2.0%
   NET SALES        111,132  124,468 139,404 160,315 535,318   100.0%
                                                                 0.0%
      COST OF SALES   70,013   78,415  87,825 100,998 337,251    63.0%
                                                                 0.0%
GROSS PROFIT         41,119   54,455  69,391  90,301 255,266    47.7%
                                                                 0.0%
EXPENSES                                                         0.0%
   SALARIES          32,700   32,700  32,700  32,700 130,800    24.4%
   PAYROLL TAXES      4,905    4,905   4,905   4,905  19,620     3.7%
   FRINGE BENEFITS    2,289    2,289   2,289   2,289   9,156     1.7%
      SUBTOTAL LABOR 39,894   39,894  39,894  39,894 159,576    29.8%
                                                                 0.0%
STORE RENT           6,000    6,000   6,000   6,000  24,000     4.5%
UTILITIES            1,200    1,200   1,200   1,200   4,800     0.9%
MAINTENANCE          1,500    1,500   1,500   1,500   6,000     1.1%
DEPRECIATION         2,250    2,250   2,250   2,250   9,000     1.7%
ADVERTISING          4,500    2,000   1,750   1,500   9,750     1.8%
POSTAGE AND FREIGHT  1,111    1,245   1,394   1,603   5,353     1.0%
INSURANCE              750      750     750     750   3,000     0.6%
TELEPHONE              450      450     450     450   1,800     0.3%
EXCISE TAXES           556      622     697     802   2,677     0.5%
MISCELLANEOUS          450      450     450     450   1,800     0.3%
   SUBTOTAL NONLAB   18,767   16,467  16,441  16,505  68,180    12.7%
                                                           0     0.0%
TOTAL EXPENSE        58,661   56,361  56,335  56,399 227,756    42.5%
                                                                 0.0%
NET PROFIT          (17,542)  (1,906) 13,056  33,903  27,510     5.1%
```

Figure 9-8. *The budget spreadsheet with all formulas completed*

fending cell, press BACKSPACE and then press ↵ or one of the arrow keys.

PROTECTING CELL CONTENTS FROM ERASURE

After you've done hours of laborious planning, experimenting, and keypunching to enter a spreadsheet and figure its formulas, you'll probably want to insure that certain cells can't be erased or altered accidentally. This prevents you or someone else from typing into the wrong cells, deleting them, clearing them, or copying into them.

Protecting your entire spreadsheet from alteration is a one-step process. You just choose Options/Protect. Now none of the cells can be altered. Also, you'll find that many of the commands on the Format and Edit menus will no longer work. You will only get a beep if you try to open the STYLE dialog box, for instance.

However, chances are good that you'll want to be able to alter some cells and not others. To do this you have to "unlock" the cells you want to be able to change. Here's how to do it. Let's say you want to be able to alter the number of employees and their salaries in the assumptions section of your budget spreadsheet.

1. First, you must turn off the protection switch. Choose Options/Protect. If it's on, turn it off. Otherwise press ESC to get out of the menu. You can't change individual cell protection while Protect is on.

2. Select the range B6:C9.

3. Choose Format/Style and set the Locked button off as you see in Figure 9-9.

4. Choose Options/Protect to reactivate the protection.

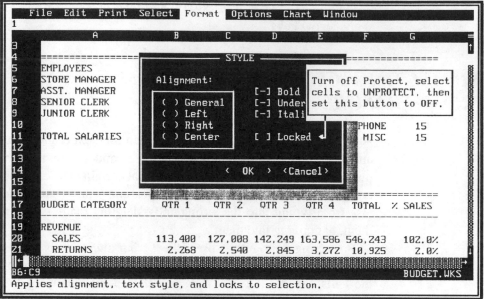

Figure 9-9. *Protecting certain cells from erasure*

Now, whenever you try to type into any one of the protected cells, the following message appears:

ERROR:
Locked cells cannot be changed

You can see whether a cell is unprotected by moving to it and choosing Format/Style. The Locked button will be set to off.

DISPLAYING YOUR FORMULAS

Another feature, just above Protect in the Options menu, is Show Formulas. This choice lets you display all the cells' formulas instead of their values. This is a very useful feature since it's easy to assume your formulas are all correct. In fact, the chances are pretty high that — at least once in a while —

you'll make an error during entry or consideration of your formulas.

How to Show the Formulas

To see the formulas, choose Options/Show Formulas. The columns double in width, allowing most formulas to be seen in full. Of course the formula bar will display the entire formula if it doesn't fit into a cell. Actually, for most formulas, doubling the width is overkill, but that's how Works does it. You will have to use horizontal scrolling to see cells to the right of the screen. Refer to Table 5-1 in Chapter 5 for a list of the navigation keys if you need to. With the formulas showing, your screen will look something like Figure 9-10.

Printing out your spreadsheet with formulas showing is a good idea, especially right after you've created a new one, since tracing errors is easier on paper. But beware: since the column widths have doubled, Works may break up your print-

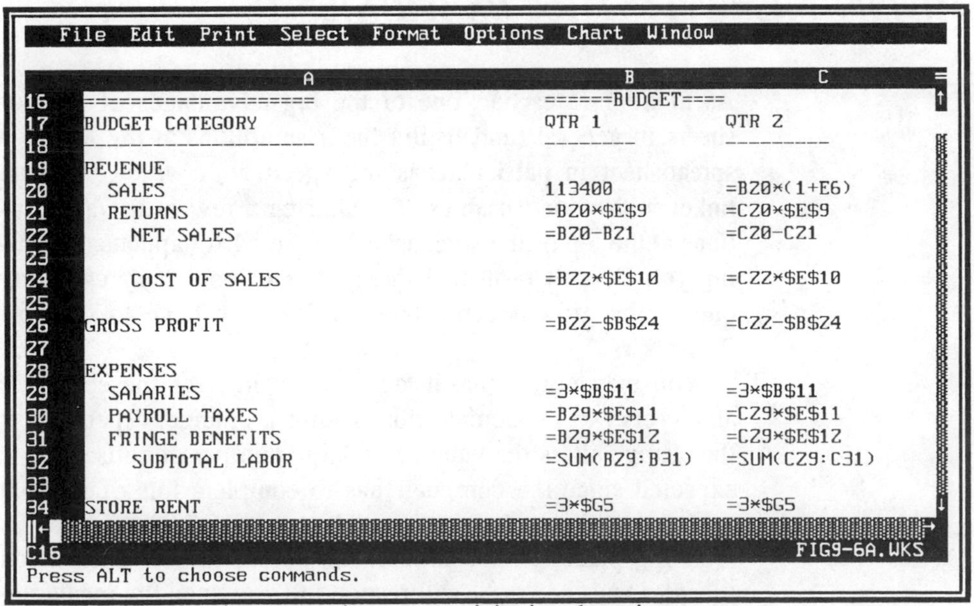

Figure 9-10. *The Show Formulas command displays formulas*

outs onto several pages. You can try printing in a smaller font (use the Print/Font command to choose). Otherwise you might have to get out your scissors and tape.

Decreasing the Column Width for Formulas

As an alternative to the scissors and tape, you can decrease the column widths while the formulas are showing. You already know how to do this, since it was covered earlier in this chapter. Once you get things adjusted to eliminate as much extra space as possible, then you print. However, when you redisplay the values, the widths will be divided by 2, requiring that you resize the columns again. One solution to this new mess is to make a copy of your spreadsheet using the Save As command. This opens the new document from which you can show the formulas, modify the widths, and print, all without modifying the original document.

RUNNING "WHAT-IF" EXPERIMENTS

As mentioned earlier, one of the big advantages of spreadsheets in general (and listing the assumptions at the top of a spreadsheet in particular) is the speed with which you can tinker with your variables. Try altering a few of the assumptions at the top of the spreadsheet to see what happens (assuming you haven't protected them). For example, try changing one of the growth percentages. (You may have to turn off Protect first.)

You may notice that it takes some time for the computer and Works to recalculate things after a change, especially if the change alters the values in a large number of cells. This is expected since the computer has to complete lots of internal mathematical calculations for each change. While this process is taking place, your computer may seem to be out to lunch (dead). Don't worry, it will respond to you once the recalculation is finished.

If you intend to alter several variables at one time and don't want to wait for the spreadsheet to recalculate each time, there is another alternative. You can postpone the recalculation until you are ready. This is done by choosing Manual Recalculation from the Options menu. When you are ready to calculate again, choose Calculate Now from the Options menu. Works informs you whenever recalculation is necessary by showing CALC on the status line. This appears after you've made any cell change that would alter another cell's value.

USING THE EDIT-POINT CYCLE

If you're the kind of person who would rather point than type, or you hate looking around the screen to see what cell address the cursor is on, you'll be interested to know that even without a mouse, there's an easier way to type in cell formulas than what we've described so far. When a formula references another cell (very common) you can use the Edit-Point cycle to type the name of the referenced cell or cell range into your formula for you.

As an example, say you want to enter the formula

=B11*B9

into the unused cell B13.

1. Move to B13.

2. Type

    =

3. Now press ↑. The status line says POINT.

4. Notice that with each press of the arrow key, the current cell's address is written into the formula you're creating in the formula bar.

5. Move to B11 and press ↵. The reference B11 gets dropped into the formula.

6. Now press F2 to enter Edit mode. Type * since that's the next part of the formula.

7. Press F2 again. EDIT disappears from the status line and you are actually in Point mode again. Press ↑ again, and POINT appears on the status line again.

8. Move to cell B9 and then press ↵. The formula is finished.

You can use Point mode any time you're editing a formula. If it doesn't seem to work for you, notice that the cursor has to be sitting just to the right of an operator before Point will work correctly. In other words, the formula has to be waiting for a cell reference, for example:

B11*___

PRINTING YOUR SPREADSHEET

You already know the basics of printing a spreadsheet because it was covered briefly in Chapter 5. However, let's run through the steps again in order to print the finished budget.

1. Press F5 and type in

   A1:G48 ↵

2. Choose Print/Set Print Area. These two steps select the range of cells you want to print.

3. At this point, you may choose the font and size via Print/Font. If you have a choice of smaller font size (such as 8) you'll probably want to use it so that more cells will fit across each page. For our spreadsheet, this shouldn't be necessary, since it's only about 70 columns wide.

4. Now open the Print menu from the LAYOUT dialog box and check that the paper size, headers, footers, and margins are set properly.

5. Choose Print/Print. Normally you can just press ↵ and begin printing. Make other changes in this box if needed. If you want the row and column headings (A B C 1 2 3) to print, turn on the Print Row and Column Labels button.

6. Turn on your printer, make sure it has paper, and press ↵. Printing should begin.

7. If you want to stop printing in the middle of the process, press ESC and wait a few seconds. A dialog box will appear asking if you want to stop printing.

The entire budget should print nicely onto one page of most printers, and look like Figure 9-1. If it doesn't fit onto one page, try resetting the left and right margins to a smaller number such as .5".

INSERTING PAGE BREAKS MANUALLY

Since large spreadsheets are often larger than a standard page, Works is designed to automatically break up a document between rows and columns as it deems necessary to print them. Works does this based on information in the Print/LAYOUT dialog box combined with knowledge about your printer and the font you've selected. You have some latitude in deciding where page breaks will occur though. The Insert Page Break and Delete Page Break commands from the Print menu let you control the location of page breaks.

To insert a page break in a specific location:

1. Select the column or row *after* which you want the page break to occur. If it's a column, Works assumes you're creating a *vertical page break;* that is, a break between

columns. If a row is selected, Works figures this is a *horizontal page break.*

2. Choose Print/Insert Page Break. A double arrow >> appears in the selection bar (left margin).

To delete a page break,

1. Select the column or row.

2. Choose Print/Delete Page Break.

Of course, you can't get blood from a stone. Works automatically tries to get as many rows and columns on a page as possible. If you need more, rather than fewer, try cutting down the margins and eliminating the headers and footers. Inserting page breaks is really intended for making them occur earlier rather than later than they would normally.

TAKING IT FROM HERE

The field of computerized spreadsheets is vast and quickly growing. Many programs, including Works' spreadsheet tool, offer too many possibilities to cover in two chapters, or even in a whole book. Bookstore shelves are lined with tomes about spreadsheets, many of which will provide the serious user with valuable tips and templates, which are ready-made and tested layouts for common business situations. Many of these templates are designed for Lotus 1-2-3, one of the most popular spreadsheet programs for the IBM PC and compatibles. Since Works is compatible with Lotus 1-2-3 version 1.A you may want to consider purchasing one of the many available books for more information. *1-2-3 Made Easy* by Mary Campbell (Berkeley-Osborne/McGraw-Hill, 1988) provides an excellent tutorial on the subject.

As mentioned in earlier chapters, you can create charts from your spreadsheet data for presentation purposes, business reports, or to more clearly see trends that might otherwise be difficult to spot when analyzing your spreadsheets. You can skip ahead to Chapter 11 to learn how to make various types of charts if you want. Then, Chapter 12 will explain how to integrate those charts into other types of documents. In any case, don't forget to save your finished spreadsheet, since it will be used later.

Finally, as stated in Chapter 1, the Works spreadsheet contains numerous "canned" formulas for expediting the design of more complex spreadsheets. For more details on the functions, operators, menu commands, and special keys used with the Works spreadsheet, turn to Appendix A.

Chapter

Expanding Your Database Skills

Ten

In Chapter 6 you learned the rudiments of the Works database, including how to create a new database, enter and edit your data, view the data in a list or a form, search and sort the data, and perform elementary querying and printing.

Now you'll have a chance to expand your knowledge of these topics. In this chapter, you'll learn about:

- Placing labels on a form

- Inserting and deleting fields and records

- More selection techniques

- Hiding certain records and fields from view

- Protecting fields from alteration

- Setting the format of fields

- Creating complex queries

- Printing professional-looking reports

To experiment with these features of the database, we'll use two different database documents. The first half of this chapter will use the Phonebk file you created in Chapter 6. The second half will use a new file that you'll have to type in. It will be an inventory list for the fictitious store for which you created a budget in Chapter 9, "Bob's House of Gadgets."

So, before going further, please open the Phonebk file.

1. Choose File/Open.

2. Select Phonebk from the list box.

3. Press F9 to switch to form view.

PLACING LABELS ON A FORM

Once the file is open and you've selected form view, your screen should look like Figure 10-1.

Even though this is a perfectly sufficient form for adding, editing, and viewing data, it could be improved. There may be times when you'll want to dress up your form view for various reasons. For example, you may want to add instructions to the

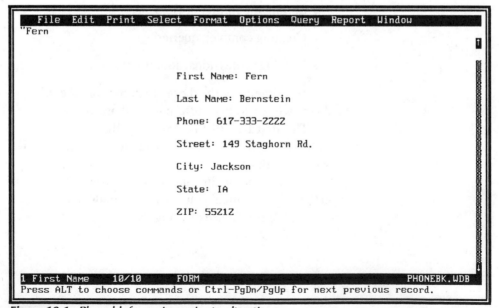

Figure 10-1. Phonebk form view prior to alteration

screen so that people less familiar with Works could more easily use the database document. If you've hired someone to enter or edit records, extra instructions may be particularly advantageous.

You can easily add text to any of your form pages (remember that there can be up to eight screens per form) from the Form Design screen. Let's change things a bit to make it easier for a novice to fill in information. You won't necessarily want to use all these changes for your forms in the future, but at least you'll know how to, just in case the need arises.

When you're finished making the changes, your screen will look like the one you see in Figure 10-2.

Turning Off the Field Names

When you created the form, Works automatically put the field names onto the form for you. Sometimes you'll want to use identifiers other than the actual field names, or you may want to change the placement of the names relative to the data cells

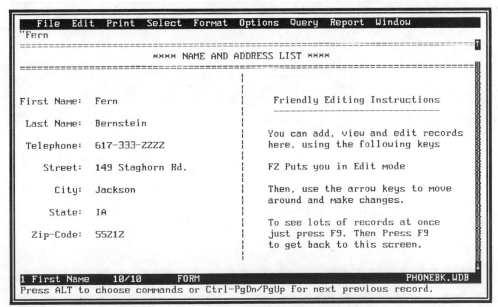

Figure 10-2. A modified form view that includes additional text

themselves. To do either, you'll have to turn off the field names.

To turn off display of the first field's name,

1. First, get into the Form Design screen by choosing Options/Design Form.

2. Move the cursor onto the First Name field. It becomes highlighted.

3. Choose Format/Show Field Name.

4. The words *First Name:* now disappear, leaving only a line which indicates the field's width. Notice that the width for actual display of data is now greater than it was before. We'll take care of that later.

5. Repeat steps 2, 3, and 4 for the rest of the fields, until they are all unnamed. Your screen will look like Figure 10-3.

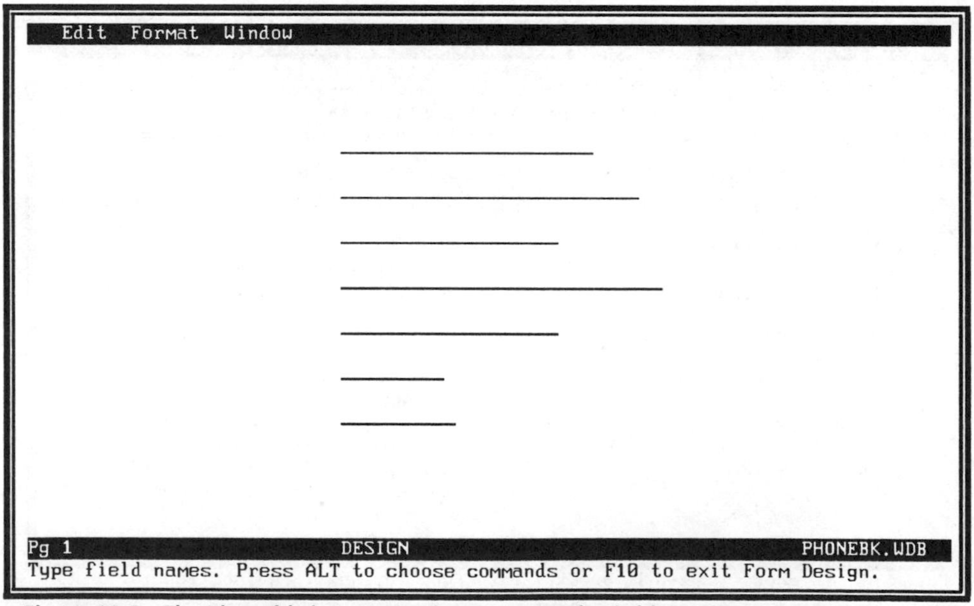

Figure 10-3. *The Phonebk form view after removing the field names*

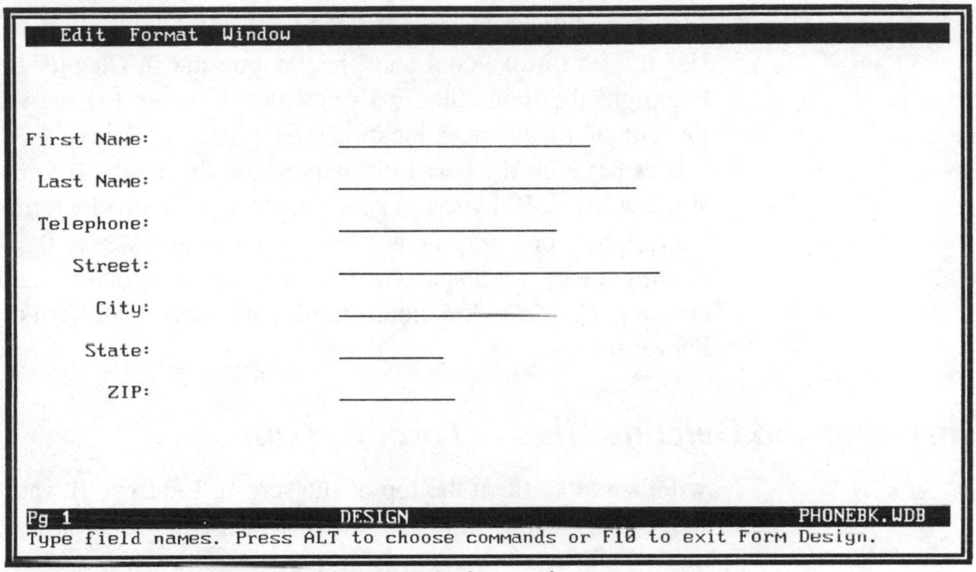

```
 Edit  Format  Window



First Name:              _____

 Last Name:              _____

 Telephone:              _____

    Street:              _____

      City:              _____

     State:              _____

       ZIP:              _____




Pg 1                    DESIGN                          PHONEBK.WDB
Type field names. Press ALT to choose commands or F10 to exit Form Design.
```

Figure 10-4. *Adding the field prompts in the new locations*

6. Next, we'll add custom prompts (labels) for each field, and line up the right sides of the prompts, rather than the left sides. Type in the prompts you see in Figure 10-4. You have to begin each prompt with a quotation mark since each one ends with a colon. Otherwise Works will try to create new fields rather than just creating prompts on the screen. In any case, the First Name prompt begins at the far left edge of the screen. Type in the others so that they all end evenly.

7. Now resize each field until it's the right length again, since turning off the names increased the size beyond what's necessary. Select each field, choose Format/Width and type in the following numbers for the indicated fields:

First Name	10
Last name	14
Telephone	14
Street	20
City	12
State	2
ZIP	5

8. Now move the fields (not the field names) over to the left. Use the Edit/Move command just as you did in Chapter 6. Highlight the field, choose Edit/Move (or press F3), move the cursor to the new location and press ↵. (Leave two spaces between the new field names and the field.) If your aim is a little off, by say, a space or two, you can adjust the line slightly one way or another by choosing Move, then moving the cursor a space or two one way or another, then pressing ↵. Move the fields until your screen looks like Figure 10-5.

Inserting and Deleting Lines in Form Design

Now let's add a title at the top of the screen. First, we'll want to move the existing lines all down a bit. This is achieved using the Edit/Insert command.

1. Move the cursor to any line above the first field.

```
  Edit  Format  Window



First Name:     _____
 Last Name:     _____
 Telephone:     _____
    Street:     _____
      City:     _____
     State:     __
       ZIP:     _____



Pg 1                     DESIGN                        PHONEBK.WDB
Type field names. Press ALT to choose commands or F10 to exit Form Design.
```

Figure 10-5. The form after moving fields to the left

2. Choose Edit/Insert. This inserts a line at the location of the cursor.

3. Repeat the command three times.

4. Oops. That looks like too many blank lines. Eliminate two of them. Choose Edit/Delete twice.

5. Now, one line from the top, enter the title

   *** NAME AND ADDRESS LIST ***

   somewhere close to the middle of the screen.

6. Add one line of equal signs (=) above the title, and another below. To do this, put move the cursor to the far left side of the screen on the first line. Press the equal sign key and hold it down until the entire formula bar is filled with equal signs. Then press ↵. Then, do the same thing two lines down, or use the Edit/Copy command to copy first line.

7. Next, put a dividing line down the middle of the screen using the *pipe* symbol (|). You may have to hunt around on your keyboard to find this one. You need to type each one in, then move down a line with the ↓ key and type in the next one.

   As you see, now there is plenty of room on the screen for typing in instructions to the data entry person, or even to remind yourself of various editing keys. As an example, you may want to add some text that is similar to what you saw in Figure 10-2.

8. Press F10 to leave the Form Design screen, and try out the new form. All the editing and navigation commands will work just as they did before.

Tip: If you have lots of fields on the screen, or don't always want to have them displayed, you can put them on one of the other eight pages of your form. Then just put a note on the first page that says something like

Need help? Just press the PGDN key for some instructions.

Tip: You can draw any character or symbol of the IBM *extended character set* on a form using the ALT key combined with the keypad numbers. This means, for example, that you can draw single- and double-line boxes around sections of your form, or foreign language and scientific characters. It will take a little work, though. Here's a short list of the key codes that you might want to experiment with if you need lines and boxes in your forms:

Key Code	Draws
ALT-196	Single horizontal lines
ALT-179	Single vertical lines
ALT-205	Double horizontal lines
ALT-186	Double vertical lines

To use one of the codes, press the ALT key and hold it down. Then, in sequence, type in the three numbers on the keypad. When you release the ALT key, the character will appear. If drawing a line, type the code in this manner, over and over until the line is the length you want. Then press ↵. This way, you've created a single line that's easy to move around the screen using the Move command, should you need to. For the other codes you may want to use, particularly corners for boxes, you should refer to a chart of the IBM extended character set, often found in books about the IBM PC.

INSERTING AND DELETING FIELDS

It's seldom the case that one plans accurately enough in advance to completely avoid later modifications to a database's structure. So you can expect to have to add or delete fields from a database from time to time. For example, say we wanted to add a field for a work phone number in addition to the phone number field already present. Perhaps a field for a company name could be added too. Fields can be added and deleted from either the form view or the list view. To demonstrate this, let's consider each view separately.

Inserting and Deleting Fields in Form View

To insert and delete fields in form view, you have to be on the Form Design screen. So first, you select Options/Design Form. Once there, you already know how to create a new field since that's how you entered your Phonebk fields originally. You simply move the cursor to the position of the new field, type in the field name followed by a colon, and press ↵. If you forget the colon, it won't work.

Deleting a field is just about as easy. You simply highlight the cell you want to delete (not necessarily the field name) and choose Edit/Delete.

Warning: Deleting a field from a database will erase all the data that was stored in the field. Works will warn you that you are about to delete all the data in that field and ask for an OK. If you are sure you want to trash the field, choose <OK>. Otherwise, press ESC or choose < Cancel >.

Inserting and Deleting Fields in List View

List view works a little differently. First let's insert a new field.

1. Get into list view by pressing F9.

2. Move to any record in the Phone field and choose Select/Field. The whole field becomes highlighted as you see in Figure 10-6.

3. Choose Edit/Insert. A new field is inserted before the selected field, pushing all fields to the right over by one

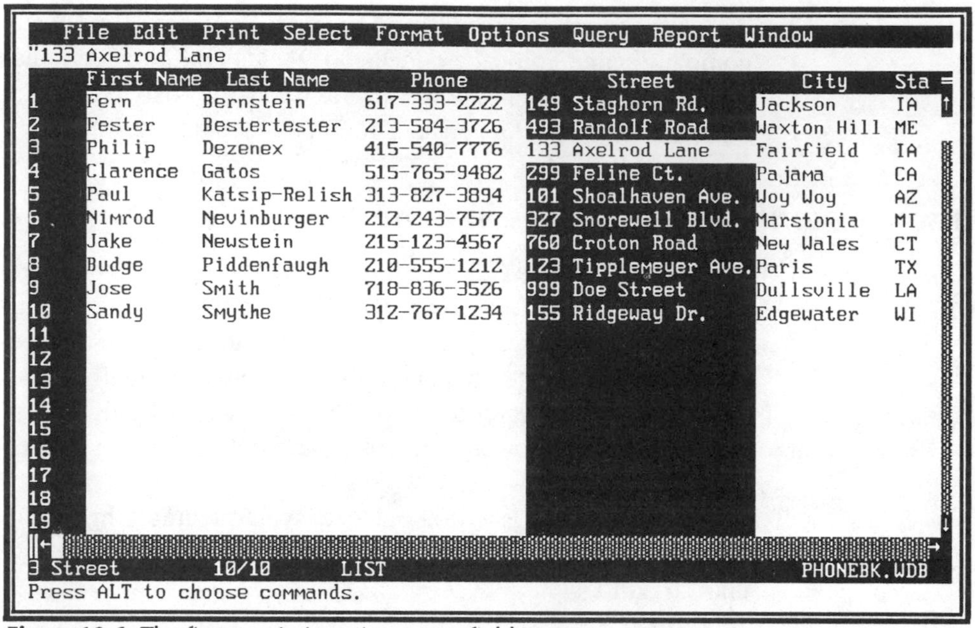

Figure 10-6. The first step in inserting a new field

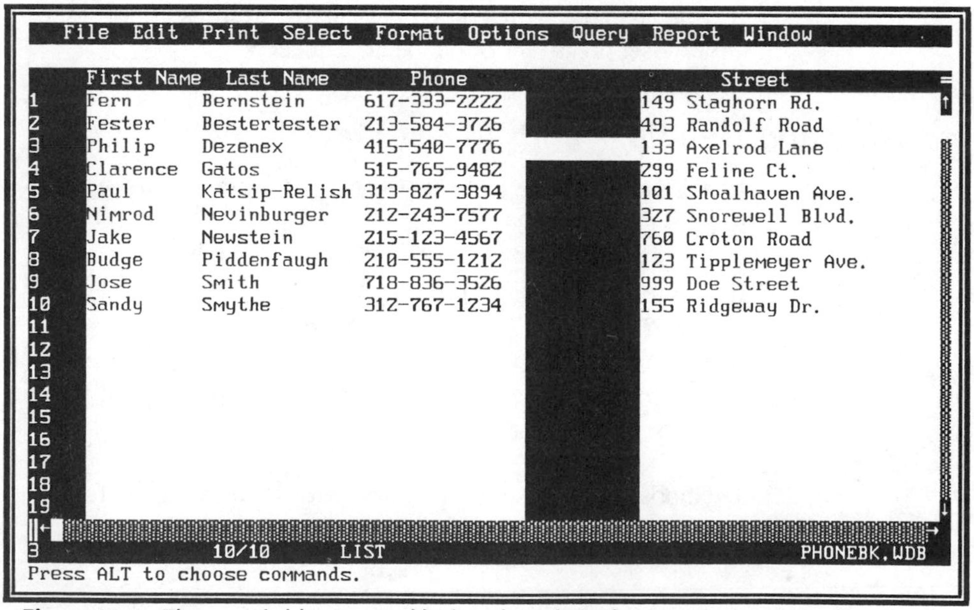

Figure 10-7. The new field is inserted before the selected one

field. All fields to the left remain unmoved. The new field is now selected and your screen looks like Figure 10-7. You can continue adding fields this way if you want.

4. Give the new field a name by choosing Edit/Name and typing in a name. Give it the name *Test*. Incidentally, you can use the Name command to change the name of any existing field while in list view.

5. Press F9 to switch to form view. Notice the new field was added to the form, down at the bottom of the screen.

6. Go back to list view and select the new field again.

7. Delete the field by choosing Edit/Delete. The field is deleted from both the list and form view. The gap is filled in by the fields to the right, which move back to their original positions.

Works inserts the number of fields you have selected prior to choosing the Insert command. So, another way of inserting more than one field is to select several fields and then insert. To select multiple fields, put the cursor in the field before which you want the new fields to be inserted. Press SHIFT → until the number of fields you want to insert are highlighted. Choose Select/Field to select all the fields. Then choose Edit/Insert. Multiple field deletion works the same way.

Warning: Deleting multiple fields will cause total loss of data in hidden fields if the hidden fields fall into the selected range of the fields you delete. (We'll see more about this in the section entitled "Hiding Specific Records and Fields.")

INSERTING AND DELETING RECORDS

So much for inserting and deleting fields. Inserting and deleting records is another matter. It's not uncommon to want to insert a record here or there in a database. Normally, adding a new record to the end of a database will suffice, particularly if you intend to sort the records, since the sorting process will rearrange the records anyway. In unsorted databases, though, or in cases when you don't want to re-sort, you can move to the intended insertion point and pop in a new record.

Naturally there will also be times when records will become outdated and you'll want to purge them from a given database, assuming that editing them won't suffice. Deleting a record or records from a database erases them permanently. There is no way of reversing the erasure except to type the record in again.

In the following sections, we'll show you how to insert and delete records in form view and list view.

Inserting and Deleting Records in Form View

In form view, the Edit/Insert command inserts one record and the Edit/Delete command deletes a record. Try these examples to learn how it's done.

1. Get into form view.

2. Jump to record 3, Philbert Dezenex.

3. Choose Edit/Insert. A new, blank record is inserted, and appears on your screen. But where was it inserted— before or after Philbert?

4. Press F9 to find out. As you probably expected, the new record was inserted before the record you were on, just as fields were inserted in the last set of exercises.

5. Press F9 again. Choose Edit/Delete. The new record is deleted, and Philbert's record is pulled to its old spot as record number 3. (Check the status line for the record number.)

Inserting and Deleting Records in List View

Let's try the same steps from list view now.

1. Press F9 to get to list view.

2. Place the cursor anywhere on record 3.

3. Choose Select/Record. The whole record becomes high-lighted, as you see in Figure 10-8.

4. Choose Edit/Insert. A new blank record is inserted above the previously selected one, as you see in Figure 10-9.

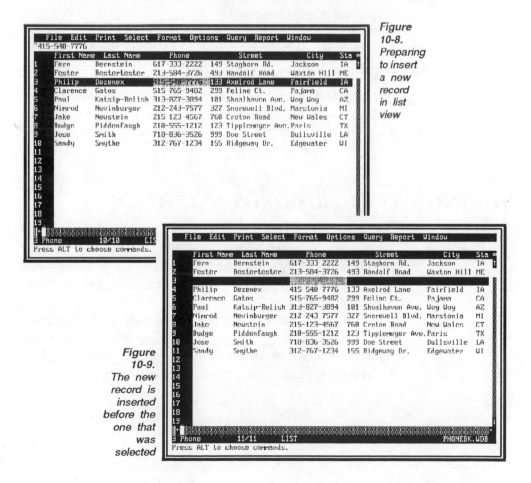

Figure 10-8. Preparing to insert a new record in list view

Figure 10-9. The new record is inserted before the one that was selected

5. Deleting a record is just as simple. Delete the record you just added by selecting it (it may already be selected at this point) and choosing Edit/Delete. The record disappears and record 4 becomes record 3 again.

Inserting and Deleting Multiple Records

You can insert or delete more than a single record. For example, say you want to insert three records after record 4.

1. Select records 5, 6, and 7.

2. Choose Edit/Insert. Three records will be inserted below record 4 and above record 5.

3. Now delete the three blank records using the Edit/Delete command.

Warning: Deleting multiple records can be dangerous. There is no Undo command to reverse your decision. Be careful when using this command.

HIDING SPECIFIC RECORDS AND FIELDS

There may be times when you'll want to turn off certain records temporarily so that they won't show up in list or form view or even in reports. They won't be printed using the Print command, either.

Recall from Chapter 6 that one way to hide specific records is to run a query. Any records not matching the query are hidden until you execute the Show All Records command again. The records matching the query are then displayed.

How to Hide Selected Records with Hide Record

Another command, Hide Record, lets you arbitrarily turn off a record or selected records. Try these steps to see how it works.

1. Move the cursor to any cell in record 8.

2. Choose Query/Hide Record. Record 8 disappears, but all the other records keep their original numbering. Notice that the record numbers along the left side of the screen jump from 7 to 9, implying that record 8 is there somewhere.

3. Just for fun, hide records 2 through 4 now by selecting all three rows at one time, and then choosing Query/Hide Record.

4. Now your screen shows only six records, because four are hidden. If you switch to form view, the same six records will be available for editing or viewing, but the hidden records will be skipped over.

How to Display Only the Hidden Records

But what if you wanted to see the hidden records again? As you know, the Show All Records will return them to visibility. But you may want to work with *only* the hidden records, not all the records. This can be really useful when you want to manually pick a few records out of a large database to work with, particularly if Query won't do the job. Here's how.

1. Make sure you're in list view.

2. Choose Query/Switch Hidden Records. You see only the records you had hidden before: records 2, 3, 4, and 8.

3. Now choose Query/Show All Records to return things to normal.

How to Hide Fields

You may notice that there is no Hide Field command. However, since you can only get a limited number of fields on the screen, it's likely that you'll want to turn off a field or two occasionally. One solution is to move the unwanted field(s) way down to the right-hand end of the database. But then you have to move the field(s) back to their original location(s) later, which is a hassle. There's an easier way. Here's an example:

1. To hide the Phone field in your database, select that field.

2. Choose Format/Width and set the width to 0.

   Voilá! The Phone field disappears and now you can see the entire address without having to pan the screen to the right.

3. Switch to form view and notice that this operation had no effect on the form.

4. Switch back to list view, and set the width of the Phone field to 14 again. Whoops! How do you select a field you can't see? You have to use the GO TO dialog box. Press F5 to get the dialog box. Skip over the record number part and select Phone from the list box, and press ↵. Nothing appears to happen since the field is still invisible.

5. You can still set the width, though, to make the field reappear. Choose Format/Width and enter 14. The field miraculously reappears.

Tip: If you wanted to take this technique to the hilt, you could have two entirely different sets of fields on the form and list views. Remove fields from list view as you just did. Then remove fields from form view by placing them on another page of the form (one of the eight allowable screens), using the Move command.

Unlike hidden records, hidden fields will still show up in reports. But they will show up in a standard printout, which will look very much like your screen display. Thus, hiding a field is a good way to customize a quick printout.

Caution: Hiding a field can result in unintentional loss of data in that field if you subsequently delete multiple fields by selecting a range that includes the hidden field within it. Be careful when hiding fields that you do not accidentally wipe them out of your database.

CREATING THE INVENTORY DATABASE

Before we can experiment further, you will need some new material to work with. Even though you could use the Phonebk database for most of the following exercises, a slightly more sophisticated database would be better. Close the Phonebk file

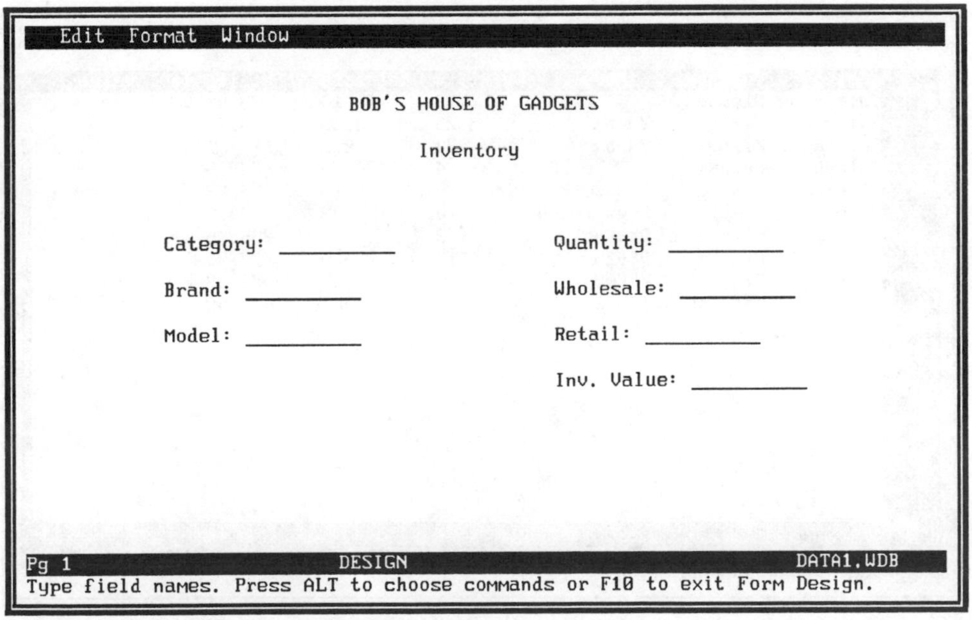

Figure 10-10. *The inventory database structure*

now (save the changes) and open a new database document. Lay out the form as you see in Figure 10-10. Make sure you enter the fields in the following order, or else they will be in the wrong order in list view.

Category
Brand
Model
Quantity
Wholesale
Retail
Inv. Value

Now add the data as you see it in Figure 10-11, and save the file under the name INVENTRY. Notice there's nothing in the last field. Don't worry about that yet.

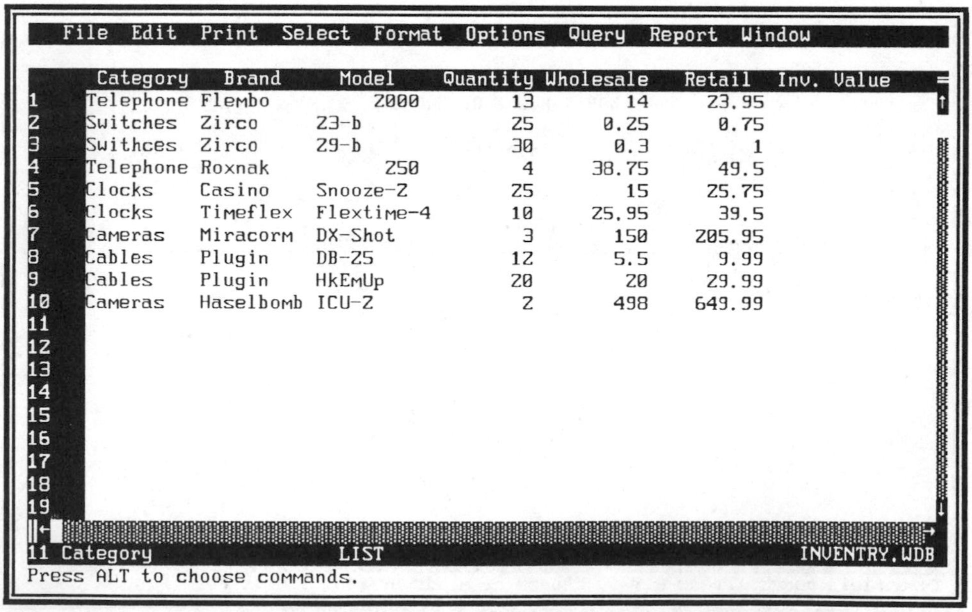

```
 File  Edit  Print  Select  Format  Options  Query  Report  Window

      Category    Brand      Model   Quantity Wholesale    Retail  Inv. Value
1    Telephone Flembo          2000       13        14     23.95
2    Switches  Zirco     Z3-b           25      0.25      0.75
3    Swithces  Zirco     Z9-b           30       0.3         1
4    Telephone Roxnak          Z50        4     38.75      49.5
5    Clocks    Casino    Snooze-Z       25        15     25.75
6    Clocks    Timeflex  Flextime-4     10     25.95      39.5
7    Cameras   Miracorm  DX-Shot         3       150    205.95
8    Cables    Plugin    DB-Z5          12       5.5      9.99
9    Cables    Plugin    HkEmUp         20        20     29.99
10   Cameras   Haselbomb ICU-Z           2       498    649.99
11
12
13
14
15
16
17
18
19

11 Category              LIST                            INVENTRY.WDB
Press ALT to choose commands.
```

Figure 10-11. *Initial layout of the data in the INVENTRY file*

FORMATTING FIELDS

Obviously the first thing we have to do is fix the formatting of some fields.

1. Change the format of the Model field by selecting it and choosing Format/Style. Choose Right alignment.

2. Now select the last three fields, Wholesale, Retail, and Inv. Value and set their formatting to Dollar, with two decimal places. Actually you only have to select a cell in each field, not the entire range of cells to set the formats. Your fields are now formatted as you see in Figure 10-12.

Logical and Other Formats

Incidentally, while we're on the subject of formatting, note that the formatting choices in the database are identical to

```
 File  Edit  Print  Select  Format  Options  Query  Report  Window

      Category    Brand      Model   Quantity Wholesale   Retail  Inv. Value
1    Telephone Flembo        2000         13    $14.00    $23.95
2    Switches  Zirco        Z3-b         25     $0.25     $0.75
3    Swithces  Zirco        Z9-b         30     $0.30     $1.00
4    Telephone Roxnak        250          4    $38.75    $49.50
5    Clocks    Casino     Snooze-Z       25    $15.00    $25.75
6    Clocks    Timeflex  Flextime-4      10    $25.95    $39.50
7    Cameras   Miracorm    DX-Shot        3   $150.00   $205.95
8    Cables    Plugin       DB-25        12     $5.50     $9.99
9    Cables    Plugin       HkEmUp       20    $20.00    $29.99
10   Cameras   Haselbomb    ICU-Z         2   $498.00   $649.99
11
12
13
14
15
16
17
18
19

11  Quantity              LIST                            INVENTRY.WDB
Press ALT to choose commands.
```

Figure 10-12. The new database after field formatting

those in the spreadsheet, including the *logical* type. Logical fields are used to store yes or no information. When formatted as Logical, a cell will display the word True if it contains numbers other than zero, and False if it contains a zero. As an example application of Logical fields, consider a customer database in which you want to record whether each customer's credit is good (true) or bad (false). Later, this information could be used in a query to ferret out all customers with bad credit, overdue bills, or other problems.

For more information on the various formats, please refer to Appendix A.

USING CALCULATED FIELDS

The last field, Inv. Value (Inventory Value) was left blank because that is going to be a *calculated* field. A calculated field is like a spreadsheet cell with a formula in it that references other cells. The formula you type into a database cell is called a *field formula*. You can have one formula per database field, and Works automatically copies the formula into all cells of the field.

Field formulas can contain items as shown in the following table:

Formula item	Explanation
Operators: * / + and -	For example, =Units*Pounds
Operands:	The thing that gets "operated on," such as a number or name of a field containing a number or word.
Functions:	Identical to the spreadsheet functions, these include functions such as trigonometric functions (SIN, COS, TAN, and so on).

For example, a typical field formula might be

=Retail*.06

which would calculate tax. Of course formulas can be complex too, such as

=((Gross income) - (Cost of Sales))/4*.25

In the case of our database, the formula is very simple, but it will serve as a typical example. The Inv. Value field will report the amount of money tied up in a given inventory item. It will be calculated by multiplying the quantity of each item in stock by the wholesale price of that item.

To enter the formula for the field, move the cursor to any cell in the last field and enter **=quantity*wholesale**. Works instantly calculates the field, plugging in the following values:

Inv. Value

$182.00

$6.25

$9.00

$155.00

$375.00

$259.50

$450.00

$66.00

$400.00

$996.00

As you may surmise, the calculated field will work very much like a spreadsheet's formula field does. For instance, you can now move to the Quantity field, change some values, and see the effects immediately in the Inv. Value field. (Be sure to change them back to their original values if you experiment.)

Some Rules About Using Field Formulas

Once you start throwing in lots of functions and references to other cells, your formulas can get pretty complicated, just as they can with spreadsheets. Unfortunately, we don't have the space to cover the details of complex formula construction in this book, but we can give you the basics.

Formulas are processed by Works using standard algebraic methods. That is, from left to right with innermost parentheses evaluated first. Multiplication and division are calculated before addition and subtraction.

Functions consist of the function name, a pair of parentheses, and additional *arguments* (in most cases). Arguments are values upon which the functions are intended to operate and are separated from those functions by a comma. Arguments must be numbers or equations that result in a number when they are calculated. References to other fields are acceptable as arguments if they contain numbers or formulas that result in numbers.

For details about functions, please refer to Appendix A.

PROTECTING FIELDS FROM ERASURE

You can protect certain critical fields so that during the process of using a database you don't accidentally erase or modify their data. This is just like protection in the spreadsheet tool, except it can't be done on a cell-by-cell basis, only on a whole field at a time.

As in the spreadsheet, protecting the whole database is a one-step process, whereas protecting individual cells takes two steps.

How to Lock All Fields

Assuming that none of the formats (locked or unlocked) of fields in your database have been altered, they'll be formatted as locked by Works. This means that when you activate protection, they will lock, preventing alteration to the field's data.

So, to lock all the fields in a database, just

1. Choose Options/Protect.

2. Once you activate Protect from the Options menu, they're all locked. Trying to change a field results in an error message in a dialog box.

   Error: Locked Cells cannot be changed

How to Lock Specific Fields

So, the process of locking only specific fields requires the following steps:

1. Select the field(s) you want to *unlock*.

2. Choose Format/Style.

3. From the STYLE dialog box, set the Locked check box on. This unlocks the field(s).

4. Choose Options/Protect to set protection on. This step must be done last or you will get a beep when you attempt step 2.

5. If you later want to make a change to a locked field, just choose Options/Protect again, to turn off protection.

If you decide later that you want to remove specific field or fields from the list of those that are locked, just select the field(s) in question, choose Format/Style, and set the Locked check box off.

CREATING COMPLEX QUERIES

In Chapter 6 you learned the basics of creating queries. Recall that queries allow you to question the database so that only certain records (those meeting the query criteria) show. Criteria, as you will recall, are essentially logical formulas, generating either a true or a false result. If all the criteria in a specific record are true, then that record is displayed. All other records are hidden from view and from subsequently generated reports as long as the query is in force.

In Chapter 6 you created some relatively simple queries that used a single field in the criteria. However, like calculated field formulas, queries can range from the simple to the extraordinarily obtuse. But more often than not, simpler queries will perform day-to-day tasks such as showing you everyone whose names fall between D and M, or who lives in certain ZIP code ranges.

There will be times, though, when you'll want to construct a slightly more complex query for listing such things as inventory items that cost more than $200 each and whose quantity exceeds 20, or houses within a certain ZIP code range whose price falls between $150,000 and $200,000 and that have negative termite records.

First, a little theory about how query criteria are strung together to form complex queries. There are two ways to combine criteria:

- More than one criteria applied to a single field. For example:

  ZIP : >19087 & <45309

- Criteria applied to multiple fields. For example:

  Last name: >"A" & <"D"

  and

  ZIP : >19087 & <45309

Operator	Effect
=	Equal to
<>	Not equal to
<	Less than
>	Greater than
<=	Less than or equal to
>=	Greater than or equal to
*	Wildcard (any length)
?	Wildcard (single character)
|	Or ("Fred" *or* "Jim")
&	And ("Smith" *and* "Jones")
~	Not (people *not* living in GA.)

Table 10-1. *Operators for Use in Queries*

Table 10-1 presents the list of operators that you can use to construct queries.

Now let's try some practical examples using the inventory database. Each exercise entails choosing Query/Define first. In each case, we've shown the field(s) you have to type entries into on the Query screen, what the exact entry is for each, and the result on the List screen after you press F10 to apply the query.

Note: In some cases you will have to delete the query set up from a previous example before going to the next one. This is indicated where it is necessary.

To see all the data about items that are switches:

Category: **Switches**

Category	Brand	Model	Quantity	Wholesale	Retail	Inv. Value
Switches	Zirco	23-b	25	$0.25	$0.75	$6.25
Switches	Zirco	29-b	30	$0.30	$1.00	$9.00

To see all the data about items that are clocks:

Category: **Clocks**

Category	Brand	Model	Quantity	Wholesale	Retail	Inv. Value
Clocks	Casino	Snooze-2	25	$15.00	$25.75	$375.00
Clocks	Timeflex	Flextime-4	10	$25.95	$39.50	$259.50

To see all the data about items that are switches or clocks:

Category: ="Switches"|="Clocks"

Category	Brand	Model	Quantity	Wholesale	Retail	Inv. Value
Clocks	Casino	Snooze-2	25	$15.00	$25.75	$375.00
Clocks	Timeflex	Flextime-4	10	$25.95	$39.50	$259.50
Switches	Zirco	23-b	25	$0.25	$0.75	$6.25
Switches	Zirco	29-b	30	$0.30	$1.00	$9.00

To display all items with more than 5 and fewer than 15 units in stock, first you must choose Edit/Delete Query. Then enter

Quantity: >5&<15

Category	Brand	Model	Quantity	Wholesale	Retail	Inv. Value
Telephone	Flembo	2000	13	$14.00	$23.95	$182.00
Clocks	Timeflex	Flextime-4	10	$25.95	$39.50	$259.50
Cables	Plugin	DB-25	12	$5.50	$9.99	$66.00

To see all items with more than 5 and less than 15 units in stock and that have a retail price of over $15.00 (note that you don't enter the $ sign in the retail entry):

Quantity: >5&<15

Retail: >15

Category	Brand	Model	Quantity	Wholesale	Retail	Inv. Value
Telephone	Flembo	2000	13	$14.00	$23.95	$182.00
Clocks	Timeflex	Flextime-4	10	$25.95	$39.50	$259.50

Using Wildcards in Queries

You may remember the wildcards ? and * from Chapter 6. We used them as search criteria in that chapter, but they can also be employed with the Query command. Below are two examples.

To see all the items whose categories start with a C, first choose Edit/Delete Query. Then enter

Category: **C***

```
Category   Brand      Model       Quantity Wholesale   Retail   Inv. Value
Clocks     Casino     Snooze-2       25     $15.00    $25.75    $375.00
Clocks     Timeflex   Flextime-4     10     $25.95    $39.50    $259.50
Cameras    Miracorm   DX-Shot         3    $150.00   $205.95    $450.00
Cables     Plugin     DB-25          12      $5.50     $9.99     $66.00
Cables     Plugin     HkEmUp         20     $20.00    $29.99    $400.00
Cameras    Haselbomb  ICU-2           2    $498.00   $649.99    $996.00
```

To see all the items whose Brands have an *i* as the second letter:

Brand: **?i***

```
Category   Brand      Model       Quantity Wholesale   Retail   Inv. Value
Switches   Zirco      23-b           25      $0.25     $0.75      $6.25
Switches   Zirco      29-b           30      $0.30     $1.00      $9.00
Clocks     Timeflex   Flextime-4     10     $25.95    $39.50    $259.50
Cameras    Miracorm   DX-Shot         3    $150.00   $205.95    $450.00
```

Additional Rules of Querying

In this section, we provide a few other rules and examples for your reference.

For a simple condition, no quotation marks are necessary in the query fields. This is clear from the examples in the last section, where you queried for clocks and switches. You just type in the words or numbers you are looking for and run the query.

However, when you begin constructing complex formulas (that is, with more than one condition in a field), you have to use the rules shown in Table 10-2 for each type of criteria. Note that you must use single quotation marks around dates, and double quotation marks around text.

Criteria	Example
Numbers	<30
	=3405
	<30&>20
Text	="Jones"|="Smythe"
	="Jones"&="Smythe"
	="Jones"|="Smythe"|="Harris"
Dates	='June, 10, 1980'
	='6/10/80'

Table 10-2. Criteria Rules for Constructing Queries

Combining Multiple Field Criteria in One Field

Normally, you will want to type the relevent query criteria or formulas into the field that the formula is associated with, as we did in the exercises in the section "Creating Complex Queries." For example, if you want to query for "Smith"|"Jones", you'd type the formula into the Last Name field.

There may, however, be times when you'll have to type multiple formulas into a single query form field. For example, say you wanted to see Smiths whose ZIP codes were less than 43000 and Joneses whose ZIP codes were more than 85000.

This would be impossible to do using the normal method:

Field   Formula

Last Name = "Smith" | = "Jones"
ZIP   <43000 &>85000

since this would show the Smiths with ZIP codes above 85000 as well as below 43000. The same would be true of the Joneses. To handle this type of situation, you need to enter the entire formula on a single line and enter it into a single query field.

Such a formula can include references to any fields in your database, and needn't be entered into any one particular field. Works will allow you to stipulate the name of the field you are referencing if you include the field name in the query formula. For example, here's how you would enter the formula for our last query into any query field:

    =(Last Name="Smith"&age<30)|(Last Name="Jones"&age>35)

Note: If this formula were entered into the Last Name query field, you could omit the references to Last Name, since Works will assume that any unreferenced formula pertains to the field into which you have entered the formula. Thus, the formula could be entered as

    =(="Smith"&age<30)|(="Jones"&age>35)

Reversing the Criteria

Sometimes you'll want to reverse the effect of a query to see all records that don't match the query criteria instead of seeing those that do. For example, suppose a query displayed all insurance policy holders with good driving records. After examining those, you might decide that you want to display those policy holders that have bad driving records. There are two ways to do this.

You can use the Switch Hidden Records command to display currently hidden records while hiding the visible ones. You learned about this command earlier in this chapter, in the section entitled "How to Display Only the Hidden Records."

The second approach to the problem, which is particularly useful if you don't need to switch between seeing hidden and visible records often, is to alter the "to reverse the" criteria, causing the exact opposite of the normal formula.

Here's how you would change the driving record formula. (Assume the word *Good* was used to indicate a good record.)

Field	Formula	Effect
Driving Record	Good	Shows good drivers
Driving Record	<>"Good"	Shows bad drivers

A slightly different modification is necessary for more complex formulas or for dates and numbers. The *Not* operator, represented by a tilde ($\sim$), is used to reverse compound formulas. Other formulas would employ the <= or >= signs for reversal. Here are some examples to refer to when constucting your own queries:

Formula	Reversed formula
200	<=200
Jones	<>"Jones"
="Jones"	<>"Jones"
<'3/6/53'	>='3/6/53'
=Units>10&Price<300	=~Units>10&Price<300

Don't forget that if your query has a formula in more than one field, you'll have to reverse each formula to get an exact reversal of records. On the other hand, by reversing only a selected field's formulas you open up other possibilities.

REPORTING

For many serious database users, the real payoff for all the time spent entering and editing data is the generation of reports. In fact, reporting on data is one of the primary reasons for the existence of computerized databases. There are so many day-to-day business requirements for complex printed reports that many offices regularly buy programs costing three or four times that of Works just to generate them.

Some database programs require customized programming in a computer language to create decent reports. Works, however, has a built-in *report generator* that makes it relatively easy to do so. With the Works report generator, you can print your reports either on paper or to the screen. By printing to the screen, you can easily fine-tune a report, and try it again to immediately examine the effects.

The Works report generator lets you create a variety of sizes and types of reports, complete with formatting, calculations, subtotals, totals, summary statistics, and explanatory text. The report generator is to the database what charting is to the spreadsheet. You can create up to eight different reports, then modify cells in the database, then run the reports again to see the effects. Changes to the database are automatically reflected in the reports.

In this section, you will create a small database report from the inventory list. In the process, you will learn most details of report generation.

There are two ways to create a report. You can have Works create the report for you, taking care of the details. This is called *speed reporting*. Secondly, you can design the report from scratch, controlling the extra details yourself.

Speed Reporting

Since speed reporting is easier than creating your own report from scratch and will produce acceptable results for most occasions, let's look at it first.

1. From list view in the INVENTRY database choose Query/Show All Records. This returns all the records to view.

2. Choose Report/New. In a few seconds, the report screen appears (notice the word REPORT on the status line). Your screen should look like Figure 10-13.

3. Choose Report/New. Works now presents you with about three screens of information, separated by a message asking you to press ↵ for each new one. On the screen, the effect of the report is a little tough to judge because Works

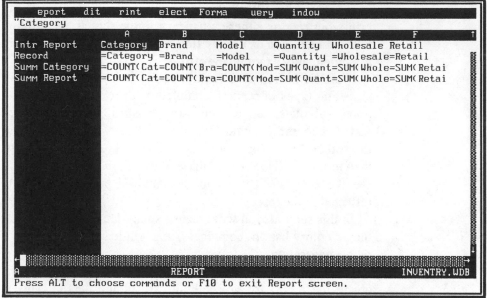

Figure 10-13. *Creating the speed report*

couldn't fit it within the 80-column width of a single screen. Even if you printed it out, it would require some work with tape and scissors to piece it together. If you did print it out and stick it together, or use a printer that could print out a slightly wider report, it would look like this:

```
Category   Brand      Model      Quantity  Wholesale  Retail      Inv. Value
Cables     Plugin        DB-25        12      $5.50      $9.99        $66.00
Cables     Plugin        HkEmUp       20     $20.00     $29.99       $400.00
        2             2         2      32     $25.50     $39.98     $2,832.75
Cameras    Miracorm   DX-Shot          3    $150.00    $205.95       $450.00
Cameras    Haselbomb  ICU-2            2    $498.00    $649.99       $996.00
        2             2         2       5    $648.00    $855.94     $1,446.00
Clocks     Casino     Snooze-2        25     $15.00     $25.75       $375.00
Clocks     Timeflex   Flextime-4      10     $25.95     $39.50       $259.50
        2             2         2      35     $40.95     $65.25       $634.50
Switches   Zirco         23-b         25      $0.25      $0.75         $6.25
Switches   Zirco         29-b         30      $0.30      $1.00         $9.00
        2             2         2      55      $0.55      $1.75        $15.25
Telephone Flembo         2000         13     $14.00     $23.95       $182.00
Telephone Roxnak          250          4     $38.75     $49.50       $155.00
        2             2         2      17     $52.75     $73.45       $337.00
       10            10        10     144    $767.75  $1,036.37     $2,898.75
```

Interpreting the Speed Report

What Works has done is rather intelligent, actually. First it sorted the database on the first field, Category. It used Category for the sort, rather than using a different field, by virtue of Category's position in the database. By default, Works will use the first field for sorting. Luckily (actually, we planned it), the first field was most reasonable for this purpose.

Having the categories sorted then allowed Works to create subtotals for each category of items in the inventory. Notice that each type of item (cables through telephones) is broken out into a separate section. Since the first three fields are not numerical, Works couldn't calculate any subtotals. Instead it reports the number of records in that section. That's what all the 2s are about. This is called a *count* rather than a *sum*.

The remaining fields show subtotals for the number of items (32 cables, 5 cameras, and so on), wholesale price, retail price, and inventory value for each type of item.

The last line of the report presents a grand total for all fields.

| 10 | 10 | 10 | 144 | $767.75 | $1,036.37 | $2,898.75 |

From this you can see that you have $2,898.75 tied up in 144 items in stock.

Note: If your report has a couple of lines of extra zeros before the grand totals, it means that your database has a few additional blank records at the end of the file. Delete them by selecting the blank records and choosing Edit/Delete.

Defining a Report from Scratch

The speed report isn't bad, especially once you get used to reading it. The layout isn't perfect, though, and there should be some labels or horizontal lines indicating where the subtotals are. You may also want to add a title, date, and/or explanations about items on the pages as well.

Also it's not uncommon to need additional *break fields*. The Category field was the break field in the speed report. But what if you wanted items under each category subtotaled by brand, and then by model number under each brand?

All of these changes require getting into the nuts and bolts of report generation. As with forms and queries, the first step in creating a report is to define it. You use the Works report definition screen to define a report.

Row Types

The primary structure of a report is defined by *report rows*. Each line in your printed report corresponds to a type of row in the report definition. There are 11 possible types of rows, as shown in Table 10-3.

If you look at the report definition screen for the speed report, you will see that only four of these possible row types were used.

Row Type	Explanation
Intr Report	Prints at the beginning of a report
Intr Page	Prints at the top of each page
Intr 1st breakfield	Prints at the beginning of 1st break field
Intr 2nd breakfield	Prints at the beginning of 2nd break field
Intr 3rd breakfield	Prints at the beginning of 3rd break field
Record	The actual data from each record
Summ 3rd breakfield	Prints the subtotal of the 3rd break field
Summ 2nd breakfield	Prints the subtotal of the 2nd break field
Summ 1st breakfield	Prints the subtotal of the 1st break field
Summ Page	Prints subtotals of all fields for the page
Summ Report	Prints subtotals of all fields for entire report

Table 10-3. Row Types in a Report

Intr Report
Record
Summ 1st Breakfield (Category)
Summ Report

Here's the gist of the steps you should follow to soup up a report definition.

- ♦ **Step 1** First, decide how many break fields you want: 1, 2, or 3. Then you'll have to sort your database accordingly, since Works needs the records organized in proper sequential order before it can figure the subtotals for each field. If you want two breaks, you'll have to do a two-level sort (two fields). For three breaks, you need three sorts.

  To do the sorting, choose Query/Sort from the Report screen. Your screen should now look like that shown in Figure 10-14.

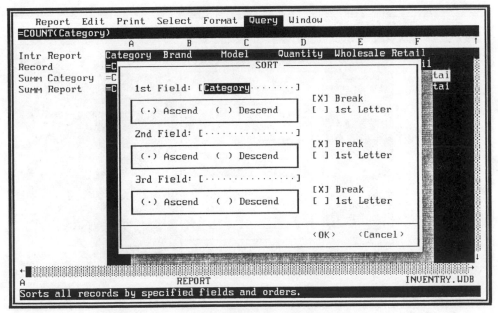

Figure 10-14. *Setting the sort order and summary field breaks*

Notice that this screen has an extra section on it from the one explained in Chapter 6 (please refer to that chapter if you need help on sorting). In this box, two additional check boxes are added for each field to be sorted:

[X] Break

This causes a break whenever a break field changes.

[ ] 1st Letter

This causes a break only when the first letter changes.

The setting you choose here for each field determines how often you will see breaks and resulting sums and counts (or other statistical computations). Choosing 1st Letter results in larger groupings, and is the default.

Finally, decide whether you want each field to be sorted in ascending (A to Z, 1 to 9) or descending (Z to A, 9 to 1) order.

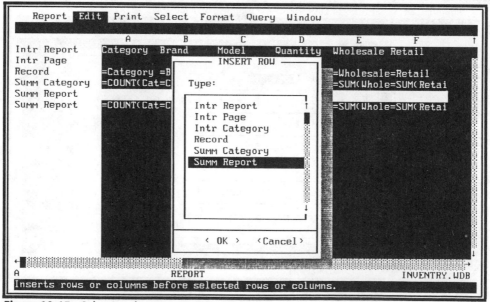

Figure 10-15. *Selecting the report row type*

◆ **Step 2** The next step is to insert whatever additional rows you want in the report. To insert the rows, you use the same technique required for inserting records into the list view of the database. That is, first you select the row you want the new row to precede. Then choose Edit/Insert. However, as shown in Figure 10-15, you'll now see a dialog box giving you a list of row types you can choose from, as you see in Figure 10-13. Select the row type you want.

Rows must be in a certain order in a report. For example, you can't have a total at the top of the report, with subtotals below it. Works will correct any error you make in placing row types, so you don't have to worry about it. The names of the new row types are shown over to the left of the screen. You can have as many rows in a report as you want.

◆ **Step 3** Once the row additions are complete, you have to tell Works exactly what information you want to assign to each row type. This is done by entering definitions into each cell of the row in question. You insert data into the cells just as you would in the database.

For example, in our speed report, the following cell definitions were inserted by Works' speed report generator:

```
Intr Report    Category Brand    Model    Quantity Wholesale Retail
Record         =Category =Brand   =Model   =Quantity =Wholesale=Retail
Summ Category  =COUNT(Cat=COUNT(Bra=COUNT(Mod=SUM(Quant=SUM(Whole=SUM(Retai
Summ Report    =COUNT(Cat=COUNT(Bra=COUNT(Mod=SUM(Quant=SUM(Whole=SUM(Retai
```

This looks like a giant mess because the cells are too short to display the complete contents. But if you move the active cell around on the screen and read the formula bar, it will make more sense because you'll see the complete formulas.

Here's a brief description of what's going on, to help you figure out how to create your own cell formulas in your rows. The Record row instructs Works to print the contents of the six fields, one after another. Thus =*Brand* means "print the contents of the brand field for each record, starting at the beginning and moving on down through the database until the end." The Record row is the only row that prints the actual data in the database, incidentally. All other rows are either printing titles or statistics based on the database records that the Record row prints.

You can enter numbers, formulas, and text into the cells. As an example, look at the speed report. Here you'll see how the Summ Category row uses typical formulas.

=COUNT(Category)   =COUNT(Brand) =COUNT(Model)

means "on this line, count up the number of records in the current subdivision." Or, when SUM is used, as in

=SUM(Quantity) =SUM(Wholesale) =SUM(Retail)

it means "on this line sum the dollar amounts in the current division."

Although the speed report entered the formulas into these cells automatically, you'll have to do it manually, or with the aid of commands in the menus. The Edit menu has three commands to help you enter data into the cells, and eliminate typos. These are shown in the following table:

Command	Action	Example
Field Name	Drops the name of any field into the cell	"Model
Field Value	Drops the value of any field into the cell	=Model
Field Summary	Drops one of seven statistical formulas into the cell	=SUM(Model)

The seven statistical formulas you can use are shown in the next table.

Formula	Explanation
SUM	Mathematical addition of numbers in the group
AVG	Average of the numbers in the group
COUNT	Number of items in the group
MAX	The largest number in the group
MIN	The smallest number in the group
STD	Standard deviation of the numbers in the group
VAR	Variance of the numbers in the group

When you choose any of these from the Edit/Field Summary dialog box, make sure you select a field from the list box section first. Only then will something happen when you choose a statistical formula.

Printing the Report

Before moving ahead to print the report you design, you may want to do several things. First, since creating reports that look right takes a fair bit of experimentation, you'll want to view your report a number of times on the screen, and fine-tune a bit each time. Use the Report/View command or press SHIFT-F10 to do this. Remember that fields which would exceed the screen's 80 columns will wrap to the next screen, though, depending on your printer, they may not actually print out that way.

Once things are basically the way you want them, you can spruce them up with formatting. Use the commands from the Format menu to set the style of individual fields or rows. For example, you might want to underline the field names at the top of each column, or print the grand totals on the bottom line in bold. If your printer has different fonts, you can use those too. Just select the fields whose font you want to choose, and make the selection from the FONT dialog box.

Next, don't overlook the use of horizontal and vertical page breaks to break up your report into separate pages as you would like. For example, you may want to print a separate page for each new category of items, expenses by company division, change of letter for Last Name, or similar break field. Choosing Print/Insert Page Break from the Report definition screen inserts a break above or to the left of the selected record or field. You have to select the entire field or row before choosing the command.

You can apply a query to limit the records that will be included in the report. Finally, take the standard steps of setting up the layout box with a header or footer, the page size, and so on. As usual, a footer containing the page number is already included as a default.

Before you're through, save your file. The reports you design (up to eight of them) will be saved along with the database. This way you can use and modify them any time that your database is open.

Chapter

Creating Charts

Eleven

As mentioned in Chapter 9, Works lets you graphically chart out the data in a spreadsheet to convey the meaning of your numbers visually rather than numerically. By plotting your numbers in a chart, you can more easily spot trends and relationships, or communicate your findings to others.

Without computers, chart making can be an expensive and tedious job, often requiring special skills, tools, and personnel. Worse yet, any alteration of the charted data sends the art staff back to their drawing boards to start again, from scratch.

With Works, you can quickly whip up charts from within the spreadsheet tool, either while you're creating a document or after it's completed. Then you can jump between viewing the chart and altering the data in the worksheet and see the effects immediately displayed in your charts.

Works lets you create eight basic types of charts, as shown in Figure 11-1.

♦ **Bar** The bar chart, sometimes referred to as the *histogram,* consists of vertical boxes or bars arranged side by side. The height of each bar corresponds to the value it represents.

♦ **Stacked bar** The stacked bar chart creates a single vertical bar for each set of related values. Each bar is divided into sections by horizontal lines. The resulting

345

bar represents the grand total, or sum of the values.

- **100% bar** The 100% bar chart is a style of stacked bar that displays each segment in a bar as a percentage rather than as individual units.

- **Line** The line chart shows related information as a series of horizontal lines in a "connect the dots" fashion. Typically these are used to display changes over a period of time.

- **Area line** Much like a stacked bar, the area line chart uses the line below it (rather than the X-axis) as its starting point. Thus, the end result is a grand total of one related set of data.

- **High-Low-Close** This type of chart is styled after the stock market charts you see in the newspaper that show you three values — a high value, a low value, and a closing value.

- **Pie** The old, familiar pie chart is simply a circle sliced into wedges, each representing a value in a single list of numbers.

- **X-Y** Sometimes called a scatter chart, this type of chart plots points against an X and a Y axis to display the relationships between pairs of numbers.

GETTING READY

Designing a chart takes some forethought, just as creating a database or a spreadsheet does. You'll need to consider in advance just what message your chart should convey to the observer. Generally speaking, it's a good idea to make charts as simple as possible. Don't try to include too much data or other information (such as labels) into a single chart. It's better to

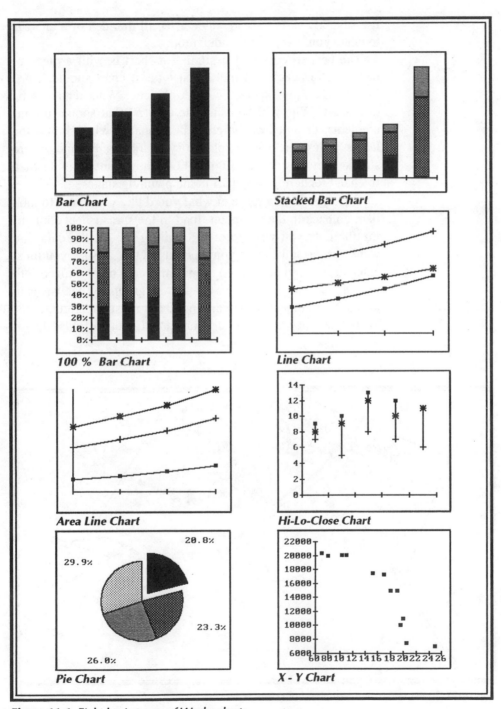

Bar Chart

Stacked Bar Chart

100 % Bar Chart

Line Chart

Area Line Chart

Hi-Lo-Close Chart

Pie Chart

X - Y Chart

Figure 11-1 *Eight basic types of Works charts*

use several charts instead, since after all the idea of a chart is to make your data easily understood.

The best way to start designing a chart is with a piece of paper and a pencil in hand. What type of chart should it be? Pie, bar, X-Y, or one of the other choices? What data will be displayed? Who will be using the chart? What should the increments, or units, of the chart be? Finally, what should the labels, titles, or other explanatory markings be and where should they be placed? Figure 11-2 shows an example of a freehand rendering of a chart in the planning stages.

Once you have a sense of what you'd like your chart to look like, go back to the computer, load in the spreadsheet containing the data you want to chart, and dig in. All the data you want to chart must be in your spreadsheet. If it isn't, you must enter it. Also, to be charted, your data must be organized into ranges that can be easily selected in groups. That is, each group of numbers you want to chart must be contiguous. Works cannot jump around your spreadsheet to find data for the chart.

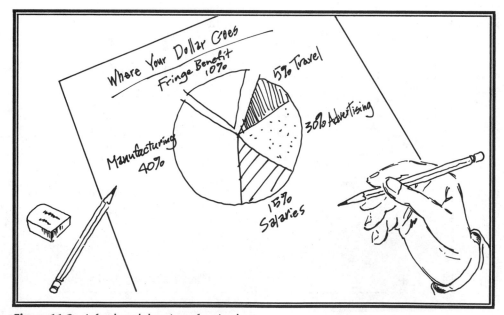

Figure 11-2. A freehand drawing of a pie chart

Opening the Budget File

We'll be using the Budget spreadsheet from Chapter 9 as data for charts in this chapter, so you should find that file and load it into Works using the File/Open command.

It's likely that your bank, prior to loaning you some capital to open your proposed branch store, will request a meeting with you. Naturally the loan officer will want to see some convincing figures on the expected revenues and profits before making the loan. What better opportunity to try out some creative chart making to emphasize your point?

CREATING YOUR FIRST BAR CHART

For openers, let's chart your estimated gross profits over four quarters, since you expect those figures to grow radically. You should show this type of growth using a line chart or a bar chart with time plotted from left to right, and profits charted vertically, as in Figure 11-3.

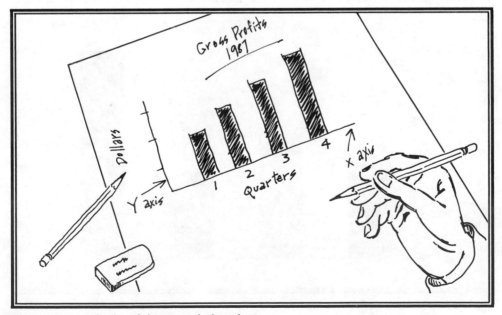

Figure 11-3. *A freehand drawing of a bar chart*

Here's how to create the new chart.

1. Select the range B26:E26 since this is the range we want to chart.

2. Choose Chart/New.

   This tells Works that you want to create a new chart. CHART appears on the status line, indicating you are on the Chart screen. This is where you define your chart. Notice that the menu bar changes, too.

   As a default, Works assumes that you want to create a simple bar chart, so you don't have to make any other changes before creating your first example on screen.

3. Choose Chart/View (or press SHIFT-F10) to display the chart. In a few seconds, the spreadsheet will vanish, being replaced by the bar chart, as you see in Figure 11- 4. This is called the chart view.

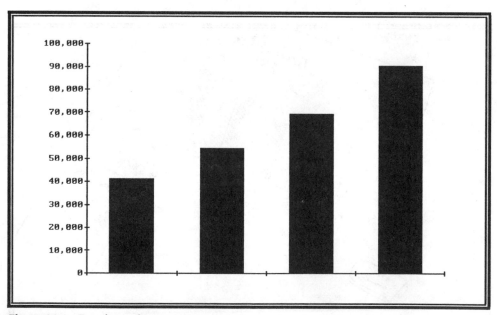

Figure 11-4. *Bar chart of B26 to E26*

Exactly how the chart looks will depend on your hardware. On some systems the chart will appear in color, on others, it will show up only in black and white, green and white, amber and white, or various intensities of these colors.

Notice that the default chart has no titles, axis labels, or data labels. These are options that you have to add manually if you want them. We'll get to that soon.

Notice also that Works is smart enough to *scale* the chart reasonably, from the lowest value to the highest value in the range, so that the chart looks good. On the Y-axis (the vertical line on the left), tick marks are computed and labeled automatically by Works in whatever it considers to be the most logical manner. You can adjust this later if you want.

Adding Some Labels

You can see just from glancing at this chart that the first year's growth has been relatively steady over the four quarters. To the casual observer, though, this chart means next to nothing without some labels to clarify the significance of the axes.

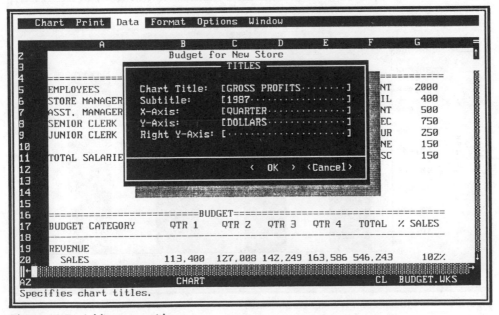

Figure 11-5. Adding some titles

1. Press ESC. This erases the chart view and returns you to the Chart screen.

2. Choose Data/Titles. A dialog box appears. Fill it in as you see in Figure 11-5.

   (Leave Right Y-Axis blank, since we're not using a right Y axis.)

3. View the chart again by choosing Chart/View or pressing SHIFT-F10. Now your chart looks like Figure 11-6.

One last thing you may want to do is have the exact amounts of each quarter's profits displayed on the chart. Here's how to do that.

1. Make sure the cells B26:E26 are still selected.

2. Choose Data/Data Labels. A dialog box appears. The first line, 1st Y-series, should be highlighted.

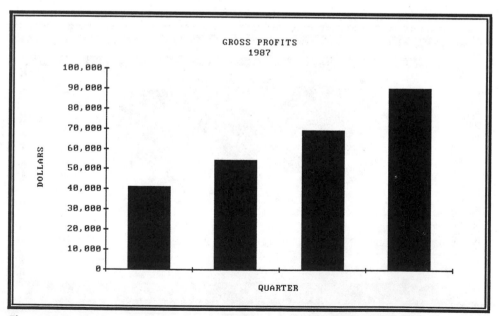

Figure 11-6. *The bar chart with labels and titles*

3. Choose <Create>. This plugs the selected range of cells (B26:E26) into the chart's *Y-series*.

A Y-series is simply a number of associated data elements (numbers) that you want to chart. In this chart, we plotted only one series of values (gross profits for four quarters), so we only have one Y-series. Works automatically plugged the selected cells' values into the 1st Y-series, but, as you will see later, you can plot up to six Y-series on a single graph.

4. View the chart again.

5. Now your chart shows the exact dollar amounts of each bar as in Figure 11-7.

NAMING AND SAVING YOUR CHART

Once you've created a chart, it is stored on disk whenever you save your spreadsheet. All aspects of the chart are saved, including a descriptive name that you can assign. Each spread-

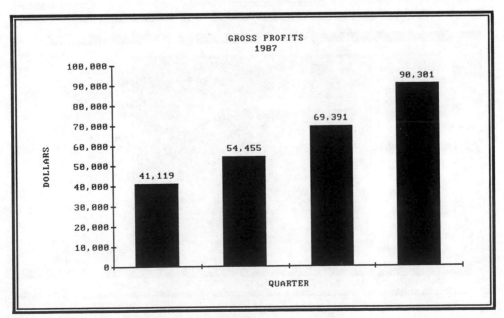

Figure 11-7. *Dollar figures appear at tops of bars*

sheet can have as many as eight charts stored along with it. You switch between charts using the Chart menu.

How to Give Your Chart a Name

Works assigns a default name to each chart you create, so you don't have to name a chart if you don't mind the default names (Chart1, Chart2, and so on). But if you use the default names you'll have to view each chart to know what's on it. To avoid that inconvenience, name your charts descriptively. In this case, we'll name the chart Profits, Bar, via these steps:

1. Press ESC to erase the chart view and return to the Chart screen.

2. Now name the chart by choosing Chart/Charts.

A dialog box appears, listing the names of all the charts associated with the current spreadsheet. Only Chart1 appears, as shown in Figure 11-8, since you've only made one chart.

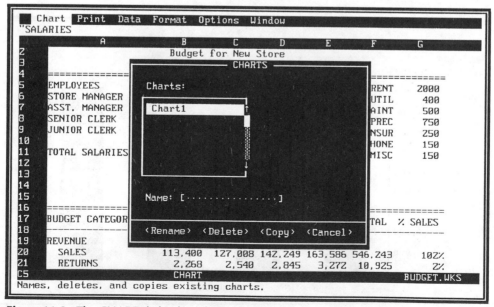

Figure 11-8. The CHART dialog box showing one chart

3. Move to the Name field and enter

   Name: [Profits, Bar......]

4. Now when you open the Chart menu, the new name appears at the bottom of the menu, with a mark beside it, indicating that this is the active chart.

How to Save a Chart on Disk

As with any other kind of Works document, make a habit of saving your charts regularly during a session as a precaution against an accidental loss of data in case of a hardware or software malfunction. So, before we continue, save the chart on disk now using the following steps:

1. Press F10 to exit the Chart screen and return to the spreadsheet.

2. Choose File/Save to save the spreadsheet and the newly named chart.

How to Delete Unwanted Charts

Sometimes you'll want to delete unwanted or outdated charts from a spreadsheet to eliminate confusion when selecting which charts to view. You use <Delete> in the CHARTS dialog box to do this. Here are the steps, even though we're not going to delete any charts now:

1. Choose Chart/Charts.

2. In the list box, select the chart name you want to delete.

3. Choose <Delete>.

The selected chart will no longer appear on the Chart menu, making room for other charts. (Remember, only eight charts per spreadsheet are allowed.)

Copying Charts for Later Modification

Often you'll want to try experimenting with a chart once you've defined its essentials. Maybe you want to try presenting the same data in a different format (pie chart, line chart, or other chart), or alter the titles and labels, or make other modifications. A good way to do this is to copy the existing chart to a new chart that you can then fiddle with.

These steps will copy the Profits bar chart to a new chart called Chart1.

1. Choose Chart/Charts. The CHART dialog box appears.

2. Highlight Profits, Bar. Move to the Name area and type in **Net Sales vs. Profits**. Then choose <Copy>.

ADDING A SECOND Y-SERIES

Now open the Charts menu and notice that a new chart called Net Sales vs. Profits has been created by Works and automatically selected as the active chart. This is the new copy of the chart you were working on. Let's modify it.

Add another set of bars to display net sales for each quarter. This way we can see the relationship between net sales and gross profits on a single chart.

1. Choose Chart/Define to get back into the Chart screen. This is necessary if you want to make changes to the chart itself. (You can alter data from the spreadsheet level and see it reflected in the chart, but more on that later.)

2. Select cells B22:E22 (net sales for the four quarters). There isn't a Select menu, so you will have to use the mouse or SHIFT-arrow keys to make the selection.

3. To make these values show up as a second set of bars, you have to assign them to a second Y-series. Do this by choosing Data/2nd Y-series.

4. Now, using Data/Titles, change the Chart Title to

Net Sales vs. Profits ↵

Leave everything else in the TITLES dialog box the same. Notice that as you typed, the title scrolled left within the box. Titles may be very long if you wish, though how much fits on the screen or on your printouts depends solely on the font sizes you use in your chart.

5. View the chart now. It should look like Figure 11-9.

Not a bad-looking chart, only you can't tell what each of the sets of bars represents, and also the data labels on the first Y-series are overlaying the bars of the second Y-series. Let's fix that now.

1. Press ESC.

2. Choose Data/Data Labels. The first line of the series reads

1st Y (B26:E26)

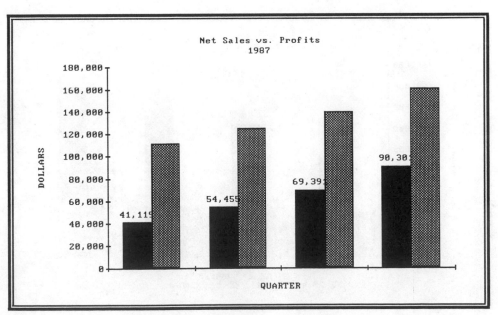

Figure 11-9. *A bar chart with a second Y-series*

3. Choose <Delete> to remove the labels from the chart.

Next, to clarify what each set of bars is for, you'll have to add some *legends*. Legends, sometimes called keys, are the little patterned or colored boxes at the bottom of the chart used to clarify what the various bars represent.

1. Choose Data/Legends. The 1st Y-Series comes up highlighted.

2. In the Legend area, type **Gross Profits** ↵.

3. Repeat step 1, but press ↓ to select 2nd Y-Series, and in the Legend area, type in **Net Sales** ↵.

4. Now view the chart. It should look like Figure 11-10.

You can see now that gross profits have risen slightly in comparison to net sales. Also, you can see from the chart that gross profits appear to approximately equal 50 percent of net sales.

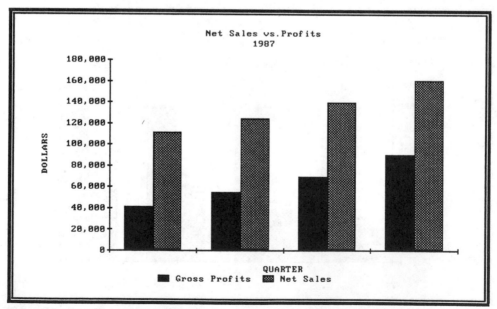

Figure 11-10. *Chart with two legends*

Incidentally, instead of typing in the legend for each Y-series yourself, you can specify the address of a cell containing the label you want to use.

CREATING A LINE CHART

Let's try viewing the currently displayed data in a line chart instead of the bar chart layout. As you will see, jumping from one chart format to another is a simple process. First, copy the existing chart to a new one named Profits, Line using the steps detailed above in the section "Copying Charts for Later Modification."

1. Choose Format/Line.

2. Choose Chart/View.

Suddenly the same data is represented as points along two lines. Let's fill out the picture a little by adding another line, representing Cost of Sales, to the chart.

1. Select B24:E24.

2. Choose Data/3rd Y-Series.

3. Choose Data/Legends.

4. Press ↓ twice to highlight 3rd Y.

5. Enter the legend

   Cost of Sales ↵

Adding Grid Lines

Now add some *grid lines* to make the chart easier to understand, and change the title.

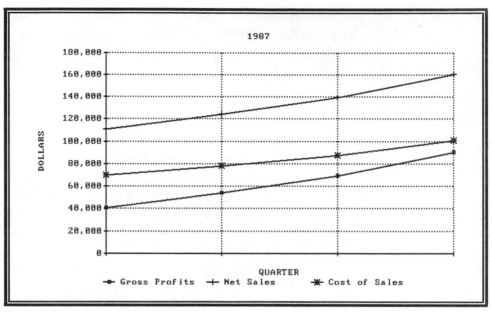

Figure 11-11. *Line chart with grid showing*

1. Choose Options/X-Axis. A dialog box appears.

2. Turn on the Grid lines check box and press ↲.

3. Repeat the process using the Options/Y-Axis command.

4. Choose Data/Titles and erase Chart Title: by pressing the BACKSPACE key once.

5. Press ↲.

6. View the chart. Your screen should now look like Figure 11-11.

Though we plotted only three sets of data, you can see from the DATA dialog box that you can plot up to six Y-Series if you want to.

MAKING A PIE CHART

Next to bar charts, pie charts are probably the most popular display format, particularly when the intention is to portray parts as a percentage of the whole. Pie charts can only display a single Y-series, however, so there are certain limitations to this type.

Let's try charting out the store's labor expenses to get an idea of the relative proportions of each category.

1. Choose Chart/New.

2. Select cells F29:F31.

3. Choose Data/1st Y-Series.

4. Choose Format/Pie.

5. View the chart.

Notice that percentages are shown around the circle's perimeter. Since pie charts show a Y-series as portions (percentages) of a whole (100 percent), these markings will always display whenever you create a pie chart.

Adding Labels to the Pie Chart

Now add labels to the chart to communicate what each slice represents. Since you already have the labels in the spreadsheet (in column A), you don't have to type them in yourself. Just select the cells containing the labels you want to use and assign them to the X-axis. (Actually an X-axis doesn't really exist in a pie chart, but this technique does the trick anyway.) Use the Data menu to make the assignment.

1. Select A29:A31.

2. Choose Data/X-Series.

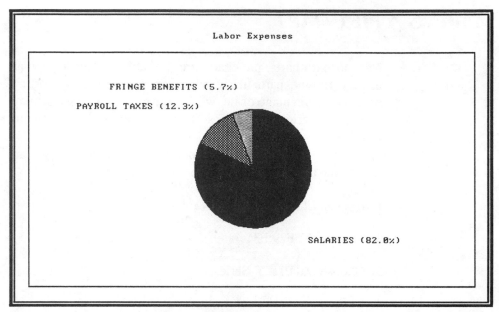

Figure 11-12. Pie chart with border and labels

3. Now add a few finishing touches. Choose Data/Titles and for the chart title, type in

Labor Expenses

4. Finally, let's add a border around the perimeter of the chart. To do this, choose Options/Show Border.

5. Redraw the chart. It should look like Figure 11-12.

Now the percentages appear in parentheses after each slice's label. Probably the first thing you noticed was that the pie is reduced in size. This is the trade-off you make when adding the labels. Also, depending on your setup and your chart, the percentage labels may overrun one another, or you may find the lettering looks too large compared to the graph. Overrunning text can often occur when adjacent pie sections are small, and thus are very close to each other. Try choosing Options/Format for B&W if you're using a color graphics adapter

(CGA) card in your computer. This may shrink the numbers enough to prevent an overlap.

Another solution is to rearrange the data in the spreadsheet so that small slices aren't next to each other in the pie. It may help to know that Works starts drawing a pie chart at the 12 o'clock position, working clockwise.

A final solution can be the use of the Explode command (which we'll explain in the next section), to move one of the slices out of the pie a little bit.

Exploding Sections of the Pie

Occasionally you'll want to emphasize a specific slice of a pie chart by *exploding* it: pulling it slightly out of the circle. You use the Format/Data Format command to do this. Say we want to emphasize the Fringe Benefits slice.

1. Choose Format/Data Format. A dialog box that lets you set up the appearance of each slice (color, pattern, and so on) pops up. Since Fringe Benefits is the third cell in our selection (from top to bottom), that corresponds to slice three of the pie.

2. Press ↓ twice to highlight 3.

3. Turn on the Exploded check box.

4. Choose <Format> (not <Format All> since we don't want to explode all of the slices) and press the SPACEBAR to format that slice.

5. View the chart. It should look like Figure 11-13.

6. Finally, using the Chart/Charts command, name your pie chart "Labor, pie" for future use.

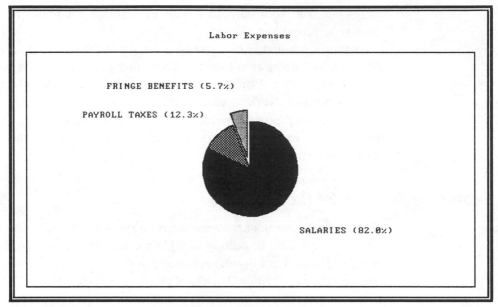

Figure 11-13. *Pie chart with a section exploded*

MAKING A 100-PERCENT BAR CHART

The 100% bar chart is a bit like a pie chart in that values are displayed as a percentage rather than as individual units of measurement. Thus, the scale on the Y-axis lists percentage, not units such as dollars, days, or pounds. Another way of thinking of this chart (and of the stacked bar charts of the next section) is to visualize piling grouped bars on top of one another instead of next to one another. Unlike pie charts, 100% bar charts plot multiple Y-series, not a single one. Each element in a Y-series is assigned to its own bar, so you need at least two series to convey any relevant information.

The big advantage of this type of bar is that as with a standard bar chart, more than one bar can be plotted at a time. It's like being able to plot multiple pie charts simultaneously. This type of chart is most useful for transforming an existing multiple-bar bar chart into a form that conveys percentage relationships of grouped bars instead of their absolute values.

As an example, let's convert the Net Sales vs. Profits chart to 100% bar format.

1. From the Chart screen, choose Chart/Charts and select the Net Sales vs. Profits chart.

2. Choose Format/100% Bar.

3. Choose Options/Y-Axis and set Gridlines on.

4. View the chart. It should look like the chart in Figure 11-14.

You can easily extract some useful information from this chart. For example, you can see that profits were about 27 percent of net sales in the first quarter, and rose to about 36 percent by the last quarter of 1987.

You may want to add labels to each section of each bar by selecting the appropriate cells and choosing Data/Data Labels, selecting the Y-series, and then <Create>. A label will appear

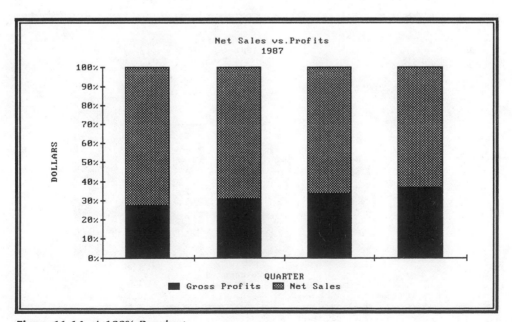

Figure 11-14. A 100% Bar chart

at the top of each bar in the series you select. One idea is to label the actual numerical value of each section of the bar. This way the Y-axis indicates percentage and the label reports actual amounts. Another use for a label would be to convey what's represented by each section, such as "Salaries" or "Expenses."

MAKING A STACKED BAR CHART

The stacked bar chart is similar to the 100% bar chart but in this type of chart, actual values of Y-series elements are displayed rather than their relative percentage of a whole. In effect, each bar displays a grand total of each set of associated bars. And instead of using the X-axis as the starting point for each new Y-series, Works uses the top of the bar that is being built upon. Thus, two grouped Y-series elements of sizes 300

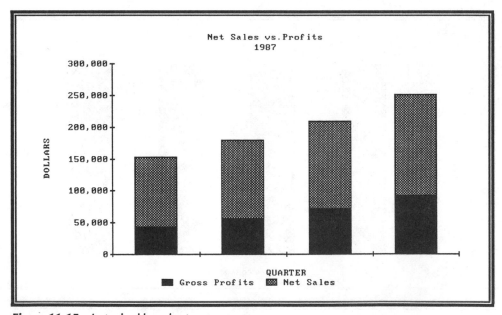

Figure 11-15. A stacked bar chart

and 500 result in a bar that shows a grand total of 800. Let's redisplay the 100% bar chart you just created in the form of a stacked bar.

1. Press ESC if the last chart is still on screen.

2. Choose Format/Stacked bar.

3. View the chart. It should look like that in Figure 11-15.

MAKING AN AREA LINE CHART

The area line chart works much the same way as the stacked bar chart. As in the stacked bar chart, each Y-series is computed and plotted using the line below it as its X-axis. The result is a cumulative or grand-total effect, with one Y-series

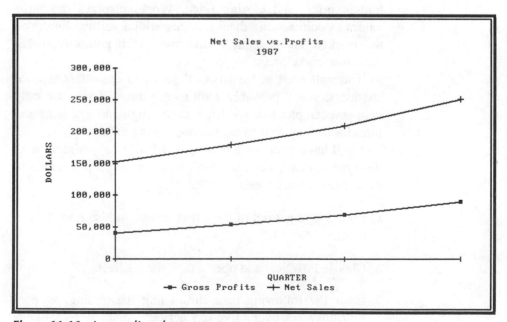

Figure 11-16. *An area line chart*

adding to the previous one. The only significant difference is that data values are displayed as points along a line instead of as bars.

Try switching the last chart to area line format via the following steps:

1. Press ESC if the last chart is still on your screen.

2. Choose Format/Area line.

3. View the chart. It should look like that in Figure 11-16.

MAKING A HIGH-LOW-CLOSE CHART

High-low-close charts are typically used to report the selling prices of stocks, commodities, and mutual funds. As the name implies, this type of chart normally displays three Y-series of data, corresponding to an item's highest trading price, lowest trading price, and closing price. Works displays the three values as points, tying them together with a vertical line. You use markers and legends to indicate which points represent high, low, and close.

You will need at least two Y-series to draw this type of chart, and you'll probably want to use three. If you use only two, you can plot low and high prices, high and low temperatures for the day, and so on, but not closing values.

We'll have to create a new spreadsheet to experiment with this type of chart, since we don't have any appropriate data in the existing spreadsheets.

1. Press F10 to get out of the Chart screen and back to spreadsheet.

2. Choose File/New and open a new spreadsheet.

3. Enter the following data chronicling the trading price of Frazmus stock over a five-day period:

	A	B	C	D	E	F
1		Monday	Tuesday	Wednesday	Thursday	Friday
2	High	9	10	13	12	11
3	Low	7	5	8	7	6
4	Close	8	9	12	10	11

4. Choose Chart/Define.

5. Select Format/Hi-Lo-Close.

6. Select the range B2:F2 and choose Data/1st Y-Series to assign those numbers to the first series.

7. Select the range B3:F3 and assign it to the 2nd Y-Series.

8. Select the range B4:F4 and assign it to the 3rd Y-Series.

9. Select the range B1:F1 and assign it to the X-Series. This will create weekday labels on the horizontal axis.

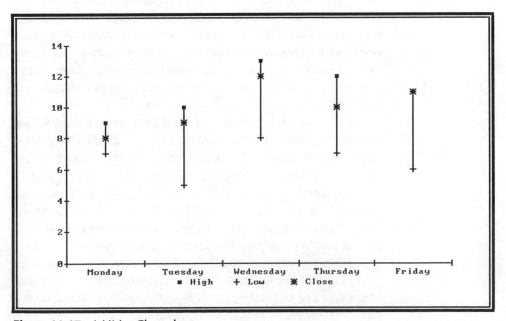

Figure 11-17. *A Hi-Lo-Close chart*

If you view the chart now, you'll see five vertical lines on the screen, each one with three dots on it. Now enter legends to show what the dots correspond to.

1. Choose Data/Legends.

2. Enter **High** as the legend for the first Y-series.

3. Repeat the process for the two other series, entering the legends **Low** and **Close** for 2nd-Y and 3rd-Y respectively.

4. Add titles if you want to.

5. View the chart. It should look something like Figure 11-17.

Making an X-Y chart

X-Y charts, often called *scatter charts*, are used for statistical analysis because they can depict correlations between two sets of data. For example, you might want to show auto insurance rates as a function of drivers' ages, or a company's stock prices as correlated to its profits. Of course, there are many other applications, notably in scientific studies where cause-and-effect relationships in experimental environments are analyzed.

To plot an X-Y graph, you need two sets of data whose relationship you want to display. One set of data is plotted against the Y-axis, the other against the X-axis. Each value is plotted as a dot, or *data point*, on the chart. If there is perfect positive correlation between the X and Y data, the data points form a 45-degree line starting in the lower-left corner of the chart. Perfect negative correlation results in the opposite effect; that is, a 45-degree line starting in the lower-right corner and rising toward the upper left. If there is very little correlation, the data points are evenly distributed across the chart. Other types of correlation, such as logarithmic, have their own characteristic patterns such as arcs or S-curves.

Let's create an X-Y chart showing the correlation between wolf and deer populations as they change over time. We'll use data from a fictitious research study.

1. Open a new spreadsheet and enter the following data:

	A	B	C	D	E	F	G
1		Dec	Jan	Feb	Mar	Apr	May
2							
3	WOLVES	20342	20021	17505	14996	10005	7412
4	DEER	7521	10301	15231	18021	19547	20500

2. Choose Chart/New.

3. Choose Format/X-Y.

4. Select B3:G3 and assign it to the 1st Y-series.

5. Select B4:G4 and assign it to the X-series (using Data/X-Series).

6. Enter the following information for the titles:

Chart Title:	[Wolves vs. Deer..............]
Subtitle:	[Population Correlation....]
X-Axis	[Deer.............................]
Y-Axis	[Wolves..........................]

7. View the chart. It should look like Figure 11-18.

The chart clearly indicates the negative correlation between wolf and deer populations.

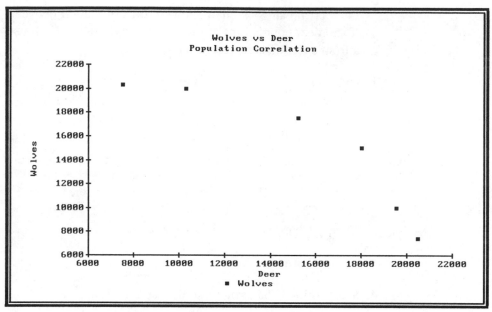

Figure 11-18. An X-Y chart

COMBINING LINES AND BARS ON A CHART

A choice from the Options menu lets you place bars and lines on the same graph. This is useful when you want to emphasize one series while leaving others to play a background role in the appearance of your chart. Here's how:

1. Make up your line or bar chart as you usually would, with as many Y-series as you need.

2. Choose Options/Mixed Line & Bar.

3. A dialog box appears, letting you decide which series you want to display as lines and which as bars. Just set the buttons in the box.

4. View the chart.

FINE-TUNING YOUR CHARTS

Once you get the hang of chart making, you will probably want to embellish your creations to make them more professional looking for presentations or simply to render them more legible. Works provides numerous options for fine-tuning your charts along these lines. None of these alterations is usually required before viewing or printing a chart, since Works sets most of them automatically, but there's no replacement for a good eye. Once you actually look at a chart the first time, chances are you'll want to change it at least a little.

Table 11-1 lists all the changes you can make and indicates where you must be to do them.

The most common alterations you'll want to make are to change the fonts, change the patterns and colors, add a border, add grid lines, and alter the scale of one or both of the axes. It's also likely that you'll want to add labels along the horizontal axis that are based on cells in your spreadsheet. Other

Alteration	Menu
Change fonts for titles	Print/Title Font
Change fonts for all other chart text	Print/Other Font
Change patterns/colors for bars, slices	Format/Data Format
Change markers for data points	Format/Data Format
Change the scale of the X-axis	Options/X-Axis
Add grid lines to the X-axis	Options/X-Axis
Change the scale of the Y-axis	Options/Y-Axis
Add grid lines to the Y-axis	Options/Y-Axis
Add a second Y-axis on the right	Options/Right Y-Axis
Add a Y-axis with another scale	Options/Two Y-Axes
Temporarily hide your legends	Options/Legend
Add a border around a chart	Options/Border
Add X-Axis labels based on cell data	Data/X-Axis

Table 11-1. Alterations You Can Make to Your Charts

options, particularly adding a second Y-axis with another scale, are rarely needed.

You already know how to add borders and grid lines from some of the examples. Let's now look at these other options.

How to Change a Chart's Fonts

You can alter the fonts used in the screen display and printouts of your charts. (See more about printing later in this chapter, in the section entitled "Printing It Out.") As with other tools in Works, the fonts available will vary, depending on your printer. After you select a printer from the Print menu (or during the installation procedure), either of the FONTS dialog boxes (there are two) will tell you what fonts are available for your printer, and in what sizes. One of the dialog boxes lets you choose the font for the title at the top of your chart. Normally you'll want that to be in larger type. The other one selects the type style for all other text on the chart, including axes titles, data point labels, scale, and legends. For display on the screen, the font called "screen" usually looks best.

To select fonts, do the following:

1. Make sure you've selected the proper printer using the Print/Select Chart Printer command. (You must do this from the Chart screen.)

2. Choose Print/Title Font. The FONT dialog box appears. Select the font style and size for the chart title.

3. Choose Print/Other Font. Then select the font style and size for all other text on the chart.

If you want to preview the approximate effect your font selections will have on your printouts, you can. You do this by choosing Options/Show Printer Fonts. Then, each time you view the chart, Works draws a reasonable facsimile of what the final output on your type of printer will be. Be forewarned, though: this increases the time Works takes to draw a chart on screen, and is largely inaccurate. However, you can use this technique to dress up charts intended for screen viewing only (for example, for presentations). If you do this, you'll have to fiddle with the Other Font sizes a bit. A good starting place is 20 point.

You will probably have to experiment a bit to determine which fonts you like best. Unfortunately there's no substitute for printing out lots of charts since the proportions and resolution of fonts on your screen will most likely differ from the final printed appearance. In general, you'll be best advised to use large sizes (around 32 or so) for titles and something a little smaller for other text.

For business charts, you should stick with simple fonts such as Helvetica, Modern, and Roman. Script fonts are generally less effective since they're less readable. The size you choose for the remainder of a chart's text depends on the type of chart and the size of the labels and legends. As you saw in the sections on pie charts and X-Y charts, too large a font size can cause larger labels, legends, and numbers to overrun one another, so you don't want to use too large a size.

How to Change the Data Format

The pattern and color of bars and pie slices and the shape of the data point markers on line charts can be set from the Format/Data Format dialog box. The box differs somewhat depending on the type of chart you're making. Pie charts have a smaller dialog box with fewer options than do line, X-Y, and bar charts.

Be aware that there are two completely separate settings (and dialog boxes) for these settings. One is for printing. The other is for screen appearance. Which one you see is controlled by the Options/List Printer Formats command. If this command is checked, your dialog boxes will report and allow alteration of the printer settings, not the screen settings. If you're trying to change a pie slice's color on the screen and nothing happens, take a look at the Options menu to see if List Printer Formats is on. The default setting for new charts will show screen formats.

Pie Charts

Changing the color and patterns of a pie chart is fairly self explanatory.

1. Just select the number of the slice you want to change, recalling that Works numbers the slices beginning at the top of the pie and then moving clockwise.

2. Choose the color and/or pattern you want for that slice.

3. Then choose <Format All> (to format all the slices the same way) or <Format> to affect only the selected slice.

If you are setting the printer formats, it's likely the only colors listed will be Auto and Black, since few printers can print in color. Works automatically assigns various hatch patterns to slices if Auto is used.

The number of colors available for screen formatting depends on your system. Again, experimentation is your best bet. With a monochrome monitor (noncolor screen) and with most printers, you'll have to rely on changing the pattern (rather than the color) of slices if Works hasn't done a good enough job automatically.

Other Types of Charts

The dialog box for other types of charts is a little more complex.

1. First you choose the Y-series you want to affect.

2. Choose the pattern and/or color you want for that series.

3. Then choose <Format All> (to format all the series the same way) or <Format> to affect only the selected series.

4. If you are working with a line or X-Y chart, you can assign a specific marker that appears at data points. The choices are as shown in the dialog box. Choosing Auto from the box allows Works to automatically assign markers as it sees fit.

How to Alter the Scaling

The Y-axes of the bar, line, X-Y and Hi-Lo-Close charts you make are labeled with numbers. These numbers indicate the scale that Works automatically calculates based on the upper and lower values in each graph's Y-series. Based on these values, Works arrives at reasonable figures for the upper and lower bounds of the Y-axis, computes the intervals in between these bounds, and labels the Y-axis accordingly. The result is that your chart is scaled in a way that allows all of your data to appear on the page and screen at once. The same automatic process occurs for the X-axis in X-Y charts.

However, there may be times when you'll want to override this feature. A typical example is when you want to *zoom* in for a close-up display of just a portion of your data so that more of the details are discernible. The Y-axis and X-axis commands from the Options menu allow you to do this.

As outlined in the next table, there are three settings in each dialog box that affect the scaling (though the X-AXIS dialog box only lets you set these values when plotting an X-Y chart):

Setting	Explanation
Minimum	Sets the lowest value on the axis (bottom of axis)
Maximum	Sets the highest value on the axis (top of axis)
Interval	Sets how many numbers Works should skip between tick marks on the axis

For example, say your data actually ranges from 0 to 20,000, but you want to chart only the data falling between 500 and 700. Fill in the dialog box as follows:

Setting	Explanation
Minimum	500
Maximum	700
Interval	25

To return the settings to normal, just type the word **AUTO** into each field.

Settings for the X-axis, and for a second Y-axis (in the case of double Y-axis charts), work the same way.

Note: Also notice that that you can see and change the current chart type from the Type option box in the Y-AXIS dialog box. This is the only way, short of viewing a graph, to see what type is currently selected (besides Pie).

PRINTING IT OUT

Your real moment of glory comes when you finally print out your charts on paper. Note, however, that some printers cannot print charts because they have no graphics capability. Generally speaking, daisywheel printers fall into this group.

On the other hand, most dot-matrix printers will be able to print charts, as will most popular brands of plotters and some laser printers. Check your printer's instruction manual and/or the Works manual if you are in doubt about your printer's ability to print charts from Works.

You can print charts from either the Spreadsheet or the Chart screen, but it's best to do it from the latter since it's then easier to make adjustments if settings aren't correct.

How to Print a Chart

Before printing, there are a few details to attend to. Assuming your chart is completed to your satisfaction, or at least finalized enough to experiment with, follow these steps to get the printer or plotter rolling.

1. Turn your printer on and make sure it's connected to the computer, is on-line, and has paper in it.

2. Choose Print/Select Chart Printer to make sure you have told Works what type of printer you have, whether you are

feeding in sheets of paper manually or using continuous feed paper, and what port your printer is connected to.

3. Choose Print/Layout if you want to alter the layout settings. (If you don't, then skip this step.)

   The LAYOUT dialog box appears, asking for details about margins, desired chart size, your paper size, and the chart's orientation on the paper. The defaults are as follows:

Top Margin:	1.0"
Left Margin:	1.3"
Chart Height:	9"
Chart Width:	6"
Page Length:	11"
Page Width:	8.5"
Orientation:	Landscape

   Landscape means the chart will be rotated 90 degrees during printing so that it runs the length of the paper rather than the width. The other orientation option, Portrait, sets the chart to print vertically on a normal page. Use the Portrait setting if you are incorporating a chart into a report and don't want the reader to have to rotate the page to read the chart. However, printing in Landscape orientation will produce a larger chart than will Portrait.

   Normally you won't have to change any of the settings, since Works will nicely place the chart in the middle of a horizontally oriented page. Occasionally you may want to shrink the chart, or place it in a specific spot on the page.

4. Once everything is set correctly, press ↵. If you didn't make any changes, just press ESC.

5. Choose Print/Print. The PRINT dialog box appears, asking how many copies you want to print, or if you want to print to a disk file instead of directly to the printer. Printing to a disk file lets you print the file out later (using the DOS COPY command), rather than waiting for the printing process now. If you print to a file, you must set the Print to

File check box on and specify the file name. See the final section of this chapter for how to print from a file.

6. Press ↵.

7. If you're printing to the printer, prepare to take a little break. The chart printing process often lasts several minutes. If you decide to stop the printing process, press ESC. You will be asked if you want to continue or abort your printout.

Printing to a Plotter

If you plan to print a chart with several colors using a plotter, there's an additional step.

1. Begin printing as described in the last section.

2. Next, you will see a dialog box:

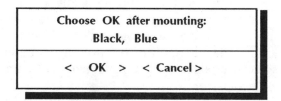

Works is trying to tell you to *mount* the correct pens on the plotter. Install the pens and press ↵. You will see this message again later if you are using multiple colors.

How to Print from a Disk File

Sometimes, especially if you're creating lots of charts, it makes sense to defer the printing of the charts until later. There are two ways to do this. As you know, you can create up to eight charts per spreadsheet. So the first technique is to design all eight charts, save them with the spreadsheet, and print them out when time allows.

The second technique prints charts from disk files. Follow these steps to create the chart print file so that you can print it later.

1. From the PRINT dialog box, you tell Works to save your chart as a disk file, give the file a name, and press ↵.

2. When you're ready to print, leave Works and return to DOS.

3. Set up your printer or plotter with paper and turn it on.

4. Use the DOS COPY command to print the file. For example, say you printed to a file called SALES. You'd then issue the command:

COPY SALES LPT1: ↵

to send the file to the printer or plotter connected to the LPT1: port. Change the port name if your printer or plotter is connected to another port.

The advantage to this technique for printing is that it lets you create more than eight charts per spreadsheet. Theoretically, you can create an infinite number of charts this way, assuming you have the disk space to hold them. The chart disk file even remains on disk in its original form after the associated spreadsheet is altered or erased. Thus, the disk storage required for the charts is minimized, but these charts will not reflect changes in your spreadsheet's data that you may make later on.

Chapter

Pulling It All Together

Twelve

Once you've created documents using Works' four basic tools, you have the option of combining them to produce a variety of documents that couldn't be achieved via any one of the tools alone. Each tool — word processor, spreadsheet, database, and communications — can be used individually for what it does best, with the resulting documents merged through Works' built-in integration ability in a number of ways.

Previous chapters have described how to copy data between documents of a single type, such as from one word processing document to another. As you have probably gathered by now, the commands used to do this within each tool are identical: you open both documents, select the section you want to copy, open the window of the destination document, place the cursor, and press ↵. That's all there is to it. Though the techniques for integration between documents of different types are a little more complex, they can result in considerable timesaving, since they eliminate the need to reenter data or to cut and paste paper.

Note: If you want to move (rather than copy) data between documents, do not use the Move command. You must instead use the Copy command, and then delete the original data. This restriction within the Works program is designed to prevent you from accidentally deleting text or data.

Figure 12-1 depicts the major avenues for sharing information between the Works tools.

383

Actually, more variations than displayed here are possible. For example, you can send and receive database and spreadsheet documents via the communications tool. However, we'll restrict the discussion of integration to its most common uses and leave to your imagination and experimentation the myriad other permutations of data transfer among the tools. This chapter will explain how to integrate word processor documents with the following:

- Text received via communications

- Spreadsheet and database cells

- Charts

- Database reports

- Database records to create form letters, mailing labels, and forms

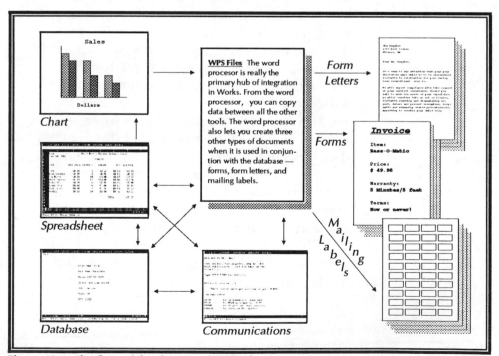

Figure 12-1. The flow of data between Works documents

Also covered in this chapter are techniques for exchanging information between the Works database and spreadsheet.

Using the knowledge gained in this chapter, you could pull together a complex, professional-looking report containing formatted text, spreadsheet charts, a database report, and portions of a spreadsheet. Figure 12-2 shows an example of such a document. Then, using a names and address list stored in a database, you could tell Works to print a personalized copy of the report for each person. As a final step, you can use the same database information to print mailing labels for each recipient's envelope. Unfortunately, Works won't lick the envelopes for you, but what do you want for less than $200?

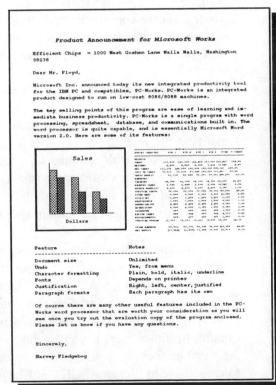

Figure 12-2.

You can combine portions of Works documents into a single integrated product

INTEGRATING WORD PROCESSOR DOCUMENTS

The word processor is really the primary hub of integration activities in Works. From the word processor, you can copy data between all the other tools and you can also create three other types of documents — forms, form letters, and mailing labels. Let's look at these capabilities one at a time, from the point of view of the word processor.

Pulling Communications Documents into the Word Processor

As detailed in Chapter 7, files created in the word processor, spreadsheet, or database tools can be sent to other computers using the Works communications tool. However, it's also the case that files you receive via a communications link can be pulled into the word processor, modified, and used in various ways.

For example, you may want to include a copy of a memo you received via electronic mail in the letter you are drafting as a response to that memo, or in some other document. Additionally, if the text you received is in the form of a list, or a table of numbers (with columns separated by tabs), you could pull it directly into a Works spreadsheet or database document. Let's look at some of these possibilities and the steps you would use to integrate communications files into the word processor.

As you know, there are two ways to receive text files via communications: through text capture and through a protocol transfer. Formatted or ASCII text files should be received using the protocol transfer. Electronic mail, stock quotes, and other wire service information should be received using text capture. In either case, if you intend to use a received file in the word processor, you'll want to insure that it's either a Microsoft Word file, an ASCII text file, or one of the file types that the conversion program provided with Works can modify. (See Appendix B for details about file conversions.)

For the purposes of this chapter, we'll assume that the file is compatible and can be opened by the Works word processor. With that in mind, the steps to pull a communications file into the word processor are simple.

1. Choose File/Open.

2. The OPEN dialog box appears. The file you want to open will not appear in the list box unless you gave the file an extension that begins with a W. If you know the name of the file, the simplest thing to do is to just type in its name. Otherwise, change the text area to read

   ```
   *.*
   ```

   and press ↵. All files on the current drive will be listed. Then select the file by highlighting it and pressing ↵.

3. Works is smart enough to realize that the file isn't a legitimate Works file and will ask you, via a dialog box, what tool you want to pull it into.

   ```
   (o) Word Processor
   ( ) Spreadsheet
   ( ) Database
   ```

   Choose Word Processor. The file will be opened just as normal Works word processor files are, and may be edited in the usual manner. However, if as you are editing you notice certain oddities or problems with the file, particularly regarding incorrect word-wrapping or margins, this may be the result of extra paragraph marks in the file. You may also see Greek letters or other strange symbols. Please refer to Appendix B of this text for suggested remedies.

Pulling Spreadsheet and Database Information into the Word Processor

Getting a section of a spreadsheet or a database to appear in a word processing document is actually quite simple, and follows the normal rules for copying data between documents.

1. First, open the source and destination documents.

2. Open the database or spreadsheet window and select the cells you want to copy. You should be in list view if copying from the database.

3. Choose Edit/Copy or press SHIFT-F3.

4. Jump to the word processor document, position the cursor where you want the data to be inserted, and press ⏎.

Works makes a copy of the selected data and drops it into the document. However, there are a couple of things to notice. First, Works automatically puts tabs between the cells in each row or record. Depending on the page layout and tab settings in your document, you may have to alter the tab settings to get the columns lined up properly.

Next, if the number of cells you want to insert is too wide to fit within your margins, Works will mess up the formatting by wrapping rows to the next line. You may want to select the whole table and, if your printer supports it, choose a smaller font size. Works will adjust the line-wraps according to the appointed size. If that doesn't work, you might try decreasing the left and right page margins (from the Print/LAYOUT dialog box) to fit more text on the page. If that doesn't work, then you'll have to decrease the number of cells you want to copy.

Copying from the Word Processor to the Database or Spreadsheet

You may want to reverse the process just outlined to send word processing files (or text files received via the communications tool) into a spreadsheet or database.

Works expects text files intended for the database and spreadsheet to have tab marks between columns and to have a paragraph mark at the end of each line of data. Recall from the word processing chapters that a tab mark looks like a little → and that a paragraph mark looks like ¶. You should use the Options/Show All Characters command to verify that the tab and paragraph marks are where they're needed. Each tab mark will tell Works to jump one cell to the right before entering the next cell's data.

Here are the steps for copying the data.

1. Open both documents.

2. Select the text area from which you want to copy.

3. Choose Edit/Copy or press SHIFT-F3.

4. Jump to the spreadsheet or database document.

5. Place the cursor where you want to insert the data and then press ↲.

Caution: Works will insert your data beginning at the position of the highlighted cell and filling to the right and down. Any cells that get in the way of the new cells will have their data overwritten. You should make sure that your selection isn't larger than the space you have allotted for it in the database or spreadsheet. As an alternative, you can select a range in the destination spreadsheet before completing the Copy. Works will fill up only the selected range.

Inserting Charts into the Word Processor

If you have a printer that can print charts, you can have Works insert your charts into word processing documents. When you print the document, the chart will automatically be inserted at a predetermined spot on the page. You can scale the chart so that it prints at a specific size, also.

To insert a chart into a document, do the following:

1. First, obviously, you have to create the chart (see Chapter 11 for details about making charts).

2. Open the spreadsheet and the word processing documents.

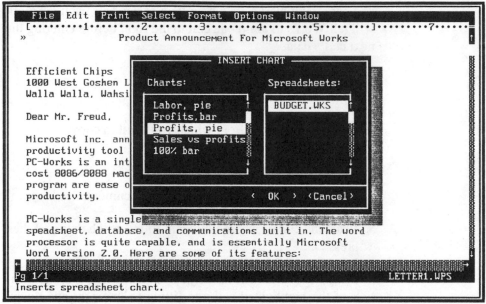

Figure 12-3. *Choosing a chart to insert into a WPS document*

3. Jump to the word processing document and position the cursor where you want the chart to be inserted.

4. Choose Edit/Insert Chart. The INSERT CHART dialog box appears, as you see in Figure 12-3.

5. From the dialog box, choose the spreadsheet. Then a list of charts associated with the chosen spreadsheet pops up in the other list box. Select the appropriate chart.

Works now pushes down the text to insert room for the chart, inserts a line like

```
>>                *chart BUDGET.WKS:Labor, pie*
```

and inserts a number of blank lines which are placeholders for the chart. You won't see the chart on the screen. It will only appear when you print the document; the blank lines on your screen indicate where it will appear. If you want to reposition the chart, you can copy or move the line just as if it were text.

You can also delete it should you change your mind about including it in your document.

Once the chart reference is inserted, you can alter the default size of the chart by putting the cursor on the chart line in the word processor file and choosing Format/Paragraph. A dialog box will pop up with the size settings in it.

```
Left Indent:  [0"......]    Chart Height: [4"......]
Right Indent: [0"......]
                                Orientation:
Space Before: [1 li....]   ( ) Landscape
Space After:  [1 li....]   ( ) Portrait
```

The left and right indents are relative to the current margins. Change the settings as necessary.

Inserting Database Summary Reports into the Word Processor

You can save a database report as a disk file for later use by the word processor or even by the spreadsheet and database, if you want. You do this using the Save As command from the Report menu, and giving the file a name. All rows but the record rows are saved in the file so you end up with a file containing all the Intr and Summ rows, that is, titles, subtotals, and totals. Obviously this is just the kind of data you want to use for preparing summary reports or making charts to display the summaries. Once the file is saved, you pull it into the appropriate word processor (or other tool) using these steps.

1. Use File/Open to open the file that you saved the summary report in. Works asks what type of file you want to open it as.

2. Choose the appropriate tool from the dialog box.

3. Open the destination file.

4. Use the normal technique for copying data between two documents.

CREATING FORMS AND FORM LETTERS

By combining word processor text files and information stored in a database file, Works can print some pretty spiffy, timesaving forms and form letters. Forms include invoices, packing slips, order forms, and the like. You can either design the form yourself or use preprinted forms that you buy from a computer supply or stationery store. A close cousin to forms is the ubiquitous form letter: a computer-generated letter with the "personal" touch. Form letters eliminate the drudgery of retyping, or at least modifying a letter over and over in order to send the same basic missive to a number of recipients.

To create forms and form letters, you first create a word processor file with the basic text you want to print. Then, using the Edit/Insert Field command, you insert special placeholders into your word processor file. Each placeholder is the name of a field in the database holding the information you want inserted into the text. Typically that database will be a name and address list, though it could include other kinds of data as well, such as credit histories, students' grades, or scientific or other numerical information.

When you are ready to print the letter or form, use the Print/Merge command. The database information is inserted into the text by Works, producing one printed letter or form for each (non-hidden) record in the database. Specifically, here are the steps you should follow to create a form or form letter and print it.

1. Create or open the database file that will hold the information you want Works to insert.

2. Create the text file that you want printed, but leave out the words or numbers that will change.

3. Each time you get to a location where you want Works to insert data from a field in the database, choose Edit/Insert Field. A dialog box appears asking which database and field you want to insert at the current cursor position. Use the

arrow keys to select the correct database and the tab key to jump to the field list. Once you select a field and press ↵, Works inserts a placeholder into the document that looks something like this:

```
<<First Name>>
```

Placeholders can be copied and moved around within your text, but make sure that you copy both sets of angled brackets along with the field name, otherwise Works won't recognize the placeholder when it comes time to print the letters or forms. You can also format the placeholders with character and paragraph format settings. When you're through editing, save the text file on disk.

When you're ready to print, follow these steps.

1. Open the word processor file and the associated database file.

2. From the word processor file, choose the Print/Merge command. The PRINT MERGE dialog box will appear, asking you for the name of the database to be used in the printing process. Choose the database.

3. Next, the PRINT dialog box appears. Choose your print options, set up your printer with ample paper, and press ↵.

Works will begin printing your forms or letters. One copy of your form or letter will be printed for each record in the associated database, beginning with the first visible record and moving through the database one record at a time. Only visible records will be used, so if you want to limit your printing to certain records, use some technique for hiding the unwanted records, such as applying a Query or using the Query/Hide Record command. Also, you may want to sort the database if you desire the forms ordered in a particular way. (For more details on sorting, querying, and hiding database records, see Chapters 6 and 10.)

When Works inserts cell data into the text, it automatically computes the word-wrapping for each line, though you won't see this on the screen. If you intend to drop very long fields into a document, this may alter the page breaks or otherwise change the page layout in ways you cannot preview on the screen. You may have to experiment by printing a few letters first.

If you are using preprinted forms, chances are you will have to do some experimenting with the settings in the Print/LAYOUT dialog box. Measure all four margins of your forms (top, bottom, left, and right) as well as the overall form width and length, and alter the settings accordingly. You'll probably have to alter the tab settings in the word processor document to align the data fields on the printed form, too. You can test the layout by printing a single form rather than the whole database via the Print/Print command rather than Print/Merge. The placeholders will be printed in place of the eventual data.

Incidentally, letters and forms may contain multiple pages, and can include data from other tools as well, such as charts or spreadsheet data, as we've detailed.

PRINTING MAILING LABELS

One of the greatest boons to people who print newsletters or do other types of bulk mailings is Works' ability to print mailing labels neatly onto various sizes of commercially available pressure-sensitive labels. Works lets you print one, two, three, or four labels per row, across a page, using the data found in fields of the database. One label is printed for each record in the database.

Of course, for printing lots of labels, you'll need a printer with a *tractor* (sprockets) that can feed the labels accurately, since printing alignment is critical. Alternatively, if you have a laser printer, you'll find that there are commercially available mailing labels for this type of printer too.

Also don't forget to sort your database by ZIP code in advance of printing if you intend to use the U.S. Postal Service's bulk mail rates, since they require you to bundle your mailings according to specific ZIP code areas.

The technique for label printing is almost identical to that for printing forms. In essence, you are creating a small form. Here are the basic steps.

1. Create a word processor document with the placeholders located in the arrangement that you want them printed in. You only have to lay out one label, even if you plan to print two, three, or four labels across the page.

2. Choose Print/Labels. The PRINT LABELS dialog box appears as you see in Figure 12-4. (This figure uses fields from the Phonebk database you created in Chapter 6.) Select the database, and set the vertical and horizontal label spacing and the number of labels.

Vertical Spacing is the distance from the top of one label to the top of the next label. Horizontal Spacing is the distance from the left edge of one label to the left edge of the next if you are printing more than one across.

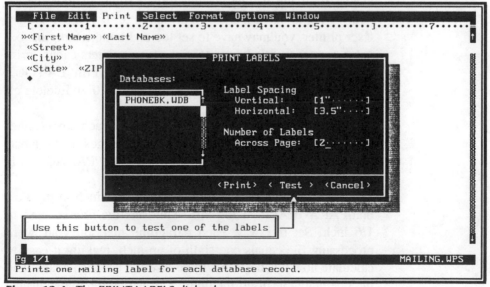

Figure 12-4. *The PRINT LABELS dialog box*

3. Choose <Test> to try printing a single row of labels, rather than the whole list. The PRINT dialog box appears. Just press ↵, and in a few seconds some labels should begin printing. Using the Test feature lets you fine-tune the placement without having to cancel the printing process each time. After the test labels are printed, you have the option of printing all of the labels, printing the test labels again, or canceling the printing process.

Fine-tuning the Mailing Labels

Chances are that it will take a little experimentation to get labels lined up properly. Unfortunately, this is almost always the case, no matter what program you are using; Works is no exception. Here are some pointers to make the job a little easier. For further explanation of the measurement descriptions, refer to Figure 12-5.

In addition to the PRINT LABELS dialog box settings, Works uses settings from the Print/LAYOUT dialog box and the Format/PARAGRAPH dialog box to determine how and where the labels print on the page.

In the LAYOUT box, specify the size of a sheet of your labels, from top to bottom and left to right. In most cases, you'll want to also set all the margins to 0. (If you are using a laser printer, you may have to set top and bottom margins to a value greater than 0, however, since laser printers cannot print right up to the edges of the paper.) Also in the Print/LAYOUT dialog box, set header and footer margins to 0 and delete all header and footer text.

If you want tiny right and left margins on each label (rather than having text print right up against the edges of the label) use the left and right indent in the Format/PARAGRAPH dialog box. You might try a 1/4 inch setting.

Another tip is to set the line spacing to 1 inch in the Format/PARAGRAPH dialog box. This sets the line spacing to 1/6 inch. Set this way, each paragraph mark in your word processing file equals one-sixth of an inch, making it easy to calculate how much space will be inserted between a label and the one below it. Insert the number of paragraph marks neces-

Measurement..How to Adjust

A	Top label margin ....Add a paragraph mark in the WPS file
B	Left indents ....Format/PARAGRAPH dialog box
C	Right indents...Format/PARAGRAPH dialog box
D	Bottom label margin ....Add a paragraph mark in the WPS file
E	Vertical spacing...PRINT LABELS dialog box
F	Horizontal spacing ....PRINT LABELS dialog box
G	Page width..Print/LAYOUT dialog box
H	Page length (between perforations).................Print/LAYOUT dialog box

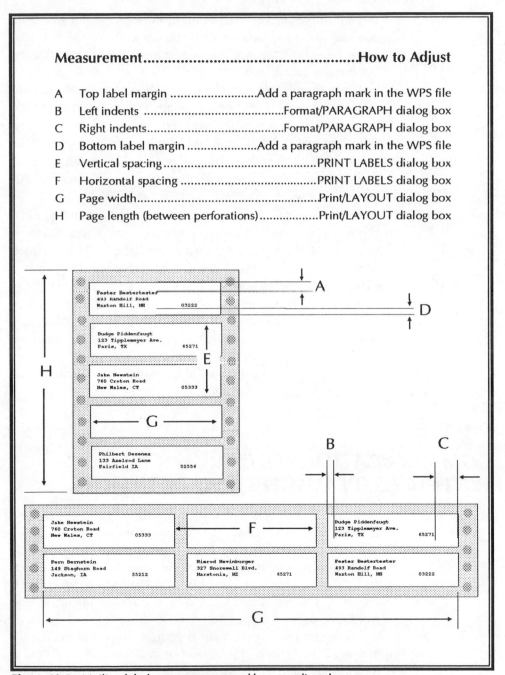

Figure 12-5. *Mailing label measurements and how to adjust them*

sary to fill the gap between them. In Figure 12-4, for example, you may need to insert a paragraph mark above the first line and another after the last line. In some cases the mark after the last line isn't necessary.

If your labels look like the information is wrapping around to the next line or data is being chopped off, try decreasing the number of labels across the page, decreasing the type size, or using a printer that can handle wider paper. Printing labels four across typically requires using a wide (132-column) printer, though three-across labels will often work fine in a normal 80-column printer.

Stationery and computer supply stores carry many types of mailing labels, most of which can be used by Works. Some of these labels allow room for your return address to be printed on them, up at the top. Since this is information that won't change from label to label, just enter your name and address as standard text into your word processing document above the field name placeholders. Of course, you'll have to adjust the spacing and layout parameters to accommodate the increased label size.

Refer to Figure 12-5 for help in determining how to set all the parameters of label spacing.

COMMUNICATIONS FILES WITH THE SPREADSHEET AND DATABASE

If the file you received via the communications tool is a list of numbers or items that are correctly formatted, they can be pulled directly into spreadsheet or database documents without going through the word processor. If they are not formatted properly, you will have to modify the formatting using the word processor first.

To determine if a document is going to import correctly, try opening it as either a spreadsheet or database, and see how it looks. If the data looks confused or misplaced, chances are that columns are separated by spaces, not tabs. This will be the case with data such as stock quotes that you download from information services.

The solution is as follows:

1. Close the file without saving the changes.

2. Then open the document as a word processing document and modify it by replacing groups of spaces (not all the spaces, mind you) with tabs. Here's how to do that.

3. First choose Options/Show All Characters so that you can see all the tabs, spaces, and paragraph marks. This way you can see what's happening.

4. Next, choose Select/Replace and type in

```
Search For:   [^s^s^w......]
Replace With: [^t..........]
```

5. Select <Replace All>.

6. After all the replacements are made, you'll then have to use the Copy command to copy the data to the spreadsheet or database, as we've explained.

COPYING DATA BETWEEN THE SPREADSHEET AND DATABASE

You can copy between the database and spreadsheet very easily, without having to worry about formatting details. As you have probably gleaned, WKS and WDB files both use the same formatting, so copying between them is a simple process.

1. Open both documents.

2. From the source file, select the area to be copied.

3. Choose Edit/Copy or press SHIFT-F3.

4. Move to the cell in the destination file where you want the copied data to begin, and press ↵. Works drops in the new cell data, filling to the right and down. In other words, the cursor location marks the upper left-hand corner of the copied data's new location.

When you copy from a database file to a spreadsheet file, Works converts database records to spreadsheet rows, and fields to columns. When copying from the spreadsheet to the database, Works does just the opposite.

Caution: As explained in the section "Copying from the Word Processor to the Database or Spreadsheet," you should be careful not to overwrite existing cell information.

SUMMARY

As I have attempted to illustrate in this chapter, using a well-integrated program such as Works adds a great deal of flexibility to your computing tasks. This chapter has covered most of the techniques you'll want to use to combine various documents created with the Works tools.

Obviously with a program as complex and capable as Works, it hasn't been possible to investigate all its arcane corners nor to include an expansive number of tips for each tool. But we hope that the essentials have been accurately and sufficiently explained to get you off and running. In the final analysis, experience — being the best teacher — will prevail and you will develop your own favorite methods and shortcuts for using Works to help you in your undertakings. In the meantime, don't hesitate to experiment. The worst that can happen is that you'll mess up a document beyond recognition. But then you can just close it without saving the changes, reopen it and try again. Also, don't overlook Appendix A as a handy reference aid during your exploits. — Good Luck!

Appendix

REFERENCE

This appendix is divided into eight sections:

- Basic Works information

- Word processor information

- Spreadsheet information

- Database and reporting information

- Spreadsheet and database functions

- Using dates and times in the spreadsheet and database

- Communications information

- Hardware and other system requirements

This appendix will not list all the commands that are available in each of the tools, since Works does that for you on its menus. The Works menus and descriptions that appear on the bottom line of your screen make it fairly clear what the purpose of each menu selection is. What will be listed here are general procedures for doing things such as copying, moving and deleting, short-cut keys, and so on. Also listed are technical specifications and other useful information about some of the tools and about Works in general.

BASIC WORKS INFORMATION

This section contains general information that applies to all of Works' tools.

To Choose a Command

1. Press ALT.

2. Press the highlighted letter of the command you want.

To Use a Dialog Box

1. Move between sections using the TAB key and SHIFT-TAB keys or by pressing (and holding down) the ALT key and pressing the highlighted letter of the section.

2. Type text into text areas.

3. Use arrow keys to select items from list boxes.

4. Use arrow keys to choose options from option boxes.

5. Use the spacebar to turn check boxes off and on.

6. Press the ↵ key to execute the command(s).

7. Press ESC to leave the dialog box without executing the command(s).

Keys Used by All the Tools

Key	Effect
F1	Help
SHIFT-F1	Tutorial

F3	Move
SHIFT-F3	Copy
F5	GO TO
F6	Next pane
F7	Repeat search
SHIFT-F7	Repeat copy or format
ESC	Terminate copy, move, or extend

Printing Headers and Footers in All Tools

The Print/LAYOUT dialog box allows you to create headers and footers to print on pages of your document. Aside from normal text, you may use the following codes to affect the formatting of your headers and footers:

Code	Effect
&l	Align following text to the left
&c	Align following text in the center
&r	Align following text to the right
&p	Print the page number
&f	Print the file name of current file
&d	Print the current date
&t	Print the time the printing occurred
&&	Print a single ampersand (&)

These codes can be combined in a single header or footer. For example, to print a header such as

Page 32   *** Potato-Sack Racing in America ***   10/10/81

enter the following line into the header area in the dialog box:

&lPage &p&c*** Potato-Sack Racing in America ***&r&d

More About the SETTINGS Dialog Box

The SETTINGS dialog box controls the appearance of tools on your screen, the units of measurement within tools, and several defaults that can vary. It also affects the creation of automatic backup files when you modify an existing file. We touched on settings in Chapter 2; here are the rest of the details.

Colors

Six color arrangements are available for your use. The Setup program initially selects an appropriate screen color option for your system. However, you may want to experiment a bit with the colors to find a setting that works best for your type of screen, or best suits your preferences. You can try one option after another to see the effects. Some settings may cause certain letters, such as letters that are supposed to be highlighted, to disappear. If this happens, try another setting.

Units

This sets the form in which Works displays and accepts units of measurement within the tools. The default is affected by the setting for Country, as we'll see in the next subsection.

Possible settings for units are shown in the following table:

Units	Abbreviation	Number/Inch	Example
Inches	"	1	.5 in or .5"
Centimeters	cm	2.54	3.88 cm
10 pitch	p10	10	5 p10
12 pitch	p12	12	5 p12
Points	pts or pt	72	48 pt

Once a given setting, such as inches, is selected from the SETTINGS box, you may enter other units as long as you specify what the units are, using the abbreviations listed. Works will make the conversion and display the measurements in the selected units.

Country

To accommodate measurement systems that vary from country to country, Works offers three Country settings. Each has its own defaults, affecting the page, date, and currency formats for all the tools.

Country Setting	Page Length	Page Width	Units	Currency	Date Order	Month Name
US	11"	8.5"	inches	$	m/d/y	Jan
Int'l A	11.69"	8.27"	inches	£	m/d/y	January
Int'l B	29.7 cm	21 cm	cm	$	d/m/y	January

WORD PROCESSOR INFORMATION

This section contains information about formatting characters and paragraphs, inserting special codes in your text, editing commands, and special Search-and-Replace codes.

Scrolling and Selection

Select text to be copied, moved, or formatted by pressing F8 or holding the shift key down, followed by one of the keys listed in the following table:

Key	Effect
←	Character left
→	Character right
↑	Character up
↓	Character down

CTRL ←	Word left
CTRL →	Word right
CTRL ↑	Paragraph up
CTRL ↓	Paragraph down
HOME	Beginning of line
END	End of line
CTRL-HOME	Beginning of document
CTRL-END	End of document
PGUP	Screen up
PGDN	Screen down
CTRL-PGUP	Top of screen
CTRL-PGDN	Bottom of screen

Mouse users have the option of selecting and scrolling via the mouse.

Formatting Characters

To format characters, use the Format menu or use the following keys. If a portion of text is selected, the format is applied to the selected text. If there is no selection, the new format applies to newly typed letters, until the format is changed. You can copy the format of some characters to other characters using the Edit/Copy Special command.

Key	Effect
CTRL-B	Bold
CTRL-U	Underline
CTRL-I	Italic
CTRL-S	Strikethrough
CTRL-SHIFT =	Superscript
CTRL =	Subscript
CTRL-SPACE	Plain

Formatting Paragraphs

To format paragraphs, use the Format menu or use the keys shown in the following table. If a portion of text is selected, the format is applied to all paragraphs that are a part of the selection. If there is no selection, the new format applies to newly typed paragraphs, until the format is changed. You can copy the format of one paragraph to other paragraphs using the Edit/Copy Special command. Paragraphs are defined as all text between two paragraph marks.

Key	Effect
CTRL-L	Left alignment
CTRL-R	Right alignment
CTRL-C	Center alignment
CTRL-J	Justified
CTRL-N	Nest
CTRL-M	Unnest
CTRL-H	Hang
CTRL-G	Unhang
CTRL-X	Normal format
CTRL-1	Single space
CTRL-2	Double space
CTRL-5	1-1/2 spaces
CTRL-O	Add one line before
CTRL-E	Add zero lines before

Normal paragraph format results in the settings listed in the following table:

Parameter	Setting
Left Indent	0
Right Indent	0
First Line Indent	0

Space Before and After	0
Line Spacing	0
Alignment	left
Keep with Next Paragraph	off
TAB Stops	every .5 inch

Word Processor Editing Keys

Key	Effect
DEL	Delete at cursor
DEL	Delete selection
BACKSPACE	Delete left

Special Word Processing Keys

Key	Name	Effect
DEL	Delete at Cursor	Deletes character at cursor location.
DEL	Delete Selection	Deletes entire high-lighted selection.
BACKSPACE	Delete Left	Deletes character left of cursor.
↵	Paragraph Mark	Creates a new paragraph and moves down one line.
SHIFT ↵	End-of-Line Mark	Lets you decide where a line breaks.
CTRL ↵	Manual Page Break	Lets you decide where a page breaks.

CTRL-HYPHEN	Optional Hyphen	Lets you designate where a word will split.
CTRL-SHIFT-HYPHEN	Non-breaking Hyphen	Holds hyphenated words together at line breaks.
CTRL-SHIFT-SPACE	Non-breaking Space	Holds words together at line breaks.
CTRL-P	Print Page	Causes a blank page to print.
CTRL-F	Print File	Prints the name of the WP file.
CTRL-D	Print Date	Prints the date the document is printed.
CTRL-T	Print Time	Prints the time the document is printed.
CTRL ;	Current Date	Inserts today's date.
CTRL-SHIFT ;	Current Time	Inserts the current time in hh:mm:am/pm format.

Special Search and Replace Characters

Type the special search and replace characters into the Search or Replace text areas for effects as outlined in the following table. To enter one of these as the search or replace character, type SHIFT-6 to get the ^ mark, followed by the character in the list that represents the special item you want to search for or replace.

Code	Finds or Replaces
^w	White space. Any combination of spaces, tabs, non-breaking spaces, new lines, paragraph marks, and hard page breaks. This cannot be used as a Replace item.
^s	Non-breaking space. Such as in *Microsoft Works* when you don't want the words to separate during line wraps.
^d	Page break
^t	TAB
^p	Paragraph mark
^n	End-of-line mark
^~	Non-breaking hyphen
^-	Optional hyphen
^?	Question mark
^^	Caret
^#	Any ASCII character where # is the ASCII character number
?	Any character

Inserting the IBM Extended Character Set into WP Documents

You can insert any symbol of the IBM extended character set into a document by holding down the ALT key and pressing the corresponding number key on the numeric keypad (not the number keys above the letter keys). For example, the code

ALT - 179

prints vertical lines.

You can use this technique to create boxes around portions of text. If you have a printer that prints these characters, such as the IBM graphics printer or equivalent, the boxes can also be printed.

You may also use the codes ALT-174 and ALT-175 to insert field name references for form letters, forms, and mailing labels in lieu of using the Insert Field command. Just type in ALT-174 (which prints double angled left brackets) followed by the field name and then ALT-175 (which prints double angled right brackets). This is a faster technique than choosing fields from the INSERT FIELD dialog box, assuming you remember the field names in the associated database.

SPREADSHEET INFORMATION

This section contains reference information about entering, editing, selecting, moving, copying, and scrolling within the Works spreadsheet tool. Spreadsheet functions are covered in of "Spreadsheet and Database Functions" in this appendix.

Special Function Keys

In addition to the keys listed at the beginning of this appendix for use with all the tools, the following function keys can be used:

Key	Effect
F2	Edit
F4	Reference
F8	Extend selection
CTRL-F8	Select row
SHIFT-F8	Select column

SHIFT-CTRL-F8	Select all
F9	Calculate
SHIFT-F10	View chart
F10	Exit chart screen

Scrolling and Selecting

Select cells to be copied, moved, or formatted by pressing F8 or holding the shift key down, followed by using the keys listed in the table below. You can also select cells by typing a range address into the GO TO dialog box (press F5 to open the box).

Key	Effect
←	Left one cell
→	Right one cell
↑	Up one cell
↓	Down one cell
CTRL ←	Left one block*
CTRL →	Right one block*
CTRL ↑	Up one block*
CTRL ↓	Down one block*
CTRL-HOME	Beginning of document
CTRL-END	End of document
HOME	Left side of sheet
END	Right side of sheet
PGUP	Screen up
PGDN	Screen down
CTRL-PGUP	Left one screen
CTRL-PGDN	Right one screen
ESC	Deselect any selection

*A block is a group of filled cells bordered by empty cells.

Entering Data into Cells

Move to the cell into which you want to enter a formula, value, or label; then use the keys as shown in the following table:

Key	Effect
↵	Enters data, remains on cell
↓	Enters data, moves down one cell
↑	Enters data, moves up one cell
←	Enters data, moves left one cell
→	Enters data, moves right one cell
CTRL ;	Enters the current date
CTRL-SHIFT ;	Enters the current time
CTRL '	Copies data from cell above
SHIFT-F7	Repeats last Copy or Format command
CTRL ↵	Enters into a cell range

If you have a block of cells selected, the following keys may save you some time. These keys only work in an area selected via SHIFT-ARROW keys.

Key	Effect
SHIFT-TAB	Enters data, moves left one cell
TAB	Enters data, moves right one cell
SHIFT ↵	Enters data, moves up one cell
↵	Enters data, moves down one cell

Editing Cell Data

To edit cell data, first move to the cell, then retype the data or press F2 to edit existing data. Then press ↵ to finalize the changes. If you press F2, Works switches to Edit mode. In Edit mode, the following keys may be used to edit the cell contents:

Key	Effect
HOME	Beginning of line
END	End of line
←	Left one character
→	Right one character
DEL	Delete at cursor
BACKSPACE	Delete character left of cursor
Type on keyboard	Insert characters
SHIFT-ARROWS	Select multiple characters

After multiple characters are selected, press DEL to erase them, or type a key on the keyboard to replace them.

Copying and Moving

To copy or move, select the range, then press the Copy key (SHIFT-F3) or the Move key (F3). Move to the new location or document and press ↵.

DATABASE AND REPORTING INFORMATION

This section summarizes the commands available in the database's list, view, form design, and report screens.

List and Report Screen Function Keys

In addition to the keys listed at the beginning of this appendix, the database tool can be controlled using the following keys:

Key	Effect
F2	Edit
F7	Repeat search

SHIFT-F7	Repeat last command
SHIFT-F8	Select column
CTRL-F8	Select row
SHIFT-F10	View report
F10	Exit reporting

Selecting Cells and Scrolling in List and Report

Key	Effect
←	Left one cell
→	Right one cell
↑	Up one cell
↓	Down one cell
CTRL ←	Left one block*
CTRL →	Right one block*
CTRL ↑	Up one block*
CTRL ↓	Down one block*
CTRL-HOME	Beginning of document
CTRL-END	End of document
HOME	Left side of database
END	Right side of database
PGUP	Screen up
PGDN	Screen down
CTRL-PGUP	Left one screen
CTRL-PGDN	Right one screen
ESC	Deselect any selection

*A block is a group of filled cells bordered by empty cells.

Form Design Screen Scrolling Keys

Key	Effect
$\leftarrow$	One space to left
$\rightarrow$	One space to right
$\uparrow$	One line up
$\downarrow$	One line down
HOME	Beginning of line
END	End of line
PGUP	Screen up
PGDN	Screen down
CTRL-HOME	Beginning of form
CTRL-END	End of form
CTRL-PGUP	Top of screen
CTRL-PGDN	Bottom of screen

Form and Query Screen Scrolling Keys

Key	Effect
$\rightarrow$ or $\downarrow$	Next cell
$\leftarrow$ or $\uparrow$	Previous cell
PGDN	Next screen
PGUP	Previous screen
CTRL-PGDN	Next record
CTRL-PGUP	Previous record
CTRL-HOME	Beginning of database
CTRL-END	End of database

Special Keys

Key	Effect
CTRL '	Copy cell above
CTRL ;	Enter current date
CTRL-SHIFT ;	Enter current time

Entering Data into Cells

Enter data into a cell from list view or form view by moving the highlight to the cell and typing. Remember that

- Formulas must begin with an equal sign (=TAX*RETAIL)

- Text needs no special treatment (Fred)

- Dates normally need no special treatment (Jan 3, 1986)

- Dates used in formulas require single quotation marks ('01/03/86')

If you have a block of cells selected, the following keys may save you some time when entering data. These keys only work in an area selected via SHIFT-ARROW keys in the list view.

Key	Effect
SHIFT - TAB	Enters data, moves left one cell
TAB	Enters data, moves right one cell
SHIFT ↵	Enters data, moves up one cell
↵	Enters data, moves down one cell

Otherwise, entering and editing data is identical to that for the spreadsheet.

SPREADSHEET AND DATABASE FUNCTIONS

Works contains 57 built-in "canned" arithmetic formulas called functions. Functions can be used in the context of either spreadsheet or database formulas. Explaining all the functions listed here is beyond the scope of this book. However, it may help the advanced user to know that Works' functions are identical to those of Lotus 1-2-3 version 1A, with the exclusion of the functions listed here.

Database statistical functions:
DAVG
DCOUNT
DMAX
DMIN
DSTD
DSUM
DVAR

String functions:
&

Logical functions:
@ISNUMBER
@ISSTRING

Special functions:
@@
@CELL
@CELLPOINTER

Date and time functions:
@DATEVALUE
@TIMEVALUE

In addition to these functions, Works includes the following Lotus 1-2-3 version 2 functions:

```
CTERM(Rate,FutureValue,PresentValue)
DDB(Cost,Salvage,Life,Period)
IRR(Guess,RangeReference)
RATE(FutureValue,PresentValue,Term)
SLN(Cost,Salvage,Life)
SYD(Cost,Salvage,Life,Period)
TERM(Payment,Rate,FutureValue)
COLS(RangeReference)
ROWS(RangeReference)
INDEX(RangeReference,Column,Row)
```

For detailed information on using these functions, you may want to refer to the Works manual (see "Database and Spreadsheet Functions"), a Lotus 1-2-3 manual, or one of the many reference books on Lotus 1-2-3. One of the most complete of these is *1-2-3: The Complete Reference* by Mary Campbell (Berkeley, Calif.: Osborne/McGraw-Hill, 1988). For information about importing Lotus 1-2-3 worksheets into Works, see Appendix B.

USING DATES AND TIMES

Dates can be entered into database and spreadsheet cells either as constants or to be used in formulas. They can be entered in a long or short form. The same holds true of times. Here are some examples.

Form	Dates	Times
Long	Dec 25, 1923	23:30:00
	Dec, 25, 1923	23:30
	Dec, 1923	
	Dec 25	
Short	12/25/1923	11:30:00 PM
	12/25/23	11:30 PM
	12/1923	11 PM
	12/25	

Works can store and manipulate dates between 1/1/1900 and 6/3/2079.

To put a date in a formula, use the short form and enclose it in single quotation marks (e.g., ='5/5/88' - '3/5/85' calculates the number of days between the two dates). Format the cell as a date to make sense of the result.

To put a time into a formula, use the Hour:Minute:Second 12-hour form and use single quotation marks around it (e.g., ='5:30:00 PM' - '3:23:00 PM' calculates the time difference). You will have to format the cell to display the result correctly, using the Date/Time format.

COMMUNICATIONS INFORMATION

As discussed in Chapter 7, for your modem to work properly with the communications tool, it has to be connected properly. Refer to the modem's installation instructions for details. In addition to the physical installation, you will also have to set the modem's internal switches to match what Works expects. The location and/or existence of these switches may vary between brands of modems, so you may have to read the modem's instruction manual to discover how the following settings are actually made. With that in mind, set up your modem as follows:

Setting	Effect
Commands enabled	Allows the modem to respond to Works
Result codes sent	Displays the results of a command to your screen
Word result codes	Displays those results in words, not numbers
Respond to DTR	Allows Works to "hang up" the phone

Characters echoed   Lets you see commands as they are sent to the modem in command state

Auto Answer disabled   Prevents the modem from answering the phone unless you tell Works to do so

Interrupt Conflicts

Your modem will not work if you assign it to a COM port that is being used by another device. Typically, your modem will be connected to the COM1 port. However, your computer may have other devices, notably a mouse or printer, connected to the COM1 port, too. If this happens, your modem will not work due to an *interrupt conflict*.

IBM PCs and compatibles have another port, COM2, that can be used as an alternative. If COM2 isn't being used by another device, you can use it for communications. With internal modems, this usually requires changing a switch or jumper on the modem board. With external modems it requires hooking the modem's cable to a different connector on the PC, or changing a switch or jumper on the serial interface board in the PC so that it is assigned to COM2 instead of COM1. After those steps are completed, load Works, open a communications document, and from the Options/COMMUNICATIONS dialog box, set the port to COM2.

Call Waiting

Many people now have a telephone service called *call waiting*. Call waiting lets you hear when someone is trying to call your phone number, even while you are already talking to another party on the same telephone line. Call waiting is a convenience to people, but can cause computers to accidentally disconnect, or to lose data during communications sessions. This happens as the result of the click that an incoming call causes on the line. If you have call waiting and find that you are regularly being disconnected in the middle of communications sessions, you will either have to run your sessions during a time when you think no one will be calling you, or turn off call waiting.

In some areas of the U.S., the local telephone company lets you temporarily turn off call waiting for the duration of a call by entering a code from your telephone. For example, in the San Francisco area, you dial *70, pause for a second, and then place your call. You can add this (or whatever sequence works in your area) to the Phone Number setting in the PHONE dialog box, so that you don't have to remember to turn off call waiting each time you run a communications setting. For example, in Oakland, California, the phone number

*70,540-1111

turns off call waiting, pauses for a moment, and dials MCI Mail.

Using an Acoustic Modem

Some modems do not connect directly into the telephone line via a cable. Instead you fit the telephone handset (receiver) into a unit that has rubber cups to hold it in place. Data is sent and received through the earpiece and mouthpiece of the telephone receiver. Since acoustic modems can't dial the phone for you, you have to use a special technique to dial the phone and use Works' communications tool as follows:

1. Open the Options/PHONE dialog box and make sure the Phone Number and Modem Setup areas are blank.

2. From the Options/COMMUNICATIONS dialog box, set the baud rate to 300 (unless your modem uses a different speed).

3. Choose Connect/Connect.

4. Dial the desired number manually, just as if making a personal call.

5. As soon as the remote computer's modem answers the phone, you should hear a high-pitched tone in your receiver, indicating that the other modem is ready to send and receive data. Immediately place the receiver into the rubber cups of your modem.

6. Continue the session in the normal way.

7. When finished communicating, you will have to terminate the call by removing the receiver from the modem and hanging it up manually.

HARDWARE AND SYSTEM REQUIREMENTS

The following table outlines the necessary hardware and software that you must have in order to run Works.

Hardware/Software	Requirements
Computer type	IBM PC/XT/AT or compatible
Memory	512K minimum
	640K recommended
Disk drives	Two 5-1/4" floppy drives (360K)
	or One 3-1/2" floppy drive (720K)
	or One hard disk
DOS	Version 2.00 or later
Screen and monitor	Color Graphics Adapter (CGA)
	or Monochrome Text Adapter
	or Enhanced Graphics Adapter (EGA)
	or PS/2 Graphics Card (VGA)
	or Hercules Monochrome Card
	or MCGA Graphics device
Mouse type	Microsoft Bus or Serial Mouse
	or compatible

Appendix

B

USING WORKS
WITH OTHER PROGRAMS

With many programs, particularly integrated applications other than Works, the documents you create cannot be used by other word processing, spreadsheet, or database programs. However, Works is an exception. Works is actually pretty good at allowing you to exchange files with people using some other popular programs. You can create files in Works that others can use, and vice versa. As a result, you may be able to take advantage of Works' simplicity and integration without sacrificing compatibility with coworkers or friends who use other programs.

This appendix outlines the steps necessary to exchange files between some popular programs and Works. It is divided into two sections.

- ♦ Exchanging word processing files

- ♦ Exchanging spreadsheet files and database files

EXCHANGING WORD PROCESSING FILES

There are two ways to exchange word processing files with other word processor programs. The first and more desirable technique is via the word processing file conversion program supplied with Works. It is called *WPTOWP* (for "Word Processor TO Word Processor") and will convert files between the following four formats:

♦ Microsoft Works format

♦ Microsoft Word format

♦ Microsoft Rich Text format (RTF)

♦ IBM's Document Content Architecture (DCA) format

Note: Early versions of Works did not include this program, but Microsoft will supply it upon request.

If the other word processing program you want to exchange data with can work with any of these formats, you should use the conversion program which is explained here. Note that many word processing programs are beginning to support at least one of the last two formats listed. Thus, even though WPTOWP can't convert, say, WordPerfect files directly, you can use the conversion program supplied with WordPerfect to create a DCA file, then use WPTOWP to convert that DCA to Works format. In other words, conversion may be a two-step process. If the other word processing package won't create or convert to one of these formats, check with your computer dealer about purchasing one of the many inexpensive conversion programs that will convert to DCA or RTF.

On the other hand, if you can't figure out a means for conversion of files to one of these formats, you'll have to use a less elegant interchange medium — a standard ASCII file. ASCII files contain the text of a document but not much of the formatting, so they can be a bit of a nuisance if you need to import or export heavily formatted documents.

The next two sections explain how to use the WPTOWP program, and how to work with ASCII word processing files.

Using WPTOWP

WPTOWP can be used in two ways: from a menu or from the DOS command line. We'll explain the menu approach here. If you want to use WPTOWP from the command line, you should refer to the Works manual, Appendix E.

To run WPTOWP follow these steps:

1. Get to the DOS prompt (A> if you have a floppy disk machine or C> if you have a hard disk). You can do this either by quitting Works via the File/Exit command, or by temporarily leaving Works via the File/DOS command.

2. Insert the disk containing the WPTOWP program into drive A (if you're using a floppy disk machine), or make sure the WPTOWP program is on the current directory (if using a hard disk).

3. Type **WPTOWP** ↵.

4. The program will prompt you for the name of the file you want to convert. Answer accordingly.

5. Next, you'll be prompted to indicate the name you want to give to the file after it's converted. This is because WPTOWP creates a new file, in the converted form, rather than overwriting (erasing) the existing file, since you might want to keep the original. If you don't stipulate a name, WPTOWP will automatically assign a new name by using the existing name and changing the extension to indicate the new file's format.

6. Then you will be prompted to indicate what format you want the file converted to. Choose the appropriate option. Here's a list showing a few popular programs and the correct choices to help you make the decision:

From	To	Use	Extension
Works	Word	MS Word	.DOC
Word	Works	MS Works	.WPS
WordPerfect	Works	MS Works	.WPS
Works	WordPerfect	DCA	.DCA

If you are converting into Works format, you can then open the file as if it were a normal Works file. If converting to a Word (.DOC) file, the new file will load into Word without difficulty. If converting to DCA or RTF, you'll have to refer to the other program's manual to determine the steps required to open the file.

Using ASCII Files

When the other word processing program you want to exchange files with doesn't support one of the formats that WPTOWP can handle, you'll have to use an ASCII file as the interchange medium. (ASCII, for American Standard Code for Information Interchange, is the most basic format that text files can be stored in, and is an older, less complete format for exchanging files.)

It's unfortunate, but true, that the standard ASCII format, though useful in that it allows text to be used in programs and computers of far-ranging different types, does not include codes for storing paragraph and character formatting, margin and tab settings, and other such details. Thus, you should remember not to waste time on this type of formatting when you intend to send an ASCII file document to another party who is using a different word processor than yours.

Exporting ASCII from the Works Word Processor

From Works, you create ASCII files via options found in the word processor's SAVE AS dialog box. This box contains three options: Works, Text, and Plain. Normally whenever you save a file, Works assumes you want to store it as a Works file, and so this is the default. When saved using this option, a word processor document has a special, proprietary format that is only usable by Works and includes all the codes for paragraph and character formatting, and the references to charts and database information that may be integrated into the document.

If you choose the Text option, only the text itself is stored in the file, but without any of the formatting listed. Also, a CR/LF (carriage return/line feed) is inserted only after paragraph marks, meaning one per paragraph. Some word processors require this type of format so that they can rewrap the lines properly after opening the ASCII file. WordStar is a common example of this since paragraph marks at the end of each line would be interpreted as "hard carriage returns," preventing reformatting of the lines once in WordStar. Upon opening a file saved as Text, it's possible that each paragraph will appear as a long single line. You may have to reform or rewrap each line to make the paragraphs reappear on the screen in a reasonable arrangement. For example, in WordStar, this would be done by typing

^Q^Q^B

which will reform the entire file.

When the Plain option is selected, Works saves the file as an ASCII file, but it adds a CR/LF at the end of every line instead of only at the end of each paragraph. It also converts all four margins (left, right, top, and bottom) and all tabs to blank spaces. Use this format for exporting to word processors that require a CR/LF after each line, or when preparing electronic mail documents to be sent through the communications tool. Typically, however, you'll want to set all the margins in the Print/LAYOUT dialog box to zero to eliminate the extra blank spaces in the margins. (You may want to leave a small right margin so that lines aren't so long that they don't fit onto the screen later.)

Importing ASCII to the Works Word Processor

To import an ASCII file into the word processor, simply follow these instructions. Of course, these steps assume the other program has an ASCII file creation option. If it doesn't, a trick you might try is having the other program print to a disk file. For example, WordStar lets you do this from its print menu. The disk file is then an ASCII file.

1. Choose File/Open.

2. Type in the name of the file and press ↵.

3. Works will present the OPEN AS dialog box. Choose Word Processor.

4. The ASCII file will open up in the word processor. Chances are that the formatting is messed up one way or another. If so, it's probably due to the existence of extra paragraph marks (CR/LFs), or spaces in the file.

5. Turn on the invisible characters by choosing Options/Show All Characters.

6. Remove the objectionable characters (typically all paragraph marks except for ones at the ends of each paragraph).

7. Format and use the file in the normal way.

Tip: You may want to automate the replacement process in large files by using the Search and Replace command. (Refer to Chapter 8 for details on using Search and Replace, and the special codes required as the Search and Replace criteria.) Basically, this is a three-step procedure.

   ♦ Insert a unique set of characters (such as %%) between each real paragraph.

   ♦ Replace all paragraph marks with nothing.

♦ Replace all occurrences of the unique set of characters (%%) with paragraph marks.

EXCHANGING SPREADSHEET AND DATABASE FILES

Spreadsheet and database files created in other programs can be used by Works if those files are ASCII files that have cells separated by tabs, by commas, or by quotes and commas (as in DIF files) and have a CR/LF at the end of each row (or record). Additionally, spreadsheets created by Lotus 1-2-3 can be used by Works without any conversion. (See Appendix A for more about specific data incompatibilities when using Lotus 1-2-3 files directly.)

Lotus 1-2-3 Files

When opening a Lotus 1-2-3 file, Works checks all the formulas in the file. If there is a function in the 1-2-3 file that Works doesn't recognize, you will see an ERROR dialog box with a message such as:

Invalid formula ignored in cell XX:XX.
Continue to display errors? Yes/No

This means Works cannot use that formula. Instead it will accept the value in the problem cell and kill the formula. Mark down the cell location so that you can reenter an acceptable formula later, using functions that Works supports.

Note also, that some 1-2-3 spreadsheets may be larger than the maximum size supported by Works. However, this will only occur if the Lotus file was created on a machine that has more than 640K of RAM and uses LIM/EMS extended memory. Chances are good that your machine does not have extended memory and thus spreadsheet size shouldn't be a problem.

Using ASCII Files

The database and spreadsheet allow you to load and save files stored in ASCII text format.

Saving as ASCII Text

When you save As Text from the SAVE AS dialog box, Works removes all formatting and formulas. Only the values themselves remain, meaning that the formulas are lost. These values are separated by commas. Additionally, double quotation marks are used to enclose labels, error values, and numbers formatted as Dollar, Percent, or Time/Date. Rows are terminated by a CR/LF. Spreadsheet column names and database field names are not written into the file. You can edit the resulting file in a word processor if necessary, or import it directly into another program that can read such a file.

1. Choose File/Save As.

2. Select the Text option.

3. Name the file. Give it a new name so you don't overwrite your existing file.

Opening as ASCII Text

As explained in Chapter 12, Works word processor files copied to the spreadsheet or database must include tabs between cells and a CR/LF at the end of each row. However, if you intend to read an externally generated ASCII file into the spreadsheet or database via the OPEN AS dialog box, the file will have to be in one of the following forms:

Type of Format	Example
Comma delimited	1,2,302,Text,5
Tab delimited	1 2 302 Text 5
	(tabs — ASCII 009 — in between)
DIF format	1,2,302,"Text",5

In any case, column or field names should not be in the file. To open the ASCII file and read it into Works, follow these steps.

1. Open the file by choosing File/Open.

2. Select Database or Word Processor from the OPEN AS dialog box.

For more information about text-file compatibilities, please refer to Chapter 7.

Trademarks

Apple®	Apple Computer, Inc.
AppleII®	Apple Computer, Inc.
COMPAQ®	COMPAQ Computer Corporation
CompuServe®	CompuServe, Inc.
CP/M®	Digital Research, Inc.
Crosstalk®	Microstuf, Inc.
dBASE®	Ashton-Tate
dBASE II®	Ashton-Tate
dBASE III®	Ashton-Tate
DEC™	Digital Equipment Corporation
DIF™	Software Arts, Inc.
Ensemble™	Hayden Software
Epson®	Seiko-Epson Corporation
Epson MX™	Epson America, Inc.
HOTSHOT™	Symsoft
IBM®	International Business Machines Corporation
IBM PC AT®	International Business Machines Corporation
IBM PC XT®	International Business Machines Corporation
LaserView®	Sigma Designs, Inc.
Lotus®	Lotus Development Corporation
Macintosh™	Apple Computer, Inc.
MCI®	MCI Communication Corporation
MicroPlan®	Chang Laboratories, Inc.
Microrim®	Microrim, Inc.
Multiplan™	Microsoft Corporation
North Star™	North Star Computers Corporation
1-2-3®	Lotus Development Corporation
Paradox®	Ansa Software
Perfect Calc™	Perfect Software
PFS:®	Software Publishing Corporation
PFS:File™	Software Publishing Corporation
Quartet™	Haba Systems, Inc.
Rolodex™	Zephyr American Corporation
Selectric™	International Business Machines Corporation
SideKick®	Borland International, Inc.
SuperCalc®	Computer Associates International, Inc.
SYLK®	Microsoft Corporation

Index

Editing
    cells, 118, 413
    data (database), 145-147
    keys, word processor, 408
    text, 73-89
END key, 37
ENTER key, 36
Entering
    data, database, 417
    data into cells, 413
    text, 66-73
Environment, 2, 33
Error messages, 52-53
Escape key (ESC), 36, 52
Exiting Works, 59
Extended character set, 410
Extensions, file, 54

F
Field criteria, multiple, 330
Field names, turning off or replacing, 305-308
Field widths, modifying, 134
Fields, 16, 126
    calculated, 322
    formatting, 321-322
    formulas in, 322
    hiding, 316-319
    inserting and deleting, 310-313
    locking, 17, 324
    moving database, 131
    protecting, 324
    rearranging in list view, 142
    sorting on, 153
File compatibility, 3, 203
File extensions, 54
    changing, 57
File menu selections, 53
File transfer problems, 203
Files, ASCII, 386, 428-433
    exchanging with other
        software, 425-433
    managing with Works, 54
    opening, 58
    saving, 54
    sending and receiving, 185-192

Floppy disk systems
    setting up Works on, 26
    starting Works with, 38
Fonts, chart, 374
Footers, 254-257
Form design, screen scrolling keys
    for, 416
Form letters, 392-394
Form view, 127, 140
    editing in, 146
    inserting and deleting fields in, 311
    inserting and deleting records in,
        314
Format codes, 226
Formats, copying, 227
Formatting
    cells, 108, 265-274
    characters, 222, 406
    fields, 321-322
    paragraphs, 208-222, 407-408
Forms, 392-394
    inserting and deleting lines
        in, 308
Forms Design mode, 132
Forms view, 17
Formulas
    copying, 290
    displaying, 294-296
    field, 324
    replicating, 112
    spreadsheet, 100
    using functions with, 289
    using in database reports, 341
Freezing spreadsheet titles, 285-286
Full screen settings, 178
Function keys, 34
    special database, 414
    special spreadsheet, 411
Functions
    built-in spreadsheet, 13
    mathematical, 101
    spreadsheet and database, 418-420
    using in formulas, 289
G
GOTO dialog box, 318
Graphs (see also Charts), 344-382

Other related Osborne/McGraw-Hill titles include:

dBASE III PLUS™ Made Easy
by Miriam Liskin

Liskin's *Advanced dBASE III PLUS™* and Jones' *Using dBASE III PLUS™* have been so successful that we're filling in the gap for beginners with *dBASE III PLUS™ Made Easy*. Learning dBASE III PLUS™ couldn't be simpler. You'll install and run the program, enter and edit data. Discover all the features of using dBASE III PLUS at the dot prompt. Each concept is clearly explained and followed by examples and exercises that you can complete at your own speed. Liskin discusses sorting and indexing, performing calculations, and printing reports and labels. Multiple databases are emphasized, and Liskin presents strategies for working with them. You'll also find chapters on customizing the working environment and exchanging data with other software. If you're curious about higher-level use, Liskin's final chapter shows how to combine the commands you've learned into batch programs so you can begin to automate your applications. (Includes two command cards for quick reference.)

$18.95 p
0-07-881294-1, 350 pp., 7³⁄₈ x 9¹⁄₄

DOS Made Easy
by Herbert Schildt

If you're at a loss when it comes to DOS, Herb Schildt has written just the book you need, *DOS Made Easy*. Previous computer experience is not necessary to understand this concise, well-organized introduction that's filled with short applications and exercises. Schildt walks you through all the basics, beginning with an overview of a computer system's components and a step-by-step account of how to run DOS for the first time. Once you've been through the initial setup, you'll edit text files, use the DOS directory structure, and create batch files. As you feel more comfortable with DOS, Schildt shows you how to configure a system, handle floppy disks and fixed disks, and make use of helpful troubleshooting methods. By the time you've gone this far, you'll be ready for total system management—using the printer, video modes, the serial and parallel ports, and more. *DOS Made Easy* takes the mystery out of the disk operating system and puts you in charge of your PC.

$18.95 p
0-07-881295-X, 385 pp., 7³⁄₈ x 9¹⁄₄

WordStar® 4.0 Made Easy
by Walter A. Ettlin

WordStar® Made Easy, the original "Made Easy" guide with 350,000 copies sold worldwide, has been so successful that Osborne has published a companion volume on the new WordStar® version 4.0. All 4.0 commands and features are thoroughly described and illustrated in practical exercises so you can put WordStar to immediate use, even if you've never used a computer before. Walter Ettlin, who has written four books and taught high school for 23 years, guides you from the fundamentals of creating a memo or report to using WordStar's calculator mode, macro commands, and Word Finder™. You'll also learn to use WordStar's latest spelling checker. *WordStar® 4.0 Made Easy* puts you in control of your software with the acclaimed "Made Easy" format now found in 11 Osborne titles. (Includes a handy pull-out command card.)

$16.95 p
0-07-881011-6, 300 pp., 7³⁄₈ x 9¹⁄₄

DisplayWrite 4™ Made Easy
by Gail Todd

Upgrading from DisplayWrite 3™ to DisplayWrite 4™? Here's the book that provides a thorough introduction to IBM's word processing software. Handle new menus, screens, and options with ease as Todd leads you from basic steps to more sophisticated procedures. The famous "Made Easy" format offers hands-on exercises and plenty of examples so you can quickly learn to produce letters and reports. All of DisplayWrite 4's new features are covered, including printing interfaces; the voice add-on; Paper Clip, the cursor control that lets you take up where you left off; and Notepad, a convenience that enables you to insert notes into documents. Todd, the author of numerous user guides and manuals, has the know-how to get you up and running fast.

$19.95 p
0-07-881270-4, 420 pp., 7³⁄₈ x 9¹⁄₄

WordPerfect® Made Easy
by Mella Mincberg

Here's the book that makes learning WordPerfect® quick, easy . . . even enjoyable. With Mincberg's follow-along lessons, this IBM® PC compatible word processing software will be at your command in just a couple of hours. Edit text, save and print a document, set tabs, format pages. You'll become a skillful Word-Perfect user as you work through practical applications. When you're ready to explore more sophisticated WordPerfect features, Mincberg is there with detailed instructions to help you run WordPerfect's spell checker and mail merge, manage files, create macros, and use special enhancements like windows and line numbering. Mincberg, author of the ever-so-useful *WordPerfect®: Secrets, Solutions, Shortcuts,* draws on her years of computer training experience to help you become an assured, savvy WordPerfect user. (Includes quick-reference command card.)

$18.95 p
0-07-881297-6, 400 pp., 7³/₈ x 9¹/₄

Microsoft® Word Made Easy, Second Edition
by Paul Hoffman

Hoffman's top-selling *Microsoft® Word Made Easy* has been revised to cover Microsoft's latest version of this widely used word processing software. Both beginning and experienced users will find a clear presentation of Word's new features, "made easy" for immediate application. Hoffman covers text outlining, spelling correction, hyphenation, creating indexes and tables of contents, and laser printers. Word's new functions, style sheets, windows, and glossaries are described in depth, and you'll find extra tips for using the mail-merge function. In the tradition of Osborne's "Made Easy" series, all techniques are explained with practical hands-on examples and are illustrated with helpful screen displays.

$16.95 p
0-07-881248-8, 300 pp., 7³/₈ x 9¹/₄

Your IBM® PC Made Easy (Includes IBM PC (DOS 2.0) And PC-XT)
by Jonathan Sachs

"In one word, OUTSTANDING! Perfect for beginning and advanced users, an excellent tutorial/reference. A very thorough guide to most facets of your IBM PC, from PC-DOS, hardware, software, resources supplies, batch files, etc. Rating: A"
(Computer Book Review)

$14.95 p
0-07-881112-0, 250 pp., 7¹/₂ x 9¹/₄

C Made Easy
by Herbert Schildt

With Osborne/McGraw-Hill's popular "Made Easy" format, you can learn C programming in no time. Start with the fundamentals and work through the text at your own speed. Schildt begins with general concepts, then introduces functions, libraries, and disk input/output, and finally advanced concepts affecting the C programming environment and UNIX™ operating system. Each chapter covers commands that you can learn to use immediately in the hands-on exercises that follow. If you already know BASIC, you'll find that Schildt's C equivalents will shorten your learning time. *C Made Easy* is a step-by-step tutorial for all beginning C programmers.

$18.95 p
0-07-881178-3, 350 pp., 7³/₈ x 9¹/₄

The Osborne/McGraw-Hill Guide to Using Lotus™ 1-2-3,™ Second Edition, Covers Release 2
by Edward M. Baras

Your investment in Lotus™ 1-2-3™ can yield the most productive returns possible with the tips and practical information in *The Osborne/McGraw-Hill Guide to Using Lotus™ 1-2-3.™* Now the second edition of this acclaimed bestseller helps you take full advantage of Lotus' new 1-2-3 upgrade, Release 2. This comprehensive guide offers a thorough presentation of the worksheet, database, and graphics functions. In addition, the revised text shows you how to create and use macros, string functions, and many other sophisticated 1-2-3 features. Step by step, you'll learn to implement 1-2-3 techniques as you follow application models for financial forecasting, stock portfolio tracking, and forms-oriented database management. For both beginners and experienced users, this tutorial quickly progresses from fundamental procedures to advanced applications.

$18.95 p
0-07-881230-5, 432 pp., 7³/₈ x 9¹/₄

The Advanced Guide to Lotus™ 1-2-3,™ Covers RELEASE 2
Edward M. Baras

Edward Baras, Lotus expert and author of *The Symphony™ Book, Symphony™ Master,* and *The Jazz™ Book,* now has a sequel to his bestselling *Osborne/McGraw-Hill Guide to Using Lotus™ 12-3.™* For experienced users, *The Advanced Guide to Lotus 1-2-3* delves into more powerful and complex techniques using the newest software upgrade, Release 2. Added enhancements to 1-2-3's macro language, as well as many new functions and commands, are described and thoroughly illustrated in business applications. Baras shows you how to take advantage of Release 2's macro capabilities by programming 1-2-3 to simulate Symphony's keystroke-recording features and by processing ASCII files automatically. You'll also learn to set up your own command menus; use depreciation functions, matric manipulation, and regression analysis; and convert text files to the 1-2-3 worksheet format.

$18.95 p
0-07-881237-2, 325 pp., 7³/₈ x 9¹/₄

Financial Modeling Using Lotus™ 1-2-3™, Covers Release 2
Charles W. Kyd

Readers of Kyd's monthly "Accounting" column in *Lotus*™ magazine already know how helpful his 1-2-3™ tips can be. Now his *Financial Modeling Using Lotus*™ *1-2-3*™ shows experienced users how to set up a data bank that can be used by everyone in the office to make more effective use of numerous financial applications. Kyd provides models for managing the balance sheet, controlling growth, handling income statements and management accounting, using Z scores for business forecasts, and more. Each model features a summary of 1-2-3 techniques, including helpful information for using the new Release 2, and explains the financial theories behind the application. You'll also find out how data for many of these financial models can be shared in the office data bank, creating an even greater resource for business productivity.

$16.95 p
0-07-881213-5, 225 pp., 7³/₈ x 9¹/₄

Using HAL™
by Andrew Postman

Using HAL™ helps you tap into the full capabilities of Lotus® 1-2-3®. Whether you're a beginning 1-2-3 user or an experienced one who demands top software performance, you'll be amazed at the increased productivity that HAL adds to 1-2-3. Postman shows you how to use HAL to execute 1-2-3 commands and functions through English phrases that you select. You'll find out about graphing with HAL and how to use the undo command, which lets you experiment with "what-if" questions without losing data. You'll also master cell relations for greater analytical abilities, linking worksheets for data consolidation, macros, and table manipulation. *Using HAL*™ gets you past the introduction so you can become thoroughly acquainted with Lotus' new 1-2-3 companion.

$19.95 p
0-07-881268-2, 380 pp., 7³/₈ x 9¹/₄

Running 4Word™
by Kay Nelson

If you've been running behind in word processing with 1-2-3® lately, now is the time to start *Running 4Word*™. Find out how to use Turner Hall's newly released 4Word™, the Add-In Word Processor™ for 1-2-3®, that lets you integrate word processing functions with Lotus' spreadsheet by pressing a computer key. You'll start with the basics of installing the program and formatting text, then work up to advanced procedures including macros and importing/exporting text and data. Practical business examples are cited so you can clearly understand how to create memos, reports, and financial documents using 4Word.

$19.95 p
0-07-881258-5, 350 pp. 7³/₈ x 9¹/₄

1-2-3®: The Complete Reference
by Mary Campbell

1-2-3®: The Complete Reference is the authoritative desktop companion for every Lotus® 1-2-3® user. All commands, functions, and procedures are explained in detail and are demonstrated in practical "real-world" business applications. Conventionally organized according to task, this essential reference makes it easy to locate information on topics such as printing, macros, graphics production, and data mangement. Each chapter thoroughly describes a 1-2-3 task and all the procedures it requires, followed by an alphabetical listing of every command or function applied. Special emphasis is placed on compatible software packages, including Report Writer™, Reflex™ and others, that you can use to extend 1-2-3's capabilities. Campbell, a consultant and writer whose magazine columns appear monthly in *IBM PC UPDATE, Absolute Reference*, and *CPA Journal*, draws on her years of 1-2-3 expertise to provide you with this outstanding, comprehensive resource.

$25.95 p, Hardcover Edition
0-07-881288-7, 920 pp., 7³/₈ x 9¹/₄

$22.95 p, Paperback Edition
0-07-881005-1, 928 pp., 7³/₈ x 9¹/₄

dBASE III PLUS™: The Complete Reference
by Joseph-David Carrabis

This indispensable dBASE III PLUS™ reference will undoubtedly be the most frequently used book in your dBASE III® library. *dBASE III PLUS™: The Complete Reference* is a comprehensive resource to every dBASE III and dBASE III PLUS command, function, and feature. Each chapter covers a specific task so you can quickly pinpoint information on installing the program, designing databases, creating files, manipulating data, and many other subjects. Chapters also contain an alphabetical reference section that describes all the commands and functions you need to know and provides clear examples of each. Carrabis, author of several acclaimed dBASE books, discusses the lastest features of dBASE III PLUS, including networking capabilities; the Assistant, a menu-driven interface; and the Applications Generator, a short-cut feature for creating database files and applications without programming. *dBASE III PLUS™: The Complete Reference* also includes a glossary and handy appendixes that cover error messages, converting from dBASE II to dBASE III PLUS, and add-on utilities.

$25.95 p, Hardcover Edition
0-07-881315-x, 600 pp., 7³/₈ x 9¹/₄

$22.95 p, Paperback Edition
0-07-881012-4, 600 pp., 7³/₈ x 9¹/₄

MAXIT™ increases your DOS addressable conventional memory beyond 640K for only $195.

- Add up to 256K above 640K for programs like FOXBASE+ and PC/FOCUS.

- Short card works in the IBM PC, XT, AT, and compatibles.

- Top off a 512 IBM AT's memory to 640K and add another 128K beyond that.

- Run resident programs like Sidekick above 640K.

- Add up to 96K above 640K to all programs, including PARADOX and 1-2-3.

- Compatible with EGA, Network, and other memory cards.

Break through the 640 barrier.
MAXIT increases your PC's available memory by making use of the vacant unused address space between 640K and 1 megabyte. (See illustrations)

Big gain—no pain.
Extend the productive life of your, IBM PC, XT, AT or compatible. Build more complex spreadsheets and databases without upgrading your present software.

Installation is a snap.
The MAXIT 256K memory card and software works automatically. You don't have to learn a single new command.

If you have questions, our customer support people will answer them, fast. MAXIT is backed by a one-year warranty and a 30-day money-back guarantee.

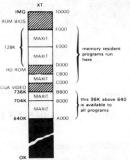

XT class machine (8088, 8086) w/640K and a CGA Color Monitor or a Compaq Type Dual Mode Display

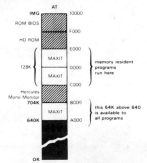

AT class machine (80286) w/640K and a Mono HERC Monitor

Order toll free 1-800-227-0900. MAXIT is just $195 plus $4 shipping, and applicable state sales tax. Buy MAXIT today and solve your PC's memory crisis. Call Toll free 1-800-227-0900 (In California 800-772-2531). Outside the U.S.A. call 1-415-548-2805. We accept VISA, MC.